To: Dean Jennifer Keene
Thank you for
all of your support.
With best wishes,
John

Latinos in Nevada

D0888901

Migration, Demography & Environmental Change:
Global Challenges

Series Editors: Tiffiany Howard and Nerses Kopalyan

With nationwide population increases driven primarily by recent immigrants and their children, the United States is currently ranked as the third most populous country and has the highest population growth of all the industrialized nations. Of particular significance is that contemporary migratory patterns have altered the country's demographics to such an extent that it is projected ethnic and racial minorities will comprise a majority of the U.S. population by 2042. Migration, Demography & Environmental Change: Global Challenges promotes works that investigate U.S. migration and population change as these factors relate to the fields of political science, public policy, history, ethnic studies, environmental affairs, sociology, anthropology, education, public health and the health sciences, as well as legal studies.

Latinos in Nevada: A Political, Economic, and Social Profile
John P. Tuman, Tiffiany Howard, David F. Damore, and Nerses Kopalyan

Latinos in Nevada

A POLITICAL, ECONOMIC, AND SOCIAL PROFILE

John P. Tuman
Tiffiany Howard
David F. Damore
Nerses Kopalyan

UNIVERSITY OF NEVADA PRESS *Reno & Las Vegas*

NATIONAL
ENDOWMENT
FOR THE
HUMANITIES

The publication is funded in part by a grant from Nevada Humanities and the National Endowment for the Humanities.

Migration, Demography & Environmental Change : Global Challenges Series
Series Editor: Tiffany Howard and Nerses Kopalyan

University of Nevada Press, Reno, Nevada 89557 USA

LIBRARY OF CONGRESS CATALOGING-IN-PUBLICATION DATA
Names: Tuman, John P. (John Peter), 1964– author. | Howard, Tiffany, author. | Damore, David F., 1970– author. | Kopalyan, Nerses, author.
Title: Latinos in Nevada : a political, economic, and social profile / John P. Tuman, Tiffany Howard, David F. Damore, Nerses Kopalyan.
Description: Reno : University of Nevada Press, [2021] | Series: Migration, demography & environmental change : global challenges series | Includes bibliographical references and index. | Summary: "Latinos in Nevada: A Political, Economic, and Social Profile provides a political, economic, and demographic profile of contemporary Latinos in Nevada. Adopting an interdisciplinary perspective, the authors examine Latino history, growth, and trends in employment, education, and health, and analyze the dynamics of political participation and civic engagement"— Provided by publisher.
Identifiers: LCCN 2020045090 (print) | LCCN 2020045091 (ebook) | ISBN 9781948908986 (paperback) | ISBN 9781948908993 (ebook)
Subjects: LCSH: Hispanic Americans—Nevada—Politics and government—21st century. | Hispanic Americans—Nevada—Economic conditions—21st century. | Hispanic Americans—Nevada—Social conditions—21st century. | Hispanic Americans—Nevada—History. | Nevada—Emigration and immigration.
Classification: LCC F850.S75 T86 2021 (print) | LCC F850.S75 (ebook) | DDC 979.3/0046800905—dc23
LC record available at https://lccn.loc.gov/2020045090
LC ebook record available at https://lccn.loc.gov/2020045091

First Printing
Manufactured in the United States of America

25 24 23 22 21   5 4 3 2 1

Contents

Illustrations

Figures

Acknowledgments

This book grew out of a research project directed by John P. Tuman and David F. Damore, and supported by Brookings Mountain West, a partnership between the Brookings Institution in Washington, DC, and UNLV. Parts of chapters 2, 3, and 4 present revised and updated material that appeared originally in working papers for Brookings Mountain West. We are grateful to Robert Lang, William Brown, and Caitlin Saladino, all of Brookings Mountain West, for their comments and suggestions. In addition, some material on civic engagement, in chapter 7, is adapted and updated from Tuman (2009). His study of Latino civic and political engagement was funded by the Woodrow Wilson International Center for Scholars.

We would like to acknowledge our former students Maria José Flor Ágreda, David Snyder, and Samantha Burtch for research assistance. Professor Jaewon Lim also assisted with analysis of the public use microdata samples (PUMS) on interstate migration. In addition, we thank two anonymous reviewers for their extensive comments on the completed manuscript, and Clark Whitehorn, former executive editor of the University of Nevada Press, for helping to bring this book to fruition. We are also grateful for the support of JoAnne Banducci in procuring a Nevada Humanities publication grant, and the assistance of Sara Vélez Mallea, Sara Hendricksen, and Iris Saltus, all with the University of Nevada Press. Paul Szydelko, our copyeditor, provided useful comments that enhanced the quality of the book. The university community has also provided a great deal of support along the way. In particular, we are thankful to our colleagues in the Department of Political Science and the Liberal Arts Dean's Office. Finally, we thank our families for support.

Latinos in Nevada

CHAPTER 1

Introduction—A History

The Southwest region of the United States has had a Hispanic presence for more than 400 years. Historical accounts reveal a long history of Hispanic settlement in the region that began with the establishment of the Spanish colonial territory of New Spain in 1521.[1] For 300 years, the Southwest, including what is present-day Nevada, was controlled by Spain, until Mexico established its independence from Spain on August 24, 1821. For more than twenty years, Mexico would retain control of the territory that now comprises the states of Texas, California, New Mexico, Utah, Arizona, Nevada, and areas of Colorado and Wyoming.[2] Mexico would eventually lose control of this territory to the United States after its defeat in the Mexican-American War of 1848.[3] And two years later, in 1850, with the first US Census that provided detailed household information, we began to have data confirming the enduring and impactful presence of Hispanics and Latinos in the Southwest, and specifically in the territory that would later become the state of Nevada.

Origins of Nevada's Early Hispanic/Latino Population

Critics and supporters of the term "Hispanic" ascribe varied meanings to the word. In New Mexico and other parts of the Southwest, many embrace the term Hispano (Hispanic in Spanish) as a term of ethnic identification. Many of those who reject the word's usage often associate it with the colonial power of Spain and its enslavement and oppression of the native indigenous population in the region. Thus, contemporary references to this group exhibit a preference for the usage of the term(s) Latino/a/x.[4] Throughout this book, the terms Hispanic and Latino will be used interchangeably, reflecting the comprehensiveness of both words, as well as acknowledging the evolution of cultural preferences. That is why in this opening chapter we begin by deconstructing the term Hispanic and contextualize its general meaning, as well as its intended meaning for the purposes of this work.

At its most basic level, Hispanic refers to the collective identity of a people with direct ethnic, sociocultural, and linguistic linkages to Spain, and by extension the Spanish-speaking countries of Latin America and the Caribbean—but excluding that of Brazil, Haiti, and all other non-Spanish speaking countries in the region. Ethnically, Hispanics are predominantly descended from the unions between indigenous Americans and early Spanish settlers. At the same time, a combination of the substantial presence of African Moors in Spain, several of whom took part in early Spanish expeditions, and the burgeoning African slave trade that began in the 1440s, has contributed to the further diversification of the Hispanic ethnic identity. As a result, Hispanics may be purely European, Indigenous, or African, a combination of two of the three groups, or a blend of all three.

Socioculturally, Hispanics reflect cultural traditions inherited from the Iberian Peninsula that were altered and transformed by the influences of indigenous and African traditions, and developed in the Americas. While no group is monolithic and there will always be variations in religious traditions, the majority of Hispanics maintain religious affiliation to the Roman Catholic Church. Finally, the primary unifier among Hispanics is the Spanish language, although the dialect varies across regions.

Mining, Ranching, and Hispanic/Latino Settlement in Nevada

Hispanic and Latino settlers established homesteads on the sites of mining discoveries in several areas in Nevada. Many of these places are easily identified in the historical record by their Spanish-origin names. In the early 1800s, the town of Montezuma was established and mined by Spaniards, and later by Mexicans. Montezuma was near Goldfield, in what is now Esmeralda County. The town was abandoned in the mid-1800s, but American miners settled there after the discovery of gold and silver in 1867.

With the 1859 discovery of the Comstock Lode in western Nevada (then Utah Territory), other settlements were quickly established in the state. Hispanics from several Latin American countries were among this first group of settlers, coming primarily from the state of Sonora in northern Mexico and from Chile. During this time period of the late 1850s, early 1860s, Hispanics of Mexican origin established the town of Guadalajara, Nevada, which was named after its Mexican counterpart. On the eastern side of the Toiyabe Range in central Nevada, the town was established on the site where Mexican settlers discovered gold and silver in the area.

During the early mining boom in Nevada, Mexicans contributed to the smelting operations for silver, bringing techniques from Mexico that included the patio process in arrastra mills.[5] Chilean immigrants also made important contributions, but by the 1860s, competitive pressures from newer mines displaced some Latino miners. In particular, the introduction of the Washoe process reduced the time required for processing, giving newer mines an edge in efficiency.[6] But Mexicans and Latinos were also central to the mining sector in other ways. Mexicans who migrated to the region provided the majority of the labor in the mining sector. As a result, the Mexican people were central to the establishment and advancement of mining interests in the state. Nevada towns such as Candelaria and Cortez were erected on profitable mining sites and largely populated by Mexican settlers; and for many decades Mexicans would retain exclusive control of the richest mines in these areas. However, by the late 1880s, Mexican control had eroded with the substantial influx of American settlers from the East and California.

Despite the displacement of Latino settlers for control of the mining industry, Hispanics played a key role in the development of Nevada's mining industry from the very beginning. With the mining boom in Nevada and the subsequent population increase, a demand for meat also rose sharply. This would lead to the establishment of some of Nevada's earliest sheep and cattle ranches, several of which were owned by Hispanics. Consequently, with the emergence of Nevada's two biggest economic industries—mining and ranching—Hispanics were instrumental in establishing some of Nevada's earliest towns as they put down roots to take advantage of the state's burgeoning economy.

Immigration to Nevada was at its peak in the 1860s, and Hispanic immigrants featured prominently in the growth and expansion of the state. Responding to population demand, cattle and sheepherders turned to ranching, and several Hispanics became owners of some of Nevada's earliest ranches.

The most notable Hispanic-owned ranch was the Spanish Ranch in northeastern Nevada. Owned by the Altube brothers, who were Basques, the Spanish Ranch was comprised of approximately 60,000 acres of land, and it was well known for being primarily run by Mexican ranch hands and general laborers. The Spanish Ranch operated under the Altube brothers from 1871, but with the death of Pedro Altube in 1905 it was sold to several private owners in 1907. The Spanish Ranch is considered one of the largest, richest, and most prominent ranching empires to ever exist in Nevada, and the lands that were originally held by the Altube brothers continue to provide livestock to Northern Nevadans.[7]

The Railroads and Nevada's Expanding Hispanic/Latino Population

The expansion of railroad lines into the Southwest spurred an increasing demand for low-cost labor. Mexican railroad workers were first hired during the 1880s to work on the Atchison, Topeka and Santa Fe Railway. At that time, only a handful of Mexican laborers were working for the railroad companies in the region, but by the turn of the century the Southern Pacific Railroad employed more than 4,500 Mexicans. The increasing number of Mexican laborers meant a significant increase in the region's overall Hispanic population as workers brought their families with them.[8] Estimates suggest that from 1910 to 1917, the United States received about 300,000 Mexicans—an average of 48,000 each year—with the majority of the migrants coming to work on the railroads.

The San Pedro, Los Angeles and Salt Lake Railroad would begin construction in 1901 in Pomona, California. The development of the interstate railroad fueled additional demand for labor, thereby leading to an influx of Mexican and Latino workers into Southern Nevada. As such, Mexicans were among the first residents of the town of Las Vegas when it was founded in 1905. And by 1911, the Dillingham Commission, which was responsible for reporting on the status of immigrants in the United States, determined that Mexican migrants were responsible for the majority of the railroad construction work that took place in the rough, largely uninhabited terrain of Nevada, Arizona, New Mexico, and Southern California.[9] By 1930, railroad crews in Southern Nevada and the surrounding areas were primarily comprised of Mexican workers, with estimates suggesting that 70 percent of the railroad labor force being of Mexican descent.[10]

For most of the laborers working on the railroads, work began to slow and disappeared entirely with the Great Depression of the 1930s; however, Mexican workers managed to maintain their predominant presence in railroad positions, despite the failing economy. This was because railroad companies paid these workers a minimal wage, and much like undocumented laborers today, in the absence of citizenship status and union protections, Mexican workers were not in any position to advocate for higher wages. With the onset of the Great Depression and the scarcity of railroad positions that were almost exclusively held by Mexican migrants, race relations deteriorated significantly among European Americans, African Americans, and Mexicans in Nevada. Despite the hardening of race relations and increasing public disapproval, Mexican workers continued to provide most of the labor in the railroad industry for more than two decades as they laid new rail and maintained existing lines in the region.

Hispanics/Latinos in Nevada after World War II

As noted, Latinos have been present in Nevada in substantial numbers since the mid-1800s. However, with the transient industries of mining and the railroad, many Latinos would only stay in one area temporarily, migrating throughout the Southwest to follow available work or opportunities. A large number of Hispanics did not begin to settle permanently in the state of Nevada until World War II when the US established the Bracero Program.

Because of the rise of unemployment, from 1929 to 1933, and again in 1936, the US government engaged in mass deportation of Mexicans. At least 500,000 Mexicans were repatriated during this period, most estimates suggest.[11] World War II created a dire labor shortage in the US, as able-bodied men were drafted and sent to war in Europe or the South Pacific. To address the growing demand for domestic labor in the US, the US government and the Mexican government signed an agreement in 1942 that came to be known as the Bracero Program. The Bracero Program was designed to be a temporary labor program whereby Mexico would provide workers for the agriculture and railroads in the US throughout the duration of the war. However, these sectors came to be dependent upon Mexican labor, even after the war ended. Because of pressure from the US labor movement, Congress terminated the Bracero Program in 1964. During its twenty-year duration, the program sponsored an estimated five million border crossings of contract workers from Mexico. Many of the Mexican guest workers eventually succeeded in obtaining legal permanent residency, while others abandoned farm work for more profitable

FIGURE 1.1. Population of Las Vegas, 1900–2010

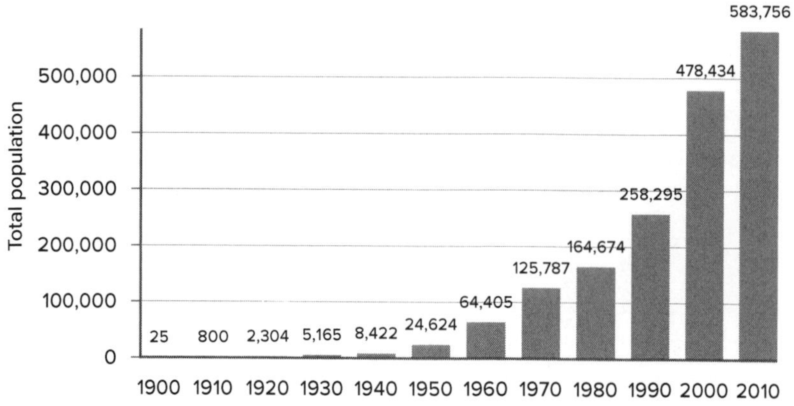

Source: US Census Bureau

employment in other US cities. Consequently, the first substantial wave of Mexican migration took place during the era of the Bracero Program, and Nevada, specifically Las Vegas, was one of the most popular places for permanent settlement.[12]

An airbase, with its defense industry employment, a magnesium factory, and a growing casino and hospitality industry came to Las Vegas and its surrounding areas during World War II. The flourishing industries and expanding population in what is now Clark County attracted more businesses to support the new residents. Many of the people who flocked to Las Vegas during this period were Hispanics, and as Las Vegas grew as a city, so did its Latino population. However, because of de facto segregation, Latinos were often relegated to menial labor jobs, working as maids, janitors, dishwashers, construction workers, and busboys in the growing Las Vegas area.

Although the population of Las Vegas has steadily increased since the city's inception, in the decades following the end of World War II, the City of Las Vegas more than doubled its number of residents (fig. 1.1). With this population growth, the racial and ethnic demographics of the city have also changed significantly. In 1950 Whites made up 92.4 percent of the city's population, and African Americans made up 6.6 percent. However, two decades later, the percentage of Whites had declined to 89.5 percent, while the Hispanic population more than tripled during that same time

FIGURE 1.2. Projected US Population Estimates, by Race/Ethnicity, 2015 and 2065

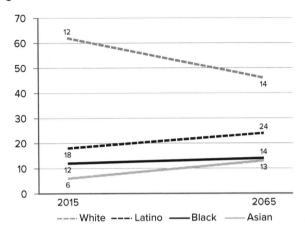

Source: D'Vera Cohn, "Future Immigration Will Change the Face of America by 2065." Pew Research Center, October 5, 2015
Note: Whites, Blacks, and Asians include only single-race non-Hispanics. Asians include Pacific Islanders. Hispanics are of any race.

period, growing from 3,174 in 1950 to 9,937 in 1970. By 1980 the Hispanic population in Las Vegas had more than tripled again to 34,998, and that increasing population trend continues today.

Conclusion: Latinos in Nevada Today

According to projections made by the Pew Research Center,[13] immigrants and their descendants will continue to account for the majority of the US population growth for at least the next fifty years. Estimates suggest that by 2065, the total US population will include approximately 441 million people—78 million will be immigrants, and 81 million will have been born to immigrant parents. The fertility rate in the US, however, is expected to remain low. As a result of immigrant-driven population growth, the demographics of the US will also continue to undergo a substantial transformation. By 2065, at least one in five of the US population will be foreign-born, and no racial or ethnic group will account for a majority of the population (fig. 1.2).

As figure 1.2 illustrates, by 2065 Hispanics/Latinos will continue to be the second-largest racial/ethnic group in the United States. Significantly,

Latinos will make up almost 25 percent of the US population. The continual rise of the US Hispanic/Latino population, in addition to changing the country's racial and ethnic demographics, will also have a sustained impact on all facets of society, including politics, education, the economy, and public health institutions. Inarguably, nowhere is the impact of the growing Latino population more evident than in the state of Nevada.

Nevada has experienced the largest population increase of any state in the country, which has resulted in its emergence as a swing state in domestic politics. Now with 47 percent of Nevadans classified as non-White, and Latinos accounting for 29 percent of the total state population in 2018, Nevada is presently a state with a majority minority population.[14] Nevada has witnessed a shift in political behavior and attitudes, largely because of its growing Latino population—a Latino population that is a diverse, multiracial collective with specific needs and objectives.

Latinos in Nevada examines the impact of the Hispanic/Latino population on Nevada—then, now, and in the future. Each chapter is thematic and, as such, we do not employ a single theoretical framework in the analysis. However, as discussed throughout the book, our analysis is broadly informed by scholarship that emphasizes the importance of structural and institutional factors, and their intersection with race and ethnicity, in shaping demographic trends, political participation, and labor market, health, and educational outcomes. Beginning with this chapter, which has briefly discussed the Latino contribution to the early development of the state of Nevada, this book highlights the societal role of Latinos in Nevada, as well as the specific implications of their growing presence in the state. In the remainder of the book, the time frame for our analysis covers 2000 to 2017, an important period of demographic, political, and economic change for Latinos in Nevada. In selected places, we also offer a brief discussion of more recent events, including the COVID-19 pandemic of 2020.

Chapter 2 picks up where we leave off, and analyzes the more recent wave of Hispanic/Latino immigration to Nevada, and how immigration has contributed to the sizeable population increase in the state. Chapter 3 shifts the focus from the demographics to political engagement of the Nevada Latino population, both at the state and local levels, but also at the national level as part of an electoral swing state. Chapter 4 assesses the economic climate in the state, the impact the Great Recession had on Nevada's Latino population, and how Latinos are faring during Nevada's contemporary economy. In chapter 5, we evaluate the broader social determinants of health, the health needs of Nevada's Hispanic/Latinos, the responsiveness of Nevada's public health institutions to this group's needs, and the resulting health outcomes for the state's Latino population. This chapter works to determine whether Nevada's Latino population has access to basic health care and if the health-care system adequately meets this group's health needs. In chapter 6, we assess how well served Latinos in Nevada are by the state's educational system by evaluating matriculation, retention, and graduation rates at every level. The concluding chapter speculates on the future of Latinos in Nevada, the role they continue to play in the politics and economy of the state, but more importantly their deepening presence in society through thriving civic institutions and groups. In this chapter, we also underline the diversity of the Latino community within the state.

Latinos in Nevada is in no way intended to provide an exhaustive analysis. Therefore, we emphasize that this analysis has a limited scope and that we did not explore all aspects of the lives and conditions of Nevada's Latino population. However, this book is among the first to provide an analysis of selected themes related to immigration and demographic change, political and civic engagement, and labor market, educational, and health outcomes among the Hispanic/Latino population in Nevada. Our goal is to highlight the past contributions, present role, and the future impact of Latinos on the Silver State.

CHAPTER 2

Immigration

Since the early 1980s, Nevada has experienced significant demographic change. In particular, the ethnic composition of the state has become considerably more diverse. Although the Asian population is one of the sources of the state's growing diversity, Nevada's Latino population has also accounted for much of the recent demographic and social change.[1] Except for brief periods following the Great Recession of 2007–2009, the Latino population of Nevada experienced sustained annual growth from 1990 to 2010. Perhaps more important, much of the growth in the Latino population has been associated with immigration, principally from Mexico and other parts of Central America.

In this chapter, we analyze data from several different sources, including the US Census Bureau's Decennial Census, the American Community Survey,[2] the Latino National Survey, and other macroeconomic data to examine the drivers of Latino population growth in Nevada. We also provide evidence from some interviews to contextualize our findings. The framework employed in our analysis is derived from structural theories that emphasize the role of economic, political, and social influences as "push" and "pull" factors in migration decisions. Push factors refer to multiple influences that may induce people to leave their country of origin, while "pull" factors may make certain destination areas attractive for immigration. We also incorporate insights from more recent theoretical work that recognizes the importance of local context and social networks in understanding why some destination cities are attractive to immigrants.[3] The first part of the chapter provides an overview of the growth in Nevada's Latino population, with a focus on the factors that have shaped migration flows from countries in Latin America and other US states. In so doing, our analysis allows us to consider what makes Nevada attractive as a "destination state" to immigrants. In part two, we examine the age structure and the concentration of the Latino population in certain metropolitan areas and counties in Nevada. From there, we move into a discussion of the impact Latin American immigration has had on the demographics of Nevada. The chapter concludes by exploring some of the implications of immigration and the growth of Nevada's Latino population.

Overview: Trends in Nevada's Latino Population

Over the course of the first decade of the twenty-first century, the Latino population of Nevada grew appreciably. The 2000 Census reported that 393,970 Latinos resided in Nevada, which represented approximately 19.7 percent of the state's total population. In 2010, Nevada's Latino population increased to 737,221, or 27.1 percent of the state population.[4] Based on the one-year estimate from American Community Survey, in 2018, the most recent year that complete data were available, Latinos comprised a total of 29 percent of the Nevada population. The number of Latinos in Nevada increased by approximately 87 percent from 2000 to 2010, although average annual growth rates slowed after the emergence of the Great Recession. This trend toward slower growth appeared to continue throughout the 2010s.

As is detailed in table 2.1, the Latino population in Nevada is also distinctive for being a relatively young population. In 2011, the most recent year for which complete age data are available, almost 48 percent of all Latino Nevadans were 24 years old or younger. Latino children 5 years old and younger comprise 10.5 percent of the state's Latino population, with larger shares between the ages of 6 and 24. In addition, the vast majority of the state's Latino population under the age of 24 is native-born. Indeed, just 13.4 percent of the Latino population ages 24 and younger were born in Latin America.[5] In part, the small weight of immigrants in the younger segments of the population may reflect the preference among many immigrants to migrate without children (or before having any children). Particularly for individuals who arrive in the US without legal authorization, the risks associated with cross-border travel are high, and migrating with children increases those risks. In addition, some immigrants might remain in the US only for limited periods of time, with the hope of returning to their home countries after earning or remitting (i.e., sending home) a sufficient amount of money; thus, they do not remain long enough to have children and start families.

TABLE 2.1. Age Distribution of Nevada's Latino Population, 2011

Age Groups	Share of Latino Population
Under 5 years	10.5%
5 to 17 years	25.6%
18 to 24 years	11.6%
24 years and younger	47.7%
25 to 34 years	16.7%
35 to 44 years	15.3%
45 to 54 years	10.4%
55 to 64 years	5.7%
65 to 74 years	2.6%
75 years and over	1.6%
25 years and over	52.4%

Source: 2011 American Community Survey

Having discussed the age structure of the Latino population, we turn now to examining the spatial concentration of the population throughout the state. Nevada's Latino population is relatively young, and it concentrates in just two counties: Clark (in Southern Nevada, which includes the Las Vegas metropolitan area) and Washoe (in Northern Nevada, which includes the Reno/Sparks metropolitan area). Data from the 2011 American Community Survey indicate that 79.3 percent of all Latinos in Nevada reside in Clark County. Over the course of the past decade, the growth trajectory of the Latino population of Clark County was also slightly higher than the pattern observed at the state level. From 2000 to 2010, the number of Latinos in Clark County went from 302,143 to 568,644, a change of 88 percent. In the same period, the share of Latinos in Clark County increased from 22 percent to 29.1 percent. An examination of patterns of residential occupancy in Clark County suggests that the majority of Latinos reside in North Las Vegas, on the eastern side of the Las Vegas valley, and, to a much smaller extent, in Henderson.

Beyond Clark County, the only other population center of Latinos in Nevada is in Washoe County. In 2011, approximately 13 percent of Nevada's Latino population was located there, with most residing in the Reno metropolitan area. The composition of the foreign-born Latino population in

Clark and Washoe Counties is similar to the pattern observed at the state level. As is detailed below, the spatial concentration of Latinos in Clark and Washoe Counties reflects in large part the economic opportunities in each county, particularly for immigrant workers.

Immigration and the Growth in Nevada's Latino Population

As many analysts have observed, a relatively large share of Nevada's Latino population is comprised of recent immigrants from Latin America. In 2011, 42 percent of Latinos in Nevada were foreign-born, but only 29.5 percent of the state's foreign-born Latinos were naturalized US citizens.[6] Migration flows from Mexico account for the vast majority (78 percent) of the total immigrant population in the Latino community in the state.[7] Nevada also attracts smaller groups of émigrés from Central America (principally, El Salvador and Guatemala) and the Caribbean (Cuba and Puerto Rico). Nearly three in ten Latin American immigrants in Nevada who are not naturalized US citizens entered the US in 2000 or later.

In part, Nevada has been attractive to Latin American immigrants (and Latinos more generally) because of the relative abundance of jobs in the state that require relatively low levels of skill and educational attainment, as well as the state's proximity to Arizona and California. Before 2008, Latino employment was concentrated in Nevada's hospitality, construction, and retail and wholesale trade sectors, as well as other low-skilled occupations. However, in the aftermath of the Great Recession, the residential home construction and hospitality sectors were hard hit, with attendant consequences for patterns of unemployment among the US and foreign-born Latino population in the state.

A number of studies have suggested that as a consequence of the recession, net migration flows from Mexico to the US declined after 2008. What remains unclear, however, is how the recession influenced net migration in states that had seen steady growth in their foreign-born Latino population, including Nevada, before the economic downturn. In the next sections, we contribute to the research literature through an examination of migration flows among Latinos in the US. Working with the data from different sources, we first examine changes in migration flows in Latin America to Nevada. Part of the analysis discusses the economic and contextual factors that make Nevada an attractive "destination state" for immigrants from Mexico and other parts of Latin America. After that, we analyze interstate

TABLE 2.2. Reasons for Immigration to US for Mexican-Born Respondents Living in Nevada and Nationally, 2005

Reason	Share of Mexican-Born Respondents in Nevada	Share of Mexican-Born Respondents Nationally
Education	6.49%	5.83%
Family reunification	9.16%	9.69%
Escape political turmoil	1.15%	0.72%
My parents brought me as a child	14.89%	13.38%
Improve economic situation	59.16%	63.57%
Other	9.16%	6.81%

Note: Authors' tabulation and analysis of Latino National Survey, adjusting for Mexican-born respondents living in Nevada and Mexican-born in the entire sample. Each state in the sample is a representative sample of the total Latino population in that state. In Nevada, the total sample size was 403; Mexican-born respondents represented 65 percent of the total sample.

migration patterns among US states and Nevada from 2007 through 2011, with a focus on the total population and the Latino population (all Latinos, and adjusting only for foreign-born Latinos). Given that the Great Recession occurred during this five-year period, the data allow us to examine how changes in Nevada's economy affected migration into and out of the Silver State. The migration partners included in the analysis are of Nevada and other US states. After this, we examine international migration from Latin American countries to Nevada.

Migration Flows from Mexico and Central America to Nevada

Although the Great Recession may have led to a temporary slowdown in migration flows from Mexico to the US, immigration from Latin America has contributed significantly to growth in Nevada's Latino population for several decades. Given the overall weight of immigration from Mexico, El Salvador, and Guatemala, it is important to understand the factors that have shaped migration flows from these countries over the past three decades. Individuals migrate for a variety of reasons, but the available evidence suggests that economic considerations are preeminent in these decisions. The data in table 2.2, which are taken from the 2006 Latino National Survey (LNS), provide a glimpse of the self-reported reasons for immigration given by Mexican-born respondents in Nevada and in other US states. It is not surprising that the most prevalent reason for migration among Mexicans in Nevada and other states was improvement of one's economic situation (59 percent of respondents in Nevada, and 64 percent of respondents nationally). In contrast, immigration as a child, family reunification, education, and to escape political turmoil were much-less cited factors for migration among Mexicans. Although the numbers of Salvadoran and Guatemalan respondents in the Nevada sample of the LNS are too small to analyze, other studies have pointed to the importance of economic factors for migrants from these two countries as well.[8]

Because the data suggest that the desire to improve one's economic situation is clearly important to understanding Mexican and Latin American flows to Nevada, the remainder of this section explores how demographic change, economic restructuring, and social and human capital have influenced evaluations of individual economic situations.[9] As noted in the introduction of the chapter, in terms of a theoretical framework, these influences may be viewed as push factors associated with outmigration from Mexico and Latin America. In what follows, we briefly discuss the role of each of these factors as inducements for outmigration.

First, because of a delay in the demographic transition, pressure for outmigration in Mexico and parts of Central America has remained strong during the past three decades. In Mexico, for example, fertility rates did not begin to decline until the mid-1970s (fig. 2.1). As a result, the number of young people in the workforce remained at high levels for a number of years. From 1970 to 1990, the share of the Mexican population ages 15 to 29 increased from 25.6 percent to 29.4 percent of the total population.[10] The share of the Mexican population between the ages of 15 and 29 remained at 28 percent of the total population in 2000, but fell (principally, after 2005) to 26.4 percent in 2010. Yet, during the period from 1982 to 2008, job creation in the formal sector of the Mexican economy was generally insufficient to absorb the number of new entrants to the labor market, resulting in a large informal sector (i.e., economic activities that are not taxed or regulated) and underemployment.[11] These problems are more pronounced in rural areas, where employment and income are more precarious than in cities.[12] Similar fertility trends are evident in El Salvador and Guatemala, two Central American countries that have also contributed to Nevada's Latino population.[13]

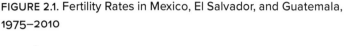

FIGURE 2.1. Fertility Rates in Mexico, El Salvador, and Guatemala, 1975–2010

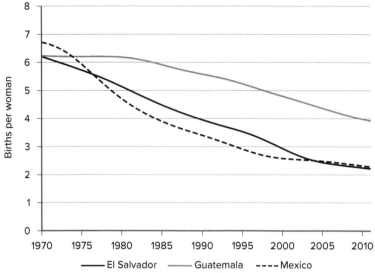

Source: World Development Indicators, Fertility Rate, Total (Births per Woman)

To be sure, as fertility rates in Mexico and Central America fall, the situation for new labor market entrants may improve—although this will also occur slowly and will be mediated by other factors (e.g., macroeconomic policy, competition from China) that are not directly influenced by demographic change.

Second, in Mexico and other parts of Central America, trade liberalization and other structural problems have created continuing pressures for outmigration. In the aftermath of implementation of the North American Free Trade Agreement (NAFTA), small-scale corn farmers in Mexico faced difficulty competing with more efficient, large-scale producers in the US. The resulting competition from cheap corn imports from the US has displaced many smallholders in Mexico. Although the Mexican government implemented a policy (PROCAMPO) designed to provide income support to farmers who are adversely affected by competition from US agricultural imports, several studies have found that the program was not adequately funded and tends to have a bias toward larger producers.[14] As a result, many small-scale farmers in Mexico exited farming and migrated in search of employment. It is important to note, however, that the impacts of trade liberalization and economic integration have not been confined to rural areas. Although North American economic integration led to the creation of manufacturing employment in Mexico, the process also produced a high degree of volatility in manufacturing employment, particularly in Mexico's in-bond export processing plants (maquiladoras) on the US-Mexico border.[15] As a result, outmigration from industrial areas in northern Mexico also occurred during the past fifteen years.[16]

In other Central American countries, such as Guatemala, El Salvador, and Nicaragua, an extreme concentration in landholdings, combined with import competition, uneven prices for commodity exports (e.g., coffee), and government repression or civil wars of the 1980s, induced migration from the agricultural sector as well.[17] Although economic conditions in Central America have been important, the significance of political upheavals should not be discounted in spurring outmigration to Nevada. For example, Geoconda Arguëllo-Kline, an immigrant from Nicaragua and current leader of Culinary Union Local 226, observed: "I grew up in Managua, Nicaragua. I lived there all my childhood until twenty-four years old. I grew up with my parents, my father and my mother. I feel great with them. Great parents...the truth is when I came to United States I came because the reason we had the revolution, for political reasons we moved to United States. We were not expecting to leave; it was like a monster surprise to leave on that day."[18]

In interviews, Guatemalan civic leaders in Las Vegas also pointed to the role of the civil war as an important factor for some Guatemalan immigrants who arrived in the 1980s.[19]

Third, despite reforms that have promoted economic openness to trade and foreign investment, annual growth in real average wages was flat or negative in Mexico and other parts of Latin America for much of this period. As one can see from the data in figure 2.2, which are from the Economic Commission for Latin America and the Caribbean, the average real wage in Mexico (as measured in constant 2000 pesos, represented by an index number) fell dramatically after 1982 and remained below its 1982 level for virtually every year from 1982 to 2010.[20] In part, the decline in real wages in the 1980s reflected the impact of government adjustment policies that were implemented after the 1982 debt crisis. However, the longer-term trend in Mexico's stagnating real wages is because of the prevalence

FIGURE 2.2. Real Wage Trends in Mexico, El Salvador, and Guatemala, 1980–2010

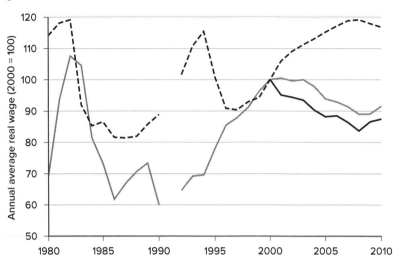

Source: Economic Commission for Latin America and the Caribbean ECLAC (2012)

of weak (or no) unions in many sectors of the Mexican economy, labor market barriers, and the absence of policies to link labor productivity and wage settlements.[21] Perhaps more important, although the trends in real wages affected many workers, the impact of real wage stagnation has (until recently) been most pronounced among workers with lower levels of education.[22] Under these conditions, incentives for cross-border migration to the US remained strong, particularly for individuals with lower levels of educational attainment.[23] Similar problems are evident in patterns of wage determination in Guatemala and El Salvador.[24]

A final factor that has shaped migration flows is the growth of informal immigration networks. Mexican immigrants, for example, have developed informal migration networks between their municipality of origin and their destination areas in the US.[25] As a form of social capital, migration networks reduce the costs and uncertainty associated with immigration. In particular, migration networks often provide information about employment opportunities and living arrangements in selected US destination cities, as well as conditions that might affect transit at different points of entry along the US-Mexico border. Research on immigrants from Guatemala found that migration networks are important, particularly given the risks for Guatemalan migrants who travel through Mexico to the United States.[26]

Nevada as a Destination State for Latin American Immigrants

Although immigrants have been a part of Nevada's social fabric before it even became a state, migration flows from Latin America grew dramatically after 1980.[27] Some immigrants in the state have arrived directly from Mexico and other parts of Latin America, but the data suggest that a (small) majority tend to reside in California, and to a much smaller degree in Arizona, before moving to Nevada. In our analysis of data from the 2006 Latino National Survey, we found that among Mexican respondents in Nevada, approximately 54 percent reported residing in another state previously. Among those Mexican respondents (in Nevada) who lived in another state, 72.5 percent responded that they had lived in California, while 5 percent reported Arizona, 3.5 percent reported Colorado, and about 2 percent each reported Texas, Utah, Illinois, and Washington.[28] Not surprisingly, once they arrive in Nevada, most Latin American immigrants search for employment in the Las Vegas metropolitan area. In addition, the LNS data suggest that 73 percent of the Mexican respondents in Nevada had resided in the state in early childhood.

Latin American immigrants choose Nevada as a destination state for reasons that are relatively straightforward. Given the skill profile of many immigrants, Nevada's two major metropolitan areas, Las Vegas and Reno, offer attractive economic opportunities. Many immigrants from Mexico and Central America have relatively low levels of educational attainment. In 2011, for example, US Census data suggest that 59.6 percent of individuals from Mexico (who were 25 years or older) residing in Nevada had less than a high school degree. In the same year, 43.6 percent of individuals (25 years and older) from Central America had less than a high school degree.

Immigrant workers with lower levels of educational attainment (table 2.3) are well matched to jobs that, despite the Great Recession, remain relatively abundant in the state. These include jobs in the service, construction, and wholesale and retail trade sectors. In 2011, 37.2 percent of the immigrants from Mexico residing in Nevada, and 52.1 percent of the Central American immigrant population, were employed in the entertainment, accommodation, and food services sector in the state. As the data

TABLE 2.3. Educational Attainment among Foreign-Born Latinos, Nevada, 2011

Educational Attainment	Latin America	Mexico	Other Central America
Less than High School Graduate	53.5%	59.6%	43.6%
High School Graduate (includes equivalency)	26.1%	24.6%	28.0%
Some College or Associate's Degree	13.8%	11.5%	18.4%
Bachelor's Degree	5.2%	3.3%	8.9%
Graduate or Professional Degree	1.4%	1.0%	1.1%

Source: 2011 American Community Survey

TABLE 2.4. Occupation of Nevada Latinos Born in Mexico and Central America, 2011

Sector	Mexico	Other Central America
Agriculture, Forestry, Fishing, Hunting, Mining	2.5%	0.6%
Construction	13.1%	5.5%
Manufacturing	7.3%	4.2%
Wholesale Trade	2.1%	1.0%
Retail Trade	6.5%	9.9%
Transportation, Warehousing, Utilities	3.0%	2.5%
Information	0.7%	0.9%
Finance, Insurance, Real Estate, Rental, Leasing	3.4%	0.8%
Professional, Scientific, Management, Administrative, Waste	11.3%	8.2%
Educational Services, Health Care, Social Assistance	5.2%	6.2%
Arts, Entertainment, Recreation, Accommodation, Food Services	37.2%	52.1%
Other Services (Except Public Administration)	7.1%	4.8%
Public Administration	0.6%	3.4%

Source: 2011 American Community Survey

in table 2.4 suggest, many immigrants from Mexico and Central America concentrate in the retail trade and construction sectors as well.

Nevada also remains attractive to immigrants because average levels of remuneration have remained well above the extant level in Mexico. The data in figure 2.3 show Mexican hourly compensation in comparison to the US (as an index number, where the US = 100). As the figure makes clear,

FIGURE 2.3. Index of Comparative Hourly Compensation Costs in Mexican Manufacturing, 1996–2011

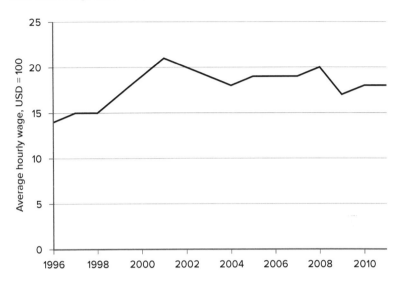

Source: US Bureau of Labor Statistics

a fairly large gap persists between the two countries despite more than a decade of closer economic integration.[29] In those sectors of the Nevada economy where immigrant workers from Mexico and Central America are concentrated (e.g., services, construction, and wholesale and retail trade), each sector's average wage in Nevada is also well above wage levels in Mexico.

For example, a highly simplified comparison of average daily wages for a construction laborer reveals that in Mexico, construction laborers were paid on average $15.83 per day in 2012, while in Nevada the corresponding daily average was $153.84 per day in the same period.[30] In other words, a construction worker's wages in Nevada might be about ten times the remuneration level in Mexico. Of course, immigrant workers in Nevada may be remunerated at closer to entry-level (or minimum) wages in construction. However, examining Nevada construction laborers' wages at the 10th percentile of wages in the sector still points to a large wage gap. In 2012, construction laborers in Nevada at the 10th percentile earned $80.32 a day, more than five times the average level in Mexico. Similar gaps in wages persist in the hospitality and service sectors in Mexico and Nevada.

Moreover, working conditions in some sectors in the Silver State have benefited from unionization. In Las Vegas, for example, Culinary Union Local 226 has a membership base of 60,000 workers, of which 45 percent are Latino. Significantly, the union estimates that a large share of its Latino membership is comprised of immigrants.[31] The economic security provided by the union is an important contextual factor for understanding why Las Vegas is often a destination city for Latin American immigrants. As Arguëllo-Kline commented: "When I moved to Las Vegas…my parents, they had already moved before me, and my brother, too…My father worked as a kitchen worker in Harrah's and my mother worked as a GRA [guest room attendant] in the Las Vegas Hilton…They only tell you, you know what? Get a union job; that's it. That was my thing; I had to be in a place where they had a union. I went to work as a guest room attendant. I cleaned rooms. I cleaned the toilets. I did my job. I feel very good about having a job where we can provide for our families and we can have health benefits for our families and everything. That's why I saw the difference between Florida and Las Vegas, different completely, the standard. I stayed in Vegas."[32]

The Culinary Union raised wages and provided health insurance and other benefits for its members, and the union's efforts have also had "spill-over" effects on wage determination in other nonunion firms in the sector.[33] Thus, even if Latin American immigrants in the Las Vegas hospitality sector are not members of the Culinary Union (or other trade unions), they may still be experiencing a higher wage floor because of the efforts of the union throughout the sector.

Finally, particularly in the Las Vegas metropolitan area, a variety of different social and economic organizations have eased the transition for immigrants. For example, a number of Mexican "hometown" associations in Las Vegas are organized around the state of origin for Mexican immigrants. The largest association is comprised of immigrants from the state of Michoacán, while smaller clubs represent Mexican immigrants from the states of Jalisco, Zacatecas, Chihuahua, Durango, and several others.[34] Likewise, the Guatemalan Unity Committee (COMUGUA) is the principal association for Guatemalan immigrants working in Las Vegas.[35] In some cases, hometown associations have coordinated their activities with the Roman Catholic Church (and its charitable institutions, such as the Catholic Charities of Southern Nevada, which provides immigration

FIGURE 2.4. Interstate Migration in Nevada (All Groups)

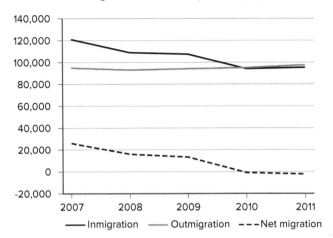

Source: US Census Bureau's American Community Survey 1-percent Public Use Microdata Sample (PUMS)

services) and other religious organizations. Through their activities, immigrant associations, the church, and other religious organizations not only prevent the cultural isolation of people from Mexico and Central America, but they also help individuals connect with consular officials and provide other forms of social assistance (e.g., classes in English and counseling).[36] In addition, a variety of retail businesses market food and other products to Latin American immigrants, while many financial institutions provide a secure means for individuals to send remittances to their country of origin. Collectively, the immigrant clubs, religious organizations, retail businesses, and other informal networks represent social capita that has reduced social isolation and, to varying degrees, helped Latin American immigrants make the transition to working and living in Las Vegas, and in Nevada more generally.

Interstate Migration Patterns among Nevada and other States and the US

Next, we examine migration patterns among Latinos in Nevada and in other US states.[37] We are particularly interested in how the emergence of the Great Recession might have influenced interstate migration flows. As illustrated in figure 2.4, during the time period under investigation, the

FIGURE 2.5. Interstate Migration Index in Nevada (Base Year, 2007=100)

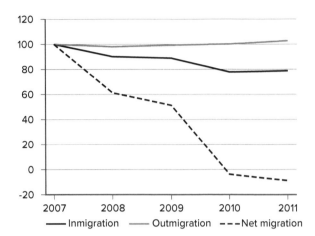

Source: US Census Bureau's American Community Survey 1-percent Public Use Microdata Sample (PUMS)

total number of migrants moving to Nevada from other states decreased sharply (going from 120,900 in 2007 to 94,100 in 2010), with a slight rebound in 2011. During the same period, the number of outmigrants from Nevada to other states increased modestly, reaching a peak of almost 100,000 in 2011. The net change caused by interstate migration, which is measured by subtracting migration inflows from outflows, shows that Nevada's migration flow switched from a net gain to loss. Most notably, in 2007, Nevada registered a net migration inflow of 26,000, but by 2011 more people migrated out of Nevada than migrated to the state (2,300 net change for 2011).

To better investigate the temporal trend in net migration flows, we present a net migration index with a base year of 2007 (2007 = 100). The index (fig. 2.5) exhibits patterns of change relative to the base year, 2007, which is also the year when Nevada's housing sector (and economy, more generally) began to decline.

The data presented in figure 2.5 indicate that from 2007 to 2010 there was a 22.2 percent decline in migration into Nevada, while outmigration began to increase in 2008 before eventually peaking in 2011 (with a 2.8 percent increase over the base year of 2007). As a consequence of decreased migration to Nevada and increased migration out of the state, the index

FIGURE 2.6. Interstate Migration of the Latino Population in Nevada, 2007–2011

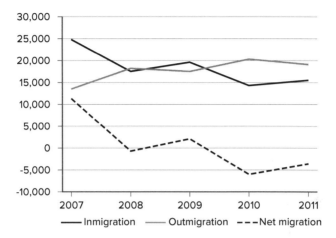

Source: US Census Bureau's American Community Survey 1-percent Public Use Microdata Sample (PUMS)

for net population change because of migration dropped significantly to its lowest point in 2011 (8.8 percent).

Interstate Migration Patterns for the US-Born Latino Population

The data presented in figures 2.4 and 2.5 are consistent with the notion that the Great Recession and the resulting economic strife simultaneously deterred migration into Nevada and caused more Nevadans to migrate out of state. As we note in the opening of this chapter and demonstrate in subsequent chapters, there is ample reason to expect that the economic downturn hit the state's Latino population particularly hard. As a consequence, it might be that Latinos, both US and foreign born, who were unable to find work in Nevada, migrated from the state, while the state's fragile economy deterred other Latinos from migrating to Nevada.

The data presented in figures 2.6 and 2.7 are consistent with these expectations, particularly during the years immediately after the onset of the recession. Specifically, as figure 2.6 makes clear, from 2007 to 2008, the total number of native- and foreign-born Latinos moving to Nevada from other US states declined by 7,300, which is equivalent to a 29.4 percent

FIGURE 2.7. Interstate Migration Index of the Latino Population in Nevada (Base Year, 2007=100)

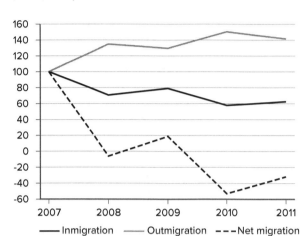

Source: US Census Bureau's American Community Survey 1-percent Public Use Microdata Sample (PUMS)

annual decrease in Latino migration to Nevada. The comparable figure for the state's entire population was a decrease of 10 percent (fig. 2.4). The number of Latinos migrating to Nevada continued to decline through 2010 before increasing slightly in 2011 (fig. 2.6). At the same time, migration of Latinos from Nevada to other states increased from 2007 to a peak of 20,300 in 2010.

As a consequence of these trends, the net Latino population change because of interstate migration shifted from a net gain of 11,300 in 2007, to a net *loss* of 700 in 2008. Continuing low levels of Latino in-migration and high levels of outmigration contributed to a 6,000 net migration decrease among Latinos out of Nevada in 2010. In the following year, the net loss fell to 3,600 because of the 8.4 percent uptick in the number of Latinos migrating into Nevada and the 5.9 percent decrease in migration from Nevada compared to 2010.

Figure 2.7 presents the change in Latino migration to Nevada relative to the base year of 2007. As can be seen from the figure, from 2007 to 2010, the index for Latino migration into Nevada fell continuously to 57.7 in 2010, indicating a 42.3 percent decline over the three-year period. The index for Latino outmigration from Nevada skyrocketed from 2007 to 2008 by 34.8 percent. The index of outmigration peaked at 150.4 in 2010,

FIGURE 2.8. Interstate Migration of the Foreign-Born Latino Population in Nevada, 2007–2011

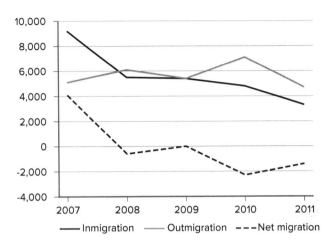

Source: US Census Bureau's American Community Survey 1-percent Public Use Microdata Sample (PUMS)

indicating a 50.4 percent increase over 2007. How did this affect the net flow? The index for net migration change plunged to its lowest point (53.1) in 2010. Although the net index value remained negative in 2011, the value was smaller compared to the value in 2010, suggesting migration flows among Latinos may be stabilizing.

Interstate Migration Patterns of Foreign-Born Latino Population in Nevada

In this section, we replicate the analysis presented in the previous two sections on interstate migration, but limit our data to Nevada's foreign-born Latino population. It is important to note that there is a significant limitation to these data in that they only allow us to capture population exchanges among localities within the US (the ACS count in-migration from foreign countries but do not consider outmigration to foreign countries).

Figure 2.8 presents the trend in the total annual migration into Nevada among foreign-born Latinos. From 2007 to 2008, the total number of foreign-born Latino migrants from other US states to Nevada fell from 9,200 to 5,500. Comparing these declines to those for Nevada's total population (fig. 2.4) and native-born/naturalized Latino migrants (fig. 2.6) indicates that the reduction in the number of foreign-born Latino migrants

FIGURE 2.9. Interstate Migration Index of the Foreign-Born Latino Population in Nevada (Base Year, 2007=100)

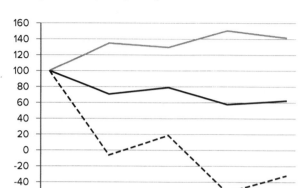

Source: US Census Bureau's American Community Survey 1-percent Public Use Microdata Sample (PUMS)

to Nevada was far larger than for these other groups. After 2008, the number of foreign-born Latinos migrating to Nevada continued to fall, reaching a low of 3,300 in 2011.

In contrast to the steady decline of foreign-born Latinos to Nevada, annual levels of migration from Nevada fluctuated from 2007 to 2011. Outmigration peaked at 7,100 in 2010. The biggest annual increase in outmigration occurred from 2009 to 2010, while the largest decline was from 2010 to 2011.

There was a net decline in migration among the foreign-born Latino population. Although the net flow was 4,100 in 2007, this changed to a net loss of 600 in 2008 (fig. 2.9). Persistent levels of migration from Nevada among foreign-born Latinos, coupled with low (and declining) levels of in-migration for this group, led to net losses of foreign-born Latino migrants in 2008, 2010, and 2011. In 2011, the net loss of 1,400 was smaller than in the previous year (2,300 in 2010), mainly because of a stabilization in the number of foreign-born Latinos migrating elsewhere.

Looking at the index of migration, one sees that migration into Nevada among foreign-born Latinos contracted by 40.2 percent from 2007 to 2008 (fig. 2.9), with the overall index declining by 64 percent from 2007 to 2011. Again, this trend suggests the foreign-born Latino population residing in other US states faced strong disincentives to migrate to Nevada.

The index of outmigration for foreign-born Latinos fluctuated annually from 2007 to 2011. The index reached its peak of 139.2 in 2010, equivalent to a 39.2 percent increase in outmigration compared to 2007. The index for net population change dropped to its lowest point of 56.1 percent in 2010. Compared to migration for all Latinos, migration from Nevada among foreign-born Latinos was less volatile, while migration into the state exhibited a rapid and consistent decline. This finding suggests that under conditions of economic turmoil, the foreign-born Latino population is less mobile compared to the total Latino population. The lack of economic resources for foreign-born Latinos—likely the result of a legacy of working in low-paid, precarious, and segmented labor markets—may explain part of this pattern.

Nevada's State Migration Partners for Interstate Migration of Latinos

Thus far, we have examined continuities and changes in migration patterns in Nevada. We turn now to an analysis of the US states that served as the major migration "partners" for Nevada. These data are presented in tables 2.5 (for migration into Nevada) and 2.6 (for migration from Nevada). For the entire study period, 2007–2011, California remained the top US state of origin for all the migrants to Nevada. Arizona ranked second in four of the five years, while Texas was second in one year, 2007. Still, the relative contribution of these second-ranked "sending" states never exceeded 10 percent of the total population migrating to Nevada.

California also served as the top state of origin for Latino and foreign-born Latinos migrating to Nevada (middle and bottom panels of table 2.5). However, compared to all Latinos, a relatively larger share of foreign-born Latinos who migrated to Nevada originated from California. The only exception to this trend occurred in 2010, when 55.9 percent of Latinos migrating into Nevada resided in California during the prior year, while the corresponding figure for the foreign-born Latino population was 50 percent. In addition, for each year from 2007 to 2010, the percentage of all migrants and foreign-born Latino migrants originating in California

TABLE 2.5. Top States of Origin for Migrants into Nevada, 2007–2011

Rank	2007 State	2007 Share	2008 State	2008 Share	2009 State	2009 Share	2010 State	2010 Share	2011 State	2011 Share
All Migrants										
1	CA	40.8%	CA	35.4%	CA	34.0%	CA	32.4%	CA	38.5%
2	TX	5.2%	AZ	5.2%	AZ	7.5%	AZ	8.5%	AZ	6.4%
3	AZ	5.1%	FL	4.3%	UT	5.2%	TX	6.0%	TX	5.5%
4	MI	4.0%	TX	4.3%	FL	4.5%	UT	4.4%	WA	4.5%
5	NY	3.9%	OH	3.9%	TX	4.3%	HI	3.4%	ID	4.0%
All Latinos										
1	CA	62.9%	CA	48.6%	CA	52.6%	CA	55.9%	CA	58.7%
2	TX	8.5%	TX	12.6%	AZ	8.7%	AZ	14.7%	AZ	8.4%
3	AZ	5.2%	AZ	4.6%	IL	6.6%	FL	4.2%	TX	6.5%
3			FL	4.6%			TX	4.2%		
Foreign-Born Latinos										
1	CA	66.3%	CA	54.5%	CA	53.7%	CA	50.0%	CA	72.7%
2	AZ	8.7%	FL	10.9%	AZ	7.4%	AZ	20.8%		
3	TX	6.5%	TX	9.1%	IL	7.4%	NJ	10.4%		
4					AZ	5.8%				

Note: US Census Bureau's ACS 1-Percent Public Use Microdata Sample (PUMS)

fell, while the trend was much shorter for native-born/naturalized Latinos (the percentage fell 2007–2008, but rebounded in 2009).

Texas, Florida, and Arizona were also second-ranked states of origin for the Latino and foreign-born Latino in-migrant population. Two unusual observations stand out, however. First, in 2010, Arizona accounted for 20.8 percent of the foreign-born Latinos who migrated to Nevada. Second, in 2011, no state other than California accounted for more than 3 percent of the foreign-born Latino population migrating to Nevada.

The data also reveal that California remained the top destination state for all three groups (table 2.6). Perhaps because of weak economic conditions in Southern California, the share of each group migrating from Nevada to California declined in 2010, but then rebounded as the economy began to recover. Compared to the total population migrating out of Nevada, a relatively larger share of Latino and foreign-born Latinos selected California as a destination state each year in the study period. This pattern may be a consequence of the prevalence of demand for low-skilled

TABLE 2.6. Top Destination States for Migrants from Nevada, 2007–2011

	2007		2008		2009		2010		2011	
Rank	State	Share	State	Share	State	Share	State	Share	State	Share
All Migrants										
1	CA	25.6%	CA	29.1%	CA	29.9%	CA	25.0%	CA	30.9%
2	AZ	7.8%	AZ	8.2%	AZ	6.8%	AZ	8.9%	AZ	6.6%
3	WA	6.1%	UT	7.2%	TX	6.7%	TX	5.9%	WA	6.4%
4	TX	5.9%	TX	5.3%	UT	4.7%	WA	5.9%	TX	5.3%
5	CO	5.0%	CO	4.2%	CO	4.1%	UT	5.3%	CO	4.6%
All Latinos										
1	CA	43.7%	CA	43.4%	CA	40.0%	CA	36.9%	CA	52.9%
2	AZ	12.6%	TX	11.0%	AZ	13.7%	AZ	9.4%	TX	8.4%
3	NM	9.6%	UT	8.2%	TX	7.4%	TX	7.4%	WA	7.9%
4	WA	7.4%	WA	5.5%	CO	5.7%	WA	5.4%	AZ	5.8%
Foreign-Born Latinos										
1	CA	45.1%	CA	47.5%	CA	46.3%	CA	36.6%	CA	42.6%
2	AZ	15.7%	TX	11.5%	CO	9.3%	AZ	11.3%	TX	14.9%
3	WA	9.8%	AZ	8.2%	AZ	7.4%	FL	8.5%	AZ	12.8%
4	OR	5.9%	FL	8.2%	IL	7.4%	NY	7.0%	WA	8.5%
5			NJ	8.2%	LA	5.6%	OK	5.6%	FL	6.4%
5					TX	5.6%	OR	5.6%		
5					WA	5.6%				

Source: US Census Bureau's ACS 1-Percent Public Use Microdata Sample (PUMS)

labor, perhaps aided by the state's proximity to Nevada and the presence of migration networks.[38]

Beyond California, several other states served as frequent destinations for migrants from Nevada. For the total population, Arizona consistently ranked as the second-place destination state. The data suggest that Texas, Utah, and Washington were also common destination states. For Latino outmigrants, Arizona, Texas, and Washington were also major migration partner states, with Arizona being the largest partner (after California) with 13.7 percent of Latinos migrating there in 2009.[39] The pattern is similar, but less clear for foreign-born Latinos. Texas and Arizona each accounted for approximately 15 percent of the destination states for foreign-born Latinos in certain years—although for Arizona, the peak (15.7 percent) was in 2007, *before* the recession.

Discussion

This chapter contributes to the research on the demography of Nevada by investigating trends in the Latino population in the state. The findings suggest that the Latino population experienced steady growth since 1980, although annual growth rates slowed somewhat from 2007 to 2011 because of the Great Recession. In addition, the findings suggest that the Latino population is a relatively young population, with close to half of the group (48 percent) aged 24 years old or younger. As with other minority population groups in the state, Latinos are concentrated in Clark and Washoe Counties, with the vast majority in Clark and residing in the Las Vegas metropolitan area.

This chapter also determined that with the onset of the Great Recession, the patterns of interstate migration among all Latinos in Nevada (both native- and foreign-born) changed in the early part of economic recovery. Both groups saw the largest one-year loss in net migration 2007–2008. The net interstate migration flow turned negative for both the native Latino and foreign-born Latino population by 2008. There was a slight recovery (i.e., a reduction in the net loss to migration) from 2010 to 2011. Yet, despite the similarity in the recovery for Latinos and foreign-born Latinos, the sources of the recovery for each group were quite different. For native-born Latinos, the stabilization in the migration flow was associated with a slight increase in immigration to Nevada and a slight outmigration from the state. However, among foreign-born Latinos, migration to Nevada continually declined, which was offset partly by a large reduction in outmigration in 2011. The underlying reason for the variation in the interstate migration behavior between these two groups remains unclear, but it might reflect the greater sensitivity of foreign-born Latinos to conditions in Nevada's housing sector (and other low-skilled employment sectors), along with greater resource constraints for foreign-born migrants who may otherwise have left Nevada.

Additionally, Nevada has remained attractive to immigrants from Mexico and other parts of Latin America because of a relative abundance of jobs that are well matched to the levels of education attainment and skill among immigrants. This includes employment in the service industry, wholesale and retail trade, and (historically) in construction. Nevada is also attractive because of the average level of remuneration in sectors where immigrants tend to work, along with the effects of various civic and religious groups that have tended to reduce the social isolation of Latin American immigrants in the state. At the same time, California remained the largest migration partner state for all groups of interstate migrants in Nevada. This suggests that there was some continuity in trends before and after the recession. However, as noted, in comparison to the total migration group, larger shares of native-born and foreign-born Latinos migrated from California, or selected California as a destination state.

Looking forward, immigration flows to Nevada are likely to continue over the short-to-medium term, although growth rates may be lower than they were in the mid-2000s. The Great Recession clearly resulted in large dislocations among immigrant workers in residential construction, hospitality, and other associated sectors, but economic recovery in these branches of the Nevadan economy resumed until the emergence of the 2020 recession, which suggests that any recent reduction in net migration flows to Nevada from Latin America may have been temporary during the last decade.

CHAPTER 3

Political Profile

Over the course of the past two decades, Nevada's Latino population has grown appreciably. As discussed in the preceding chapter, immigrants from Mexico and other parts of Latin America accounted for most of the growth in the state's Latino population during this period. Nevertheless, the number of US native-born and naturalized Latinos residing in Nevada has also increased, and this growth has altered the political landscape of the state. Indeed, the number of Latinos in the Nevada Legislature expanded steadily from 2001 to 2011 (fig. 3.1). And while recent studies have pointed to the potential significance of Nevada's growing Latino electorate, its influence on Latino political participation in the state remain poorly understood.[1]

In this chapter, we attempt to fill this gap by developing a political profile of Nevada's Latino community. We begin by examining how two important electoral institutions— redistricting and term limits—affected Latino representation from 2000 to 2013. Next, we present aggregate data detailing election turnout patterns for Nevada's Latino voters from 2000 through 2012. The third part of our analysis offers an individual-level examination of Latino participation in the 2012 election, including analysis of presidential vote preferences by gender, age, education, and income, as well as an assessment of the geography of the Latino electorate in Clark County. We conclude by examining how increased participation and mobilization of Nevada's Latino community has reshaped Nevada's political landscape. The appendix provides an overview of the data sources, including discussions of the methodological issues that the use of these data raises.

FIGURE 3.1. Number of Latinos Serving in the Nevada Legislature, 2001–2013

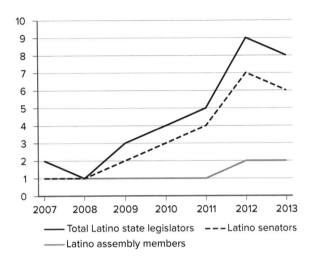

Source: The National Conference of State Legislatures, "Legislator & Legislative Staff Information"

The Institutional Context:
The Impact of Redistricting and Term Limits

Perhaps the most obvious indicator of the increased electoral weight of Nevada's Latino community can be gleaned from a comparison of the 2001 and 2011 reapportionment and redistricting processes. In 2001, despite an energetic lobbying effort by Latino activists on behalf of the almost 20 percent of Nevadans who were classified as Latino (according to the 2000 US Census), Latinos received very little consideration in the final maps of the Nevada Legislature and US House of Representatives that were used during the 2002–2010 elections.[2] Ten years later, however, with Latinos constituting approximately 26.5 percent of Nevada's population, partisan differences regarding how to ensure Latino representation caused Nevada's 2011 reapportionment and redistricting process to be completed in state court.[3] Compared to the outcome in 2001, the growth of the Latino population, and the concentration of this population in the state's two urban counties (Clark and Washoe), meant that actors in the 2011 redistricting

TABLE 3.1. Latino Composition of Nevada's US House of Representatives Districts, 2012

District	Location	Latino Population	Latino Population—Voting Age
1	Clark (Part)[1]	42.77%	36.58%
2	Washoe and Rural[2]	20.43%	16.60%
3	Clark (Part)	15.66%	22.93%
4	Clark and Rural[3]	26.63%	22.33%

Source: "United States House of Representatives Plan—Special Masters—October 14, 2011 Population Report," Dec. 2011. https://www.leg.state.nv.us/Division/Research /Districts/Reapp/2011/Proposals/Masters/CON-Masters-Tables.pdf

[1] Part refers to parts of Clark County, but not its entirety

[2] Washoe and Rural includes Washoe, Carson City, Churchill, Douglas, Elko, Eureka, Humboldt, Lander, Lyon (part), Pershing, Storey

[3] Clark and Rural includes Clark (part), Esmeralda, Lincoln, Lyon (part), Mineral, Nye, White Pine

TABLE 3.2. Percentage of the Latino Voting-Age Population Relative to the Total Voting-Age Population in the State Legislative Districts, 2012

Chamber	Less than 15%	15.1%–30%	30.1%–45%	More than 45.1%
Senate (n = 21)	9	7	4	1
Assembly (n = 42)	14	19	6	3

Source: Data from 1. "Senate Plan—Special Masters V2—October 26, 2011 Population," Dec. 2011. https://www.leg.state.nv.us/Division/Research/Districts/Reapp/2011/Final /Senate/SEN2011_Tables.pdf

2. "Assembly Plan – Special Masters V2 – Oct. 26, 2011 Population, Dec. 2011. https://www.leg.state.nv.us/Division/Research/Districts/Reapp/2011/Final/Assembly /ASM2011_Tables.pdf

process faced strong pressures to be responsive to Nevada's Latino community. Data in tables 3.1 and 3.2 illustrate this point.

Using data from the 2010 US Census, tables 3.1 and 3.2 summarize the Latino population share for Nevada's four US House of Representatives districts and its twenty-one Senate and forty-two Assembly districts in the Nevada Legislature, respectively. These tables clearly indicate that going forward, Nevada's Latinos are positioned to influence the winners and losers of a large number of seats in the Nevada Legislature and, to a lesser extent, outcomes in Nevada's first, third, and fourth US House districts.

Another institutional factor, term limits, which were imposed on the Nevada Legislature after the 2009 session, has facilitated increased representation of Latino interests in the Nevada Legislature. As figure 3.1 details, before the implementation of term limits, the number of Latinos serving in the Nevada Legislature was five. Once terms limits went into effect, a number of veteran legislators who represented districts with a heavy concentration of Latinos were precluded from running for reelection and were replaced, in a number of instances, by Latinos, many of whom were first-time candidates. As a consequence, the number of Latinos serving in the Nevada Legislature increased to nine during the 2011 session. After the 2012 election, a total of eight state legislators were Latino; two Latinos were serving in the Senate, while six members were in the Assembly.[4] In addition, two of Nevada's constitutional offices have been held by politicians with Latino roots: Governor Brian Sandoval, elected to the first of two terms in 2010, and Attorney General Catherine Cortez Masto, who was first elected in 2006 and reelected in 2010. Cortez Masto served as attorney general until 2015, and in 2016 she was elected to the US Senate, becoming that body's first Latina. Still, even with this increase in Latino representation, during the 2013 legislative session Latino representation lagged significantly behind population share. Moreover, in 2013, only one Latino presently serving in the Nevada Legislature represented a district with a Latino voting-age population that is less than 20 percent.[5] Thus, redistricting and term limits, coupled with Nevada's demographic change, have increased the opportunities for Latino representation in state government. Yet, the number of Latinos elected to office remains well below the community's share of Nevada's population.

Latino Voter Turnout

While the reelections of US Senate Majority Leader Harry Reid in 2010 and President Barack Obama in 2012 demonstrated to the national audience the importance of the Latino vote in Nevada, the results of these contests were a continuation, rather than the beginning, of efforts to mobilize and engage the state's Latino community in the electoral process.[6]

Starting in the late 1990s, the Nevada Democratic Party, organized labor, and community organizations (e.g., the Latin Chamber of Commerce, Hispanics in Politics, and clubs representing Mexican and Latin

FIGURE 3.2. Exit Poll Estimates of the Racial and Ethnic Composition of the Nevada Electorate, 2000–2012

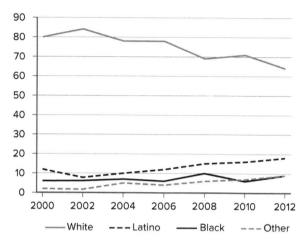

Source: Data from the Voter News Service (2000 and 2002) and National Election Pool Exit Polls (2004–2012) for Nevada

FIGURE 3.3. Current Population Survey Estimates of Latino Electoral Participation, 2000–2012

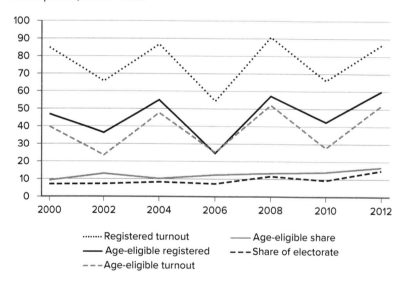

Source: 2000, 2002, 2004, 2006, 2008, 2010, and 2012 Current Population Survey by the Bureau of Labor Statistics and the US Census Bureau

American immigrants) began efforts to register and turn out Latinos who had previously been unengaged in politics. Subsequently, following the Las Vegas immigration protests in 2006, a number of groups in Southern Nevada attempted to sustain the political momentum generated by the demonstrations by urging eligible Latinos to register and vote.[7]

The data in figure 3.2, which summarize the racial and ethnic components of the Nevada electorate using exit poll data from 2000 through 2012, indicate that the result of these efforts was a gradual increase in the Latino share of the electorate. During this period, the proportion of the Nevada electorate that self-identified as Latino increased from 12 percent in 2000 to 18 percent in 2012.

Commensurate with this increase, as well as increased turnout among other minority groups, the White share of the vote in Nevada decreased from 80 percent in 2000 to 64 percent in 2012.

To be sure, the growth in the size of the Latino electorate is notable. However, as the data presented in figures 3.3 and 3.4 suggest, despite these increases, there is a large reservoir of untapped Latino voters. Specifically, figure 3.3 uses data from the election-year Current Population Surveys (CPS) to estimate a number of indicators of Latino electoral participation: the Latino share of the age-eligible population; Latino registration and turnout relative to age-eligible population; turnout among registered Latinos; and the Latino share of the electorate.

As the data in figure 3.3 indicate, Latinos who registered to vote turned out at rates ranging from 54 percent in 2006 to a remarkable 91 percent in 2008. While these values offer an optimistic view of Latino electoral participation, they are somewhat misleading as they only consider turnout among registered voters. Inspection of the share of age-eligible Latinos who registered to vote suggests that registration among eligible Latinos exceeded 50 percent for the 2004, 2008, and 2012 presidential elections, but is much lower for the midterm elections.

As a consequence, the age-eligible turnout ranges from a low of 23 percent in 2002 to a high of 52 percent in 2008 and 2012. Or put differently, in only two of the six elections during the period studied did more than half of Nevada's age-eligible Latinos vote.

The bottom two lines, which capture the Latino age-eligible population and the share of the overall electorate that was Latino, indicate that Latino turnout lags behind population share in the midterm elections but narrows for presidential elections.

FIGURE 3.4. Difference Between Vote Share and Age-Eligible Share by Race, 2000–2012

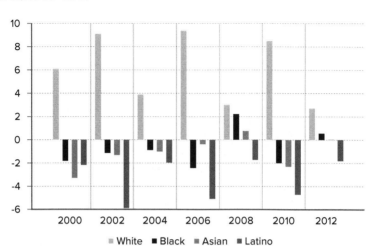

Source: 2000, 2002, 2004, 2006, 2008, 2010, and 2012 Current Population Survey by the Bureau of Labor Statistics and the US Census Bureau

To further assess these dynamics, figure 3.4 compares the difference between the share of the electorate and the age-eligible population for Whites, Blacks, Asians, and Latinos for 2000–2012 elections using the Current Population Survey data. These data allow us to evaluate the degree to which different racial and ethnic groups vote relative to their population shares. Consistent with national patterns, figure 3.4 makes clear that, on average, Whites constitute 7 percent more of the Nevada electorate than their share of the population because of their higher registration and turnout levels relative to non-Whites, particularly during midterm elections. In contrast, for most of the elections examined here, the participation of Blacks, Asians, and Latinos lags relative to each groups' share of the voting-age population. However, these differences decrease during presidential elections and in the 2012 election, as Blacks and Asians voted at levels equivalent to their share of the state's population, while the Latino vote lagged less than 2 percent behind the Latino population share.

Thus, the degree to which the preferences of White voters differ from those of other racial and ethnic groups means that White voters are exerting outsized influence on electoral outcomes in Nevada, particularly during midterm elections, even as the White share of the electorate decreases.

The 2012 Election: Taking a Closer Look

The discussion presented above allows us to assess the contours of Nevada's Latino political participation in broad strokes. Lacking from this analysis, however, is any sense of individual-level difference in Latino electoral participation in Nevada. Fortunately, for the 2012 election we were able to analyze individual-level survey data from the Nevada subsample of the *impreMedia/Latino Decisions* Election Eve Poll, which surveyed 400 Latinos in Nevada who either voted early or indicated that they were sure to vote on Election Day, to more finely parse variation in the Latino vote.

We begin by considering the partisan self-identification of Latinos who voted (or were likely to vote) in Nevada during the 2012 presidential election (fig. 3.5). Two-thirds of the sample reported that they generally think of themselves as Democrats compared to 16 percent self-identifying as Republicans. Also note that Latino voters were more likely to identify as either nonpartisans or with a minor party rather than identifying with the GOP. Not surprisingly, the Democratic registration advantage translated into significant support for President Obama in November as Obama won the votes of 80 percent of Nevada's Latinos (including 27 percent of self-identified Republicans) compared to 17 percent for Republican Mitt Romney.

As figure 3.5 makes clear, across every subcategory, Obama won comfortably. Of particular note is the almost equivalent support for Obama among male and female Latinos. Polling conducted by *Latino Decisions* in June and October suggested a small gender gap, but this did not come to fruition in November.

The vote distributions for income and education highlighted the president's overwhelming support among lower-income and less-educated Latinos. Perhaps the one bit of good news for the Republicans was found among higher-income Latinos.[8] While Obama won every income category, his margin decreased among those with family incomes greater than $60,000. Unfortunately for Republicans, just more than 20 percent of Nevada Latinos who voted in 2012 had household incomes above that level. Romney's vote share also increased among the 36 percent of the Latino electorate with some post–high school education.

Lastly, figure 3.5 suggests troubling long-term prospects for the Republican Party in Nevada. Latinos who were 29 years old or younger were the least likely to support Romney among all age groups. Moreover, not only did this cohort constitute almost a quarter of the Latino electorate, these

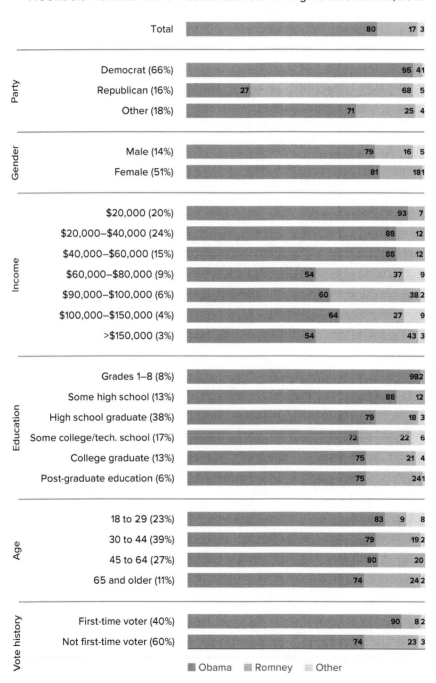

FIGURE 3.5. Variation in the Presidential Vote among Nevada Latinos, 2012

		Obama	Romney	Other
	Total	80	17	3
Party	Democrat (66%)	95	4	1
	Republican (16%)	27	68	5
	Other (18%)	71	25	4
Gender	Male (14%)	79	16	5
	Female (51%)	81	18	1
Income	$20,000 (20%)	93	7	
	$20,000–$40,000 (24%)	88	12	
	$40,000–$60,000 (15%)	88	12	
	$60,000–$80,000 (9%)	54	37	9
	$90,000–$100,000 (6%)	60	38	2
	$100,000–$150,000 (4%)	64	27	9
	>$150,000 (3%)	54	43	3
Education	Grades 1–8 (8%)	98	2	
	Some high school (13%)	88	12	
	High school graduate (38%)	79	18	3
	Some college/tech. school (17%)	72	22	6
	College graduate (13%)	75	21	4
	Post-graduate education (6%)	75	24	1
Age	18 to 29 (23%)	83	9	8
	30 to 44 (39%)	79	19	2
	45 to 64 (27%)	80	20	
	65 and older (11%)	74	24	2
Vote history	First-time voter (40%)	90	8	2
	Not first-time voter (60%)	74	23	3

■ Obama ■ Romney ▨ Other

Source: Nevada subsample of the impreMedia/Latino Decisions Election Eve Poll

voters were more than five and half times as likely to identify themselves as Democrats than Republicans. The patterns are even more lopsided for first-time voters, who accounted for 40 percent of the 2012 Latino turnout in Nevada. These voters supported President Obama at a 90 percent clip and were more than nine times more likely to self-identify as Democrats than Republicans.

In thinking about the long-term implications of these results, it is worth recalling that in 2011 approximately 48 percent of all Latinos in Nevada were 24 years old or younger (and 86 percent of this age group were born in the US).[9] If younger Latinos continue to show such a strong preference for the Democratic Party, Republicans will face an increasingly challenging environment as greater numbers of young Latinos enter Nevada's electorate.

While the data presented in figure 3.5 offer insight into variation in the voting preferences of the Latino electorate, figures 3.6 and 3.7 capture the geography of the 2012 Latino vote in Southern Nevada, which is home to roughly 80 percent of Nevada's Latino population. Specifically, each figure maps the share of the Latino voting-age population and the Latino turnout in each state Assembly (fig. 3.6) and state Senate (fig. 3.7) district in Clark County. Inspection of these figures reveals an interesting dynamic: in areas with a high concentration of voting-age Latinos (the dark-shaded districts in the top panels of figs. 3.6 and 3.7), turnout is low (the light-shaded districts in the bottom panels of figs. 3.6 and 3.7), while in areas with low concentrations of voting-age Latinos (the light-shaded districts in the top panels of figs. 3.6 and 3.7), turnout is much higher (the dark-shaded districts in the bottom panels of figs. 3.6 and 3.7).

As such, these data suggest two important aspects of Latino political participation in Nevada. First, patterns of Latino turnout are similar to other racial and ethnic groups. That is, assuming that areas in the urban core with high concentrations of voting-age Latinos tend to be populated by lower socioeconomic status Latinos and the suburbs tend to be home to higher socioeconomic status Latinos, then not surprisingly we find, all else equal, significantly higher Latino turnout in the suburbs. Second, the figures reiterate the point made above that even though electoral participation among Nevada's Latino population has increased in recent elections, a significant share of the age-eligible Latino population, particularly in areas with high concentrations of Latinos, remains untapped.

MAP 3.1. Voting-Age Population and Latino-Voter Turnout in Clark County Assembly Districts, 2012

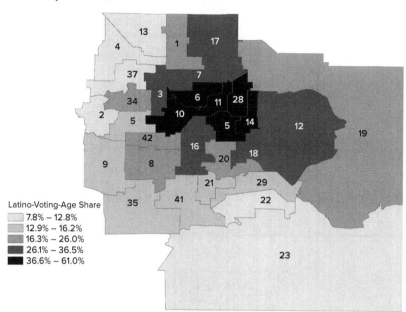

Latino-Voting-Age Share
- 7.8% – 12.8%
- 12.9% – 16.2%
- 16.3% – 26.0%
- 26.1% – 36.5%
- 36.6% – 61.0%

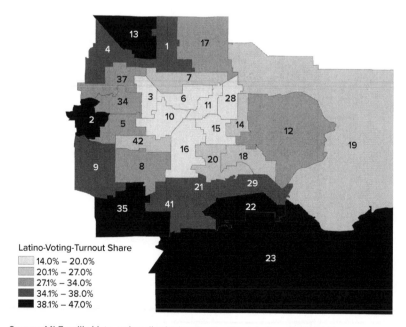

Latino-Voting-Turnout Share
- 14.0% – 20.0%
- 20.1% – 27.0%
- 27.1% – 34.0%
- 34.1% – 38.0%
- 38.1% – 47.0%

Source: Mi Familia Vota, using district level voter file data from NGP VAN

FIGURE 3.6. Perceptions of Obama's and Romney's Attitudes toward the Latino Community and Impact of Immigration-Related Issues on Enthusiasm for Obama and Romney among Nevada Latino Voters, 2012

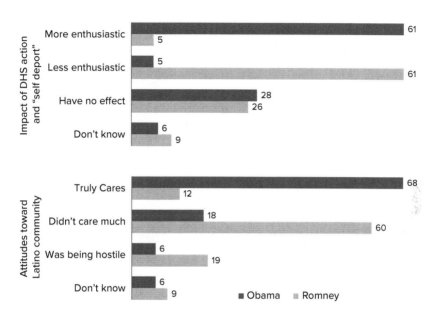

Source: Nevada subsample of the impreMedia/Latino Decisions Election Eve Poll

Collectively, the data presented in figures 3.5, 3.6, and 3.7 allow us to determine the variation in participation across a number of demographic and geographic variables. Yet, these data do not explain why President Obama won the votes of so many Nevada Latinos.

The data presented in figures 3.8, 3.9, and 3.10 provide some understanding of the drivers of the Latino vote. We begin by considering the degree to which Obama and Romney were perceived as caring about the Latino community. Specifically, the top panel of figure 3.8 summarizes the responses to two questions relevant to this point.[10]

The first question on the survey asks respondents if Obama's decision in June 2012 to stop the Department of Homeland Security (DHS) from deporting undocumented youth who attend college or serve in the military and provide them with a renewable work permit made respondents more or less enthusiastic about Obama. The second assesses if Romney's campaign statement that immigrants who cannot legally work in the United States should "self-deport" affected voters' enthusiasm for Romney.

MAP 3.2. Voting-Age Population and Latino-Voter Turnout in Clark County Senate Districts, 2012

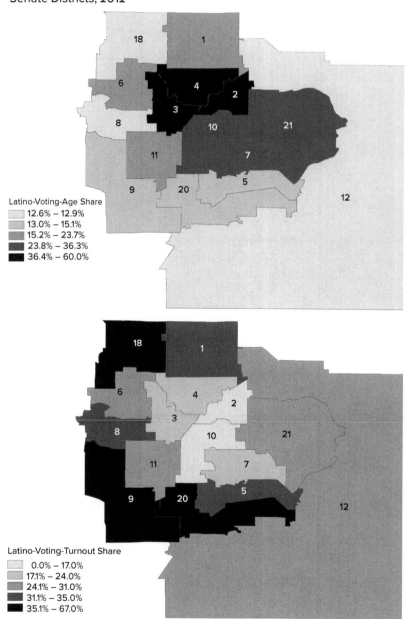

Latino-Voting-Age Share
- 12.6% – 12.9%
- 13.0% – 15.1%
- 15.2% – 23.7%
- 23.8% – 36.3%
- 36.4% – 60.0%

Latino-Voting-Turnout Share
- 0.0% – 17.0%
- 17.1% – 24.0%
- 24.1% – 31.0%
- 31.1% – 35.0%
- 35.1% – 67.0%

Source: Mi Familia Vota, using district level voter file data from NGP VAN

FIGURE 3.7. Policy Preferences of Nevada Latino Voters for Selective Issues, 2012

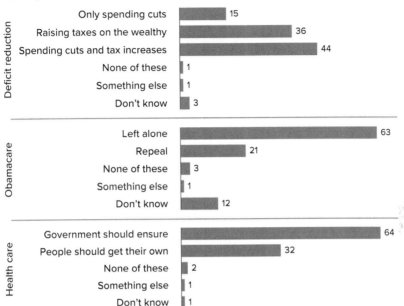

Source: Nevada subsample of the impreMedia/Latino Decisions Election Eve Poll

Obama's DHS action was quite popular among Latino voters; 61 percent of the sample indicated that the decision made them more enthusiastic about Obama. In contrast, the same share of respondents suggested that Romney's advocacy for "self-deportation" made them less enthusiastic about his candidacy. Not surprisingly, and as is summarized in the bottom panel of figure 3.8, almost four out of five Latino voters in Nevada saw Romney as either uncaring or hostile to the Latino community.

Just 12 percent responded that Romney truly cared about the Latino community. In contrast, 68 percent of voters perceived Obama as caring, with 18 percent responding that the president did not care much, and only 6 percent felt that Obama was hostile.

So while Romney did himself no favors among Latino voters in Nevada, there is also ample evidence that the Republican Party was out of step with the preference of the Latino community. Figure 3.9 summarizes respectively Nevada Latinos' preferences for deficit reduction, repealing the Patient Protection and Affordable Care Act ("Obamacare"), and the

FIGURE 3.8. Perceptions of the Most Important Problem Facing the Latino Community among Nevada Latino Voters, 2012

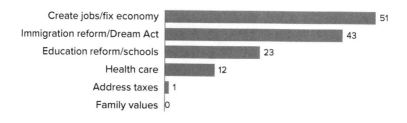

Create jobs/fix economy	51
Immigration reform/Dream Act	43
Education reform/schools	23
Health care	12
Address taxes	1
Family values	0

Source: Nevada subsample of the impreMedia/Latino Decisions Election Eve Poll

role of government in providing access to health care. For all three policies, the vast majority of Nevada Latinos held attitudes that are inconsistent with the policies advocated by the Republican Party.

In terms of deficit reduction, just 15 percent supported a solution that relies exclusively on spending cuts, 36 percent favored closing the deficit by raising taxes on the wealthy, and 44 percent preferred a combination of spending cuts and tax increases (the position Obama advocated during the campaign). The Patient Protection and Affordable Care Act was overwhelmingly popular among Nevada Latinos: 63 percent indicated that they wanted the law left as is, and only 21 percent favored its repeal.

Also, as is suggested by figure 3.9, twice as many Nevada Latinos supported a role for the federal government in ensuring universal access to health insurance rather than making individuals responsible for getting their own health insurance.

Throughout the 2012 election cycle, a common Republican refrain was that Latinos were a "natural" constituency for the GOP given the party's economic messages and its family values agenda (e.g., opposition to abortion and gay marriage). At least in Nevada, little evidence supports these claims. Specifically, figure 3.8 summarizes the responses to an open-ended question assessing the issues that Latino voters thought were the most important for their community.

Not surprisingly, economic issues and job creation were the primary concern of Latino voters, followed by immigration reform and passage of the DREAM (Development, Relief, and Education for Alien Minors) Act, and improving education, while health care was a distant fourth. Among voters who identified the economy and jobs as the most important issue, more than 77 percent self-reported a vote intention for Obama. Obama's vote share increased to 87 percent for those who identified immigration and passage of the DREAM Act as the Latino community's most important issue and 92 percent for voters concerned about education and schools. Also note how little resonance that family values (0 percent) and taxes (1 percent) have as political issues for Nevada Latinos. Beyond these results, little evidence suggests that parties emphasizing social issues will be more successful among Latin American *immigrants* who might become naturalized citizens.

For example, data from the Latino National Survey indicated that only 1 percent of Latin American immigrants residing in Nevada felt that family values/morality was the most important issue facing the Latino community. Significantly, in the same survey, no immigrant respondents rated abortion as the most important issue.[11]

In sum, based upon analysis of survey data from the 2012 election, the Republican Party had traction in few if any subpopulations in Nevada's Latino community. Much of the party's struggles with Latino voters in Nevada stemmed from the misalignment between the GOP's policy agenda and the preferences of most Latino voters in the state and the perceived insensitivity of the 2012 Republican presidential nominee, Mitt Romney, toward the state's Latino community. As noted in a later section of this chapter, the Republican Party's reputation with Latino voters in Nevada only worsened in the 2016 electoral cycle, when then-candidate Donald Trump employed unusually harsh rhetoric to characterize immigrants from Mexico and Central America. After his election, President Trump's repeated use of deprecatory language against immigrants continued to create deep concerns among Latinos.

Discussion

The above analysis has offered a profile of the Latino electorate in Nevada. The overall picture that emerges is of a voting group whose participation has gradually increased over the course of recent elections. Yet, despite these gains, a significant segment of Nevada's Latino population continues to be uninvolved in the political process.

Regarding the representation of Latino interests in Nevada's governing institutions, the number of Latinos elected to public office increased in recent election cycles, through 2013. However, much of the increase during this period was limited to the Nevada Legislature, as there were no Latinos serving on the powerful Clark County Commission, the Board of Regents, and the Clark County School District, and there were only two Latinos serving on the city councils for some of the state's largest cities, Las Vegas, Henderson, and North Las Vegas—all of which are in Southern Nevada. Since then, Latinos have maintained their presence in the Nevada Legislature, while making modest gains in the Clark County School District and the Reno City Council. Still, there is considerable room for improvement.

At the same time, as a consequence of the growth of the Latino community and the outcomes of the 2011 reapportionment and redistricting process, with additional electoral participation, Latinos are positioned to affect electoral outcomes up and down the ballot. Thus, regardless of their race, ethnicity, or partisanship, candidates competing for many local, state, and federal elective positions will need to be responsive to Latino interests if they hope to win and hold office. Moreover, the continued development of a Latino political infrastructure that is distinct from the Nevada Democratic Party and the service-based unions (e.g., Service Employees International Union and the Culinary Union Local 226) is producing a new generation of Latino leaders who are likely to run for elective offices in the near future.

Although Latino political development in Nevada has yet to be fully realized, there are clear indications that increased participation to date has had significant effects on Nevada's political environment, particularly in statewide races. Most notably, Nevada is one of four states (along with Colorado, Florida, and New Mexico) in 2012 where the Latino vote tipped the outcome for President Obama.[12] It is also unlikely that US Senate Majority Leader Harry Reid would have been reelected in 2010 without strong Latino turnout.[13]

As such, it can be safely argued that much of Nevada's Democratic tilt during the prior decade has been driven primarily by the Latino vote; and data from the 2016 *Latino Decisions* Election Eve Poll reveals that Latinos in Nevada continued their solid support of Democratic candidates.

Figure 3.9 indicates that 40 percent of Latino voters in Nevada reported that they were motivated to turn out in 2012 to support Democrats (13 percent voted to support the Republicans), and an almost equal share (39

FIGURE 3.9. Motivation for Voting among Nevada Latino Voters, 2012

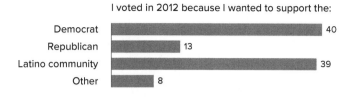

I voted in 2012 because I wanted to support the:

Democrat	40
Republican	13
Latino community	39
Other	8

Source: Nevada subsample of the impreMedia/Latino Decisions Election Eve Poll

percent) responded that they voted to support the Latino community. This finding would suggest that Nevada's Latino electorate could be persuaded to support Republican candidates in the future if their platform aligns with the values and priorities of Nevada's Latino community, specifically when it comes to immigration.

Figure 3.10, which presents findings from the 2016 Nevada subsample of the *Latino Decisions* Election Eve Poll, seems to provide support for this assertion. Fifty-three percent of respondents indicated that immigration was the most important voting issue to them, compared to the second most important issue, which was the economy and jobs, with 33 percent of respondents indicating the economy was their most important voting issue. That finding is important because it reveals that immigration is significantly more important to Latinos in Nevada than even the economy.

The importance of immigration to Nevada's Latino electorate is further highlighted when asked if they would support the GOP in the future. When posed with the question of future GOP support, 28 percent responded they would be more likely to vote for the GOP if the Republican Party passes comprehensive immigration reform. When that response is aggregated with the 18 percent who responded they are already likely to support the GOP in the future, the percentage of Nevada's Latino electorate that are likely to support the GOP is 46 percent. That is statistically equal to the percentage (47 percent) of Latinos in Nevada who responded that it would be hard for them to consider voting for the GOP in the future, i.e., likely Democrat supporters. This is significant given that even with strong Latino support for Democratic candidates, Nevada remains a swing state. There is indeed potential for the GOP to garner support from the Latino electorate, but only if the party resolves the issues surrounding immigration reform.

FIGURE 3.10. Motivations for Voting and Policy Preferences of Nevada's Latino Voters for Selective Issues, 2016

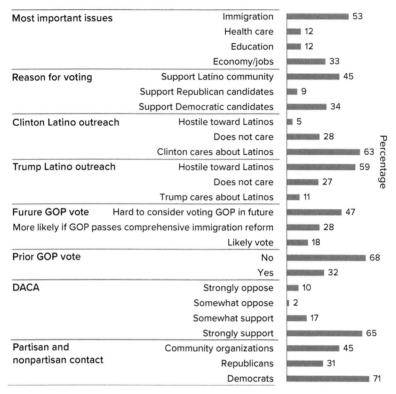

		Percentage
Most important issues	Immigration	53
	Health care	12
	Education	12
	Economy/jobs	33
Reason for voting	Support Latino community	45
	Support Republican candidates	9
	Support Democratic candidates	34
Clinton Latino outreach	Hostile toward Latinos	5
	Does not care	28
	Clinton cares about Latinos	63
Trump Latino outreach	Hostile toward Latinos	59
	Does not care	27
	Trump cares about Latinos	11
Furure GOP vote	Hard to consider voting GOP in future	47
More likely if GOP passes comprehensive immigration reform		28
	Likely vote	18
Prior GOP vote	No	68
	Yes	32
DACA	Strongly oppose	10
	Somewhat oppose	2
	Somewhat support	17
	Strongly support	65
Partisan and nonpartisan contact	Community organizations	45
	Republicans	31
	Democrats	71

Source: Nevada subsample of the 2016 Latino Decisions Election Eve Poll

At the same time, however, figure 3.10 also reveals the GOP has some work to do if it is ever going to harness the voting power of Nevada's Latino electorate. Figure 3.10 indicates that 86 percent of respondents in 2016 said they viewed Republican presidential nominee Donald Trump as hostile or apathetic to Latinos, compared to 33 percent who said they viewed Democratic presidential nominee Hillary Clinton as hostile or apathetic to Latinos. It is also significant that 71 percent of respondents said they were contacted by the Democratic Party before the election, compared to only 31 percent who indicated they were contacted by the Republican Party before the election.

Similarly, the data in figure 3.11 indicate that even when adjusting for variations in citizenship origins, gender, age, income, and education level,

FIGURE 3.11. Variation in the Presidential Vote among Nevada Latinos, 2016

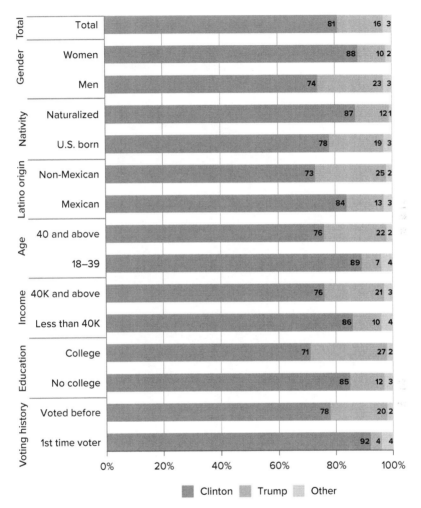

Source: Nevada subsample of the 2016 Latino Decisions Election Eve Poll

the Democratic Party commands a sizeable majority of the Latino elector-ate in Nevada. It would be difficult for the GOP to make substantial inroads into swaying this voting bloc given the party's current platform and the Trump administration's policy initiatives, which have been viewed as hos-tile toward Latin-origin immigrants. Furthermore, as Nevada's demog-raphy continues to shift and Latino voters, particularly the immense under-thirty, heavily Democratic cohort, become more engaged in politics, the GOP's ability to compete in Nevada is becoming increasingly unlikely. The under-thirty Latino cohort is embracing candidates with a progressive agenda, and their turnout was key to Vermont senator Bernie Sanders' recent victory in the state. Indeed, in the 2020 Nevada Democratic caucus, entrance poll data suggested that 51 percent of Latino voters exhibited a preference for Sanders, while former vice president Joe Biden (the party's eventual nominee and winner of the general election) garnered only 13 percent (in second place).[14] As Latino voters expand their political participation, then, we expect that Nevada will remain part of the "blue wall" of other western states.

CHAPTER 4

The Great Recession, Labor Market Conditions, and Employment

The Great Recession of 2007–2009 created a number of challenges for workers in Nevada. The crisis in the housing sector, combined with a sharp reduction in tourism, generated an increase in unemployment and a contraction in real incomes. By 2010, Nevada's hospitality sector had stabilized, but residential construction—long one of the drivers of employment in the state—continued to struggle for a number of years. Although many different groups of workers were affected by the economic crisis, Latino workers experienced some of the highest levels of unemployment in this period. The patterns that emerged during the crisis broadly illustrated how race and ethnicity mediate the process of labor market segmentation and do so in ways that pose unique risks to the economic security of Latino workers in Nevada.[1]

From 2014 to 2019, Nevada's economy recovered. Many analysts have acknowledged the improvement in the state's labor markets that started in 2014.[2] Nevertheless, little research has examined how different groups of workers fared during the recovery period. This chapter fills this gap by analyzing labor market conditions for Latinos throughout the state's economic recovery. Drawing upon state-level data from the Bureau of Labor Statistics (BLS) and other sources of data, we examine changes in Latino labor force participation, unemployment, and employment in Nevada, with a focus on the period of 2010 through 2015.[3] The BLS combines data from the Current Population Survey (CPS), along with other local and state data, to yield annual estimates for each state. We also draw on individual-level microdata from the Current Population Survey (Annual Social and Economic Supplement, for March) of each year, made available through the Integrated Public Use Microdata Series (IPUMS).[4]

FIGURE 4.1. Latino Labor Force Participation Rate in Nevada (Percent of Latino Civilian Labor Force), 2003–2014

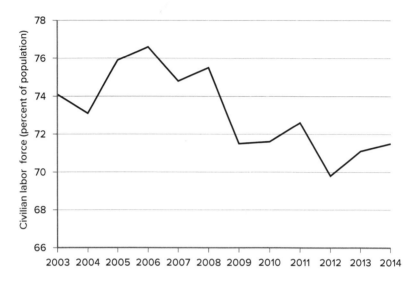

Source: Bureau of Labor Statistics, Local Area Unemployment Statistics Program (LAUS) and the Current Population Survey, *Geographical Profile and Unemployment and Employment*, selected years

In what follows, we begin with a discussion of Latino labor force participation. We then analyze trends in unemployment and the duration of long-term unemployment. After this, we examine changes in the sectoral distribution of Latino employment during the recovery period. The concluding section explores some of the larger policy implications of the findings. Although this chapter focuses on the aftermath of the Great Recession, in the conclusion we briefly touch on the COVID-19 pandemic of 2020 and its effects on Latino unemployment.

Trends in Latino Labor Force Participation in Nevada

To understand changes in labor market conditions, it is useful to begin by examining the Latino labor force participation rate. Figure 4.1, based on the BLS data, presents the trend in the Latino labor force participation rate for 2003–2014, without adjustments for gender, age, or other variables. Beginning in 2007, Nevada experienced a steep decline in the Latino labor force participation rate, which fell by 5 percentage points from 2007 to 2012. As noted in prior research,[5] although disability, retirement, college

FIGURE 4.2. Latino Labor Force Participation Rate for Men and Women, Nevada, 1997–2015

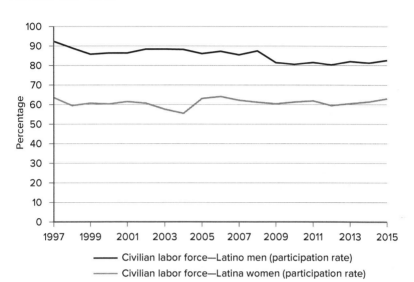

Source: Bureau of Labor Statistics, Local Area Unemployment Statistics Program (LAUS) and the Current Population Survey, *Geographical Profile and Unemployment and Employment*, selected years

attendance, and other slowly changing variables might have affected Latino labor force participation over the long run,[6] those variables likely do not explain the magnitude of the decline after 2007.

Instead, the trend was consistent with a rapidly deteriorating labor market in Nevada—driven largely by the Great Recession, a collapse of the housing markets, and small-business failure[7]—that led to an increase in job discouragement. Under these economic conditions, some Latinos (particularly foreign-born) may have dropped out of the labor market or migrated to other US states or countries. As one can see from the data in figure 4.1, after 2012, Latino labor force participation improved. However, in 2014, the most recent year for which complete data are available, the participation rate remained below the precrisis levels observed in 2007.[8]

After adjusting for the influence of gender, some continuities and changes emerge in the trends in labor force participation. Figure 4.2 presents the labor force participation rate among Latinos and Latinas in Nevada. One trend that remains unchanged is that the labor force participation for Latina women is consistently below the rate for Latino men.

However, for Latinas, labor force participation varied during the recession years and into the recovery. From 2007 through 2012, the Latina participation rate in Nevada declined somewhat, but by 2014, the rate for Latinas had rebounded to a level close to the prerecession mean observed in 2006 and 2007 (a mean of approximately 63 percent). By contrast, the pattern for Latino men was quite different. While remaining above the women's participation rate, Latino men's participation fell after 2008 and has yet to rebound to the prerecession mean rate registered in 2006 and 2007. Still, there was an uptick in the men's rate in 2015. In part, this might reflect the very recent recovery of sectors where men tend to be concentrated, including construction. Indeed, the data suggest that Latino men in Nevada are more likely to have an occupation in construction (the effect of gender on occupational choice for construction is statistically significant).[9] This evidence also suggests the effects of labor market segmentation experienced by different subgroups of Latinos in the state.

The source of the gap in Latina women's labor force participation remains unclear. Some researchers hypothesize that the lower rate of Latina labor force participation is associated with the relatively high share of foreign-born Latinas in the Latino working-age population.[10] Women's labor force participation in Latin America has increased, but the absolute level of women's participation remains below the rate for men, including in Mexico, a country that accounts for the vast majority of the foreign-born population in Nevada.[11] It is possible that the pattern observed in Latin America (i.e., lower participation rates for women) might influence immigrant women's labor force activity when they arrive in the US. In addition, given their average levels of educational attainment, Latina women—including those who are foreign-born—are more likely to have an occupation in the gaming and hospitality sector. Beyond the gaming and hospitality sector, however, Latina women with less education may face entry barriers in other industries that require more education.[12]

The Impact of the Great Recession on Nevada's Latino Community

The Great Recession had a profound impact in Nevada. The economic downturn generated high unemployment levels and led to turbulence in many sectors, particularly residential home construction and the hospitality industry. In the wake of the crisis, median home prices in Nevada plunged, while the residential foreclosure rate increased and remained one of the highest in the country during this period. By 2009, it was evident that a tightening of commercial bank lending for new mortgages,[13] combined with the impact of rising joblessness and plunging housing values, was hampering recovery efforts in the housing sector and Nevada's economy more generally.[14] As a result of these trends, residential home construction—the engine of employment growth in Nevada since 2000— came to a virtual standstill.

At the same time, the fallout from the recession throughout the United States reduced disposable incomes and led many individuals in California, Arizona, and other states to reconsider travel to Las Vegas and other parts of Nevada. Spending among tourists visiting the state also fell below pre-recession levels, placing Nevada's hospitality industry—once perceived as "recession proof"—on very insecure footing.[15] The consequences of the economic downturn were further magnified because of sharp declines in the primary revenue sources (gaming, sales, and property taxes) that are used to fund state and local government services.[16] In response, policy-makers made significant and extended cuts to education, public safety, health care, and other public sector budgets.[17]

In the section that follows we consider how the recession affected the distribution of Latino employment in different sectors of the state's economy. Additionally, we discuss how the lack of diversity in Nevada's economy and the inability of policymakers to expand federal employment retraining programs further hindered Nevada's recovery.

Trends in Unemployment

As noted at the outset of this chapter, Nevada was particularly hard-hit by the economic downturn with unemployment reaching a high of 14.5 percent in October 2010. Yet, as our analysis reveals, the impact of the Great Recession on employment did not affect all groups in the same manner.

Looking first at figure 4.3, which presents the trend in unemployment among all Latino workers in Nevada from 1997 to 2012, one can discern how the economic downturn affected Latino employment.[18] From 2002 to 2006, the unemployment rate among Latino workers in Nevada fell from 6.2 percent to 4.9 percent.[19]

However, as the first signs of trouble emerged in the housing market in 2007, the trend in unemployment quickly reversed itself. From 2007

FIGURE 4.3. Latino Employment Status in Nevada, 1997–2015

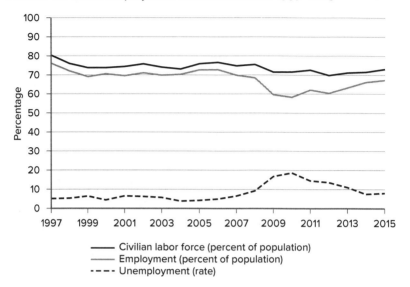

Source: Bureau of Labor Statistics, Local Area Unemployment Statistics Program (LAUS) and the Current Population Survey, *Geographical Profile and Unemployment and Employment*, selected years

to 2010, unemployment among Latinos jumped from 6.5 percent to 18.6 percent, but then started a gradual decline in the following years. Still, in 2012, Latino unemployment in Nevada remained at 13.6 percent, a rate higher than in any year before 2007 and much higher than the state rate of 9.8 percent.

In comparative terms, the unemployment rate among Latinos in Nevada was among the highest in the United States, and exceeded the unemployment rates for Latinos in almost every other western state except Washington.[20] In addition, the Latino unemployment rate in the Las Vegas–Paradise metropolitan area mirrored the trend at the state level. This finding is not surprising given that the vast majority of Nevada's Latino population and labor force is concentrated in Clark County.[21]

Beyond an examination of the aggregate data on unemployment, a fine-grained analysis reveals a more complex picture about how the Great Recession affected Latino workers throughout Nevada. First, the official unemployment data may have understated the impact of the recession on Latino employment. The method the BLS used to estimate the official unemployment rate (the "U-3 rate") does not include data on "discouraged" workers. The BLS defines a discouraged worker as "[p]ersons not in the labor force who want and are available for a job and who have looked for work sometime in the past 12 months (or since the end of their last job if they held one within the past 12 months), but who are not currently looking because they believe there are no jobs available or there are none for which they would qualify."[22]

Although data on the number of discouraged Latino workers in Nevada are not available, one has good reason to suppose that their ranks swelled after 2008. As the recession emerged, Latinos tended to be overrepresented among discouraged workers at the national level.[23] In addition, the available state-level evidence suggests that job discouragement was prevalent among Latinos.[24] The data in figure 4.3 show that after 2008, the absolute size of Nevada's Latino civilian labor force and the participation rate both declined.[25] In 2008 and 2009, the Latino labor force participation rate declined from 75.5 percent to 69.8 percent. Demographic change (reaching retirement age, outmigration), school enrollment, and disability may have played roles in declining labor force participation, but most of these factors change slowly and do not explain a steep decline occurring over a short period.[26] Rather, the pattern in the labor force data is consistent with rapid growth in discouragement that led many Latino workers to exit the labor market.[27]

Recent data support this assertion. Despite the decline in unemployment, in 2015, 8 percent of Latinos in Nevada remained unemployed—a rate above their mean unemployment rate 2004–2006 (fig. 4.4).

Second, Latinos experienced an increase in both the average duration of unemployment and in long-term unemployment of a year or more. As figure 4.5 demonstrates, the average duration of unemployment among all unemployed Latinos more than doubled, from 16.7 weeks in 2008 to 38.1 weeks in 2012. In addition, among Latinos in Nevada who were unemployed in 2008, 2 percent were unemployed for 52 weeks or longer. By 2012, 13 percent of Latinos who were unemployed in the state had been without work for 52 weeks or longer. The increase in long-term unemployment was associated with an increase in poverty among the Latino adult civilian population (which comprises both the labor force population

FIGURE 4.4. Latino Unemployment Rate in Nevada, 2002–2015

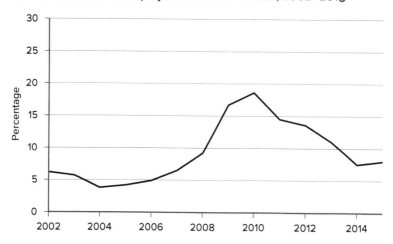

Source: Bureau of Labor Statistics, Local Area Unemployment Statistics Program (LAUS) and the Current Population Survey, *Geographical Profile and Unemployment and Employment*, selected years

FIGURE 4.5. Duration of Unemployment among Latinos in Nevada, 2006–2014

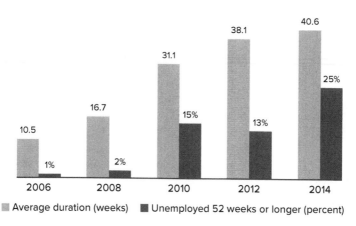

Source: Bureau of Labor Statistics, Local Area Unemployment Statistics Program (LAUS) and the Current Population Survey, *Geographical Profile and Unemployment and Employment*, selected years

FIGURE 4.6. Unemployment Rate among Latino Males, Females, Ages 16–19, in Nevada, 1997–2015

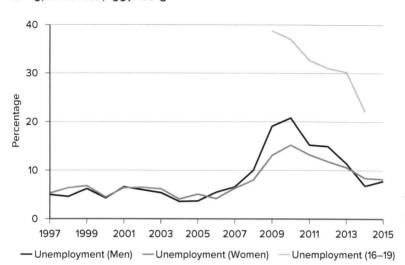

Source: Bureau of Labor Statistics, Local Area Unemployment Statistics Program (LAUS) and the Current Population Survey, *Geographical Profile and Unemployment and Employment*, selected years
Note: There are no data for Latinos age 16–19 prior to 2009.

and those marginally attached to the labor force). Indeed, from 2008 to 2012, the percentage of the adult civilian Latino population in poverty in Nevada increased from 12.35 percent to 15.6 percent.[28]

Recent data suggest that long-term unemployment continues to be a challenge for Latinos. As demonstrated in figure 4.5, among those Latinos who were unemployed in 2014, 25 percent were unemployed 52 weeks or longer—a percentage higher than what was observed in prior years. This suggests that despite a decline in overall unemployment, among those Latinos who remained unemployed, workers face unique challenges with finding reemployment (or securing lasting employment) during the recovery period. Further study will be needed to understand the barriers encountered by this group of workers.

Third, unemployment varied sharply among women and men in the Latino population. As the data in figure 4.6 demonstrate, from 2002 to 2005, the unemployment rate among female Latina workers in Nevada was slightly higher than the rate among men. However, between 2006 and 2012, the trend reversed: Latino men (fig. 4.6) were more likely to experience higher levels of unemployment. Perhaps more important, after 2008, the gap in unemployment between Latino men and women grew. For example, in 2009, 19.1 percent of Latino men were unemployed in Nevada, while the corresponding rate among women was 13.1 percent. A similar pattern was evident in 2010 (the unemployment rates of Latino men and women were 20.8 percent and 15.2 percent, respectively).[29]

Although differences in Latino men and women's labor force participation rates (and discouragement) might have had some influence on the unemployment gap, we think that the sectorial trends also played a role.[30] Job losses from 2008 to 2012 in Nevada were heavily concentrated in residential construction, a sector where Latino men were more likely to be employed before the recession. It is also important to recall that in the leisure and hospitality sectors—where women are well-represented—job losses rose initially to high levels (in 2008), but were not sustained as the sector stabilized in the following years.[31]

A fourth tendency is that unemployment was concentrated among younger workers. The unemployment rate of Latinos ages 16–19 registered at 38.8 percent in 2009, but declined to 31 percent in 2012.[32] Several factors during the downturn that hindered many young Latino workers may have caused relatively high levels of unemployment: They tend to have fewer years of educational attainment and experience, which reduces their employability. Those experiencing job loss for the first time are significantly more at risk for becoming discouraged workers. And young workers transitioning from school to work often are inadequately prepared for sectors that require more skill for entry-level positions.[33]

Finally, compared to several other groups of workers, Latinos were more likely to experience unemployment. Of course, before 2008, there had been variation in unemployment rates among Latinos and other groups in the state. However, as is detailed in figure 4.7, after the emergence of the recession, the Latino unemployment rate both increased and diverged significantly from the unemployment rates of White and Asian workers. In 2010, for example, unemployment among Latinos was 18.6 percent, while the unemployment rates of Whites and Asians were 13.9 percent and 11.8 percent, respectively. The underlying mechanisms that contributed to higher unemployment among Latinos remain unclear. As noted,

FIGURE 4.7. Unemployment Rates for African Americans, Asians, Latinos, and Whites in Nevada, 2002–2015

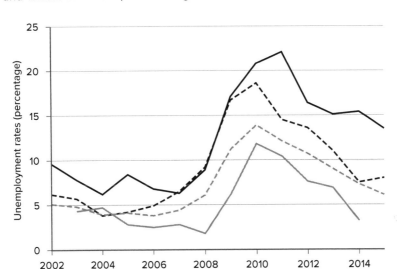

Source: Bureau of Labor Statistics, Local Area Unemployment Statistics Program (LAUS) and the Current Population Survey, *Geographical Profile and Unemployment and Employment*, selected years

Latinos were more likely to find employment in residential construction, a sector that contracted sharply during the downturn.

In addition, Latinos may have been at elevated risk for unemployment compared to others because a large share of the Latino workforce in Nevada is comprised of workers with lower levels of education attainment.[34] As the labor market weakened after 2008, employer demand for workers with lower levels of education fell, having a disproportionate impact on Latinos.[35] Indeed, the national-level CPS data suggest that in 2011 and 2012, Latinos (born in the US and abroad) with a high school degree or less had higher unemployment rates compared to Latinos with more educational attainment.[36]

The pattern of unemployment among African Americans in Nevada also demonstrates the effects of educational attainment on the risk of unemployment. In 2011, 46 percent of African Americans in Nevada possessed a high school degree or less. The data indicate that the Latino and

FIGURE 4.8. Latino Employment in Nevada, by Sectors (Percent of Latinos Employed), 2003–2014

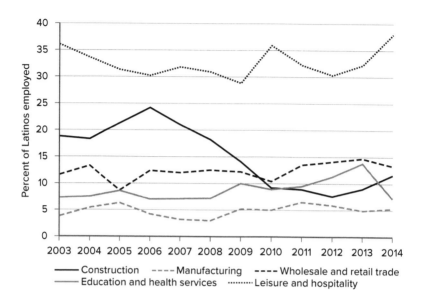

Source: Bureau of Labor Statistics, Local Area Unemployment Statistics Program (LAUS) and the Current Population Survey, *Geographical Profile and Unemployment and Employment*, selected years

African American unemployment rates were close to one another from 2009 to 2012 (and higher than the rates for other groups), which suggests that educational attainment is a cause for some of the variation in unemployment among different groups during the period in question. Also, more recent data suggest Latino and African American workers in Nevada continue to face much higher rates of unemployment in comparison to other groups of workers.

Changes in Latino Employment by Sector and Industry

The economic downturn also led to significant changes in the distribution of Latino employment in different sectors of the Nevada economy. As the data presented in figure 4.8 make clear, the change was most evident in the construction sector. As demand for residential homes plummeted in the wake of the financial crisis, construction of new homes in Clark County and other areas came to a halt. The cessation of new home building after

2008 was associated with a steep decline in Latino employment in the construction sector. From 2003 to 2006, the period when residential construction growth was strong, the percentage of Latinos in Nevada employed in construction (as a percent of Latino employment in all sectors) went from 18.8 percent to 24.2 percent (fig. 4.8).[37] However, in 2007, when the first indications of distress in Nevada's housing market became evident, there was a 3.2 percentage point decline in Latino employment in construction in the state.

This trend continued as the recession became full-blown. From 2008 to 2011, the percentage of Latinos employed in construction in Nevada fell from 18.2 percent to 8.9 percent, and continued to decline to 7.6 percent in 2012. In 2014, 11.6 percent of Latinos were employed in construction. It is worth emphasizing, however, that the figures for 2014 remain well below the peak in 2006, when 24.2 percent of employed Latinos were in construction. This suggests that despite the modest recovery in new construction during this period, Latino workers in that sector continued to face challenges.

Given the importance of construction for Latino employment, historically, and particularly for male Latino workers, the trends in construction employment signal that levels may not return to the prerecession pattern. The trend in the leisure and hospitality sector was similar, if less pronounced. In 2007, approximately 32 percent of all Latino workers were employed in the leisure and hospitality sector. The percentage fell to 28.8 percent in 2009, and then stabilized. Still, in 2014, the level remained at 30.8 percent, which was below the prerecession level registered in 2007. However, from 2012 to 2014, Latino employment in that sector (as a percentage of all Latinos employed) increased from 30.8 percent to 38 percent, respectively. In thinking about the differences between the construction and leisure and hospitality sectors, it is worth recalling that rehiring in hospitality resumed within about a year or two after the start of the recession, while hiring in construction (residential and commercial) remained very weak with many workers turning to repair work in homes purchased by investors.[38] As a result, the relative distribution of Latino workers employed in the hospitality industry stabilized after 2009, while employment in the construction sector continued to decline.

As one can see from the data in figure 4.8, in other sectors, including services, wholesale and retail trade, and manufacturing, the percentage of

Latinos employed in each sector varied slightly after the recession but did not show any clear pattern. Similar to hospitality and leisure, labor market adjustment in the service sector appeared to be relatively less severe and shorter in duration. Given the relatively low-skilled nature of some jobs in the service sector, it is also possible that some Latinos in construction may have been able to transfer successfully into some service sector jobs. Unfortunately, the CPS data are not refined enough to permit a more in-depth analysis to address this question.

Discussion

In this analysis, we assess the effects of the Great Recession on patterns of unemployment and employment among Latinos in Nevada. The findings indicate that unemployment among Latinos increased dramatically from 2008 to 2010, but then started a gradual decline. Although the modest recovery in Nevada has led to recent improvements in the state's labor market, the Latino unemployment rate in 2015 remained well above pre-recession levels. In addition, long-term unemployment among Latinos increased, while the data suggest that job discouragement (as measured by the decline in the Latino labor force participation rate) may have increased as well. Unemployment among men and young Latinos was significantly elevated. Compared to Whites and Asians, Latinos in Nevada also experienced higher rates of unemployment. In part, this outcome reflects the concentration of Latinos in economic sectors that were particularly hard hit by the recession (e.g., construction), along with the prevalence of lower levels of educational attainment among Latinos.

The findings also suggest that Latino employment in the construction sector after 2008 had a fairly steep decline. Although residential home construction in the Las Vegas valley resumed in late 2012 and early 2013, the modest recovery in new home construction continues to affect Latino employment in that sector. Latino employment decreased in leisure and hospitality, but employment in that sector rebounded through 2019.

The broader policy implication of these findings concerns the relationship between education and unemployment. Latinos and African Americans experienced much higher rates of unemployment after 2008 compared to Whites and Asians, which, as noted, may stem from variation in educational attainment. Latinos and African Americans in Nevada have lower high school graduation rates, and the data at the national level indicate that workers with less education (in particular, those with less than a high school degree) were at a significantly higher risk for unemployment during the recession.[39] Certainly, civic leaders in the Latino community have continued to emphasize the importance of education to provide pathways to mobility and to reduce the risk of economic insecurity. As Linda Rivera, a community leader in Las Vegas, commented in 2009:

> And to also bring younger people, students, into professions that previously maybe they would have shied away from? Yes. Yes. Most definitely. That's my return on my investment, is that I see them start school, finish high school, and more importantly, graduate college and then integrate into the work environment. That's been the payoff for me. That's been the biggest payoff for me. My children carry the same, more or less, passion. I think my son, he didn't, he didn't want to be a school teacher to begin with...and he's, twist fate, took him into the education arena and he was a fabulous teacher, fabulous teacher.[40]

For adult immigrants from Mexico and other parts of Central America, improving their educational attainment and training may be a challenge.[41] Still, adult Latinos born in the US and naturalized immigrants from Latin America might benefit from retraining or other adult education programs. Yet, to date there have been limited efforts to retrain displaced workers in Nevada. Most notably, between 2012 and 2014, state policymakers failed to take advantage of federal workforce training programs, such as Trade Adjustment Assistance (TAA) and Trade Adjustment Assistance Community College and Career Training (TAACCCT), specifically designed to assist displaced workers through education and job training.[42]

At the same time, for Latinos born in the United States (and children who are immigrants), improving high school graduation rates and access to higher education will provide additional skill sets and reduce the risks associated with prolonged unemployment during future downturns. What this implies, then, is that efforts to improve labor market outcomes will need to be sensitive to the performance of educational institutions in the state. However, as we discuss in chapter six, to date Nevada has done little to reform policy and funding of K-12 and higher education in the wake of the demographic change that is reshaping the state. The misalignment between the state's demography, its economic needs, and present education policy provides a significant barrier to overcoming cycles of economic boom and bust that have defined the Silver State since statehood.

An added challenge, particularly for those with less education, is the limited diversity of Nevada's economy. While the Governor's Office of Economic Development is continuing to implement the "State Plan for Economic Development," which seeks to both grow and diversify Nevada's economy, to date most of the postrecession job growth has been concentrated in the service and hospitality sectors, although there have been some positive initiatives in other sectors. For example, discussions abound regarding the rooftop solar industry, which may represent one alternative for workers who have experience in residential construction or similar industries.[43] The planned Faraday Future plant in the Apex Industrial Park near North Las Vegas, where many Latinos reside, was also a promising opportunity, but the firm canceled the investment. Still, Faraday made improvements to the land in Apex, and as of early 2020, officials in North Las Vegas and the Governor's Office of Economic Development continued to explore the possibility of attracting another original equipment manufacturing (OEM) firm to the site. If successful, the location of an OEM plant in Apex would undoubtedly expand manufacturing employment among Latinos in North Las Vegas and Clark County more generally.

To be sure, the uptick in employment during the past few years has been welcome news for many Nevadans, particularly those who have been unemployed for extended periods of time. However, the inability of Nevada to move beyond its traditional economic drivers leaves the state vulnerable to the vicissitudes of broader economic conditions and puts the state further and further behind its regional and global competitors. Indeed, in March 2020, the virtual shutdown of the state's hospitality sector, schools, and other activities in response to the COVID-19 virus has led to furloughs and layoffs, with about 206,000 workers in the gaming and hospitality sector in Nevada unemployed.[44] By April 2020, Nevada's seasonally adjusted unemployment rate had increased to 30.1 percent, before falling to 12.6 percent in September.[45] Given the concentration of Latino workers in that sector, Latinos have been at higher risk of unemployment since the pandemic emerged. Looking forward, then, efforts of state and local officials to diversify the state economy are essential to the creation of stable bases of employment.

CHAPTER 5

The Social Determinants of Health

As many public health researchers have noted, the majority of premature deaths in the US are "explained by preventable conditions and behaviors."[1] Preventable health conditions and behaviors are strongly associated with socioeconomic, behavioral, and environmental factors, which are collectively referred to as the social determinants of health. The social determinants of health are defined as "the conditions in the environments in which people are born, live, learn, work, play, worship, and age that affect a wide range of health, functioning, and quality-of-life outcomes and risks."[2] The social determinants of health are essential to understanding health disparity, disease risk, health promotion, and the quality of the systems that exist to prevent and address illness in the United States, and specifically in Nevada.

Among the states, Nevada ranks thirty-fifth for overall quality of health. Health benchmarks are key indicators of quality of life and one's overall standard of living, so Nevada's ranking in the bottom half of the nation poses several challenges for its Latino population. Economic figures for Nevada's Latino population reveal that in 2017, 19.4 percent of Latino families in Nevada lived below the poverty line, which was higher than the overall rate for Nevadans, which stood at 14.2 percent.[3] Likewise, throughout the 2010s, the percentage of Latinos under the age of 17 living below the poverty line was higher than for non-Hispanic Whites in the same age group. The average personal income (in 2018 US current dollars) for Latinos in Nevada was only $28,994, which also remained lower than the mean for non-Hispanic Whites.[4]

The tenuous economic situation for Nevada's Latino population has implications for this group's health outcomes, health insurance rates, and access to quality health care. Each aspect of the social determinants of health will be evaluated in this chapter. These include individual risks,

TABLE 5.1. Leading Causes of Death, Nevada 2014

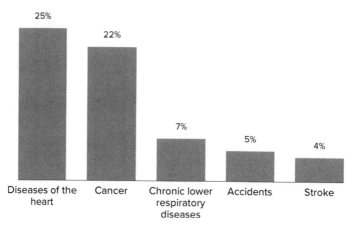

Source: Behavioral Risk Factor Surveillance System (BRFSS), Prevalence and Trends Data, 2011

FIGURE 5.2. Chronic Disease Prevalence by Race in Nevada, 2011

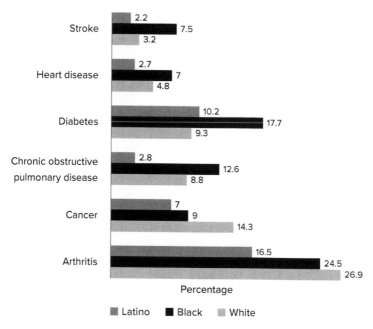

Source: Behavioral Risk Factor Surveillance System (BRFSS), Prevalence and Trends Data, 2011

such as chronic health conditions; behavioral risk, such as substance abuse, smoking, and sexual behavior; environmental risk, such as public health funding and living conditions; and finally, socioeconomic conditions, such as health-care access, health-care providers and service penetration, the diversity of the health-care workforce, and health insurance coverage.

With the social determinants of health for Latinos as our primary focus, we analyze data from a number of sources, including the US Census, the Centers for Disease Control (CDC) and Prevention, the Southern Nevada Health District, and other data sets to provide a snapshot of the health needs, challenges, and overall health outcomes for Latinos in Nevada.

Chronic Diseases

According to the CDC, chronic diseases and chronic health conditions "are among the most common, costly, and preventable of all health problems."[5] Chronic diseases represent diseases and health conditions, such as heart disease, cancer, type-2 diabetes, arthritis, obesity, and stroke. These diseases are considered chronic in nature because they persist over a long period of time, and, in some cases, the duration of an individual's lifespan. In 2014, seven of the ten leading causes of death were chronic diseases. Two of these, heart disease and cancer, together accounted for approximately 46 percent of all deaths.[6]

As the data in figure 5.1 suggest, in 2014, the leading causes of death in Nevada were heart disease, cancer, chronic respiratory diseases, accidents, and stroke. Heart disease and stroke combined accounted for almost one out of three deaths in Nevada.

Figure 5.2 provides estimates of chronic disease prevalence in Nevada, with adjustment for ethnicity and race. With the exception of diabetes, Latinos report significantly lower rates of chronic disease compared to Whites. Even in the case of diabetes, the rate of this chronic disease among Hispanics (10.2 percent) is only slightly higher compared to Whites (9.3 percent). Explanations for the relatively low rates of chronic disease among Latinos in Nevada may reflect inequities in access to routine health care, which may influence reporting in epidemiological surveillance data. However, lower prevalence rates have been attributed to the Healthy Immigrant Effect, which will be discussed in detail in the conclusion of this chapter.

Obesity, Exercise, and Nutrition

A poor diet and a primarily sedentary lifestyle are two of the most important behavioral risk factors for disease that are modifiable. According to research, an unhealthy diet and lack of exercise contribute to obesity and increase the risk for chronic disease.[7] Obesity has important implications for an individual's overall health. Obesity has been linked to several chronic health conditions, such as heart disease, diabetes, stroke, and various cancers.[8] Beyond chronic health conditions, obesity has also been linked to key health risk factors, including smoking and depression, while the health-care costs alone associated with obesity have been estimated to exceed $150 billion.[9] The economic burden of obesity extends beyond health-care costs. For example, the total economic cost of obesity in the United States, driven by related medical costs, excess mortality, and weight-related disability, is approximately $300 billion per year. However, these economic costs must also take into account lost productivity and negatively impacted quality of life because of obesity. To illustrate, recent studies have found that relative to the average individual in the US, obese patients incur:[10]

1. 46 percent increased inpatient costs
2. 80 percent increased spending on prescription drugs
3. 27 percent increased physician costs and visits, and outpatient visits

With respect to Nevada, the state had the seventh lowest rate (26.7 percent) of adult obesity in the nation in 2018.[11] Similarly, 21.7 percent of the adult population in Clark County reported not participating in any exercise or physical activity outside of work, which comparatively is better than the national average of 27.6 percent for adults nationwide. However, Nevada's adult obesity rate has steadily increased over the past two decades. In 1995, the adult obesity rate in Nevada was 13.1 percent, compared to 16.0 percent in 2000 and 26.7 percent in 2018.

Figure 5.3 indicates the rates of obesity with adjustments for race and ethnicity in Nevada. The rate of obesity among Latinos (30.6 percent) was higher than the state average (25.8 percent), and was only marginally lower than the obesity rate for African Americans in Nevada, which is 30.8 percent. The rate of obesity for Latinos is also higher than the obesity rate for Whites in Nevada, which was 26.2 percent.

FIGURE 5.3. Obesity Rate by Race in Nevada, 2016

Percentage

Source: Trust for America's Health and Robert Wood Johnson Foundation. The State of Obesity 2017 [PDF]. Washington, DC: 2017

Consistent with the high rates of obesity among Latino adults, childhood obesity among Latino youth has emerged as a key concern for public health advocates. As of 2013, 12.1 percent of adolescents in Clark County were obese, with large disparities by race and ethnicity. The obesity rate for non-Hispanic White adolescents was only 7.9 percent, compared to that of non-Hispanic Black adolescents, which was 17.4 percent, and 14.5 percent for Hispanic/Latino youth.

Two key factors that mitigate obesity-related chronic health conditions are maintaining a healthy diet and engaging in consistent physical activity. With respect to daily physical activity, Hispanic/Latino adolescents in Nevada hover around the middle of the spectrum when compared to other racial/ethnic groups. Figure 5.4 displays the levels of physical activity for Nevada adolescents across racial and ethnic groups in 2015. The data reveal that while approximately one-fourth of Latino youth surveyed reported that they met the minimum physical activity guidelines, more than one-fourth also reported spending more than three hours daily engaging in sedentary activities.

In contrast to Latino youth, Latino adults in Nevada had the second-highest rate of physical activity, and are only slightly less likely than Whites to engage in physical activity outside of work. Figure 5.5 indicates that 79.5 percent of Whites surveyed reported that they participated in exercise outside of their job, while 77.1 percent of Hispanic/Latinos reported participating in exercise outside of their job.

FIGURE 5.4. Nevada Factors Related to Physical Activity and Sedentary Behavior among Adolescents, by Race/Ethnicity, 2013

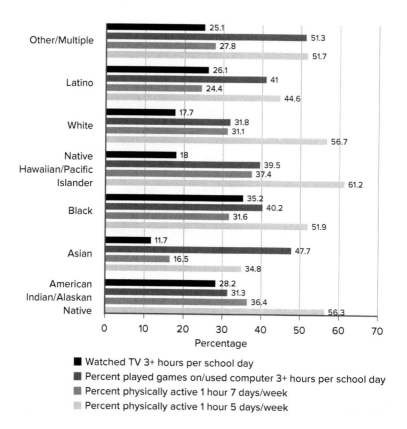

Source: Nevada Youth Risk Behavior Survey (YRBS), 2013

Maintaining a healthy and nutritious diet is equally important to that of exercise and physical activity when it comes to health promotion and disease prevention. The data reveal that in general, Hispanic youth maintain a nutritious diet. Although 14.2 percent of Hispanic adolescents report drinking one or more sodas each day, a greater percentage of Latino adolescents reported drinking of one glass of milk each day (fig. 5.6). Likewise, the percentage of Latino youth who consume vegetables three or more times a day is comparable to other groups.

Similar to their high rates of non-work-related physical activity, a high percentage of Hispanic adults in Nevada also report maintaining a healthy and nutritious diet. Government reports indicate that in comparison to

FIGURE 5.5. Nevada Percent of Adults Reporting Any Exercise Other Than Their Job, by Race/Ethnicity, 2014

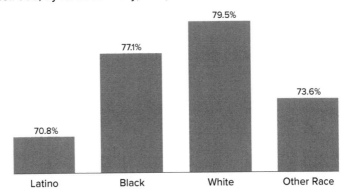

Source: Nevada Behavioral Risk Factor Surveillance Survey (BRFSS), 2014

FIGURE 5.6. Nevada Selected Factors Related to Nutrition among Adults, by Race/Ethnicity, 2013

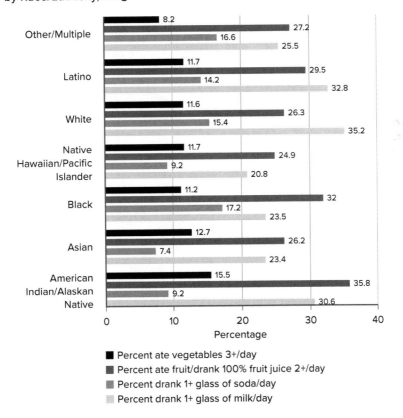

Source: Nevada Behavioral Risk Factor Surveillance Survey (BRFSS), 2013

TABLE 5.1. Percentage of Clark County School District Kindergarten and First-Grade Students Vaccinated at 36 Months of Age by Race/Ethnicity, 2009–2010 School Year

Vaccine	Asian		NA[1]		Black		Latino		White		Total
	Crude	Adj.	Crude	Adj.	Crude	Adj.	Crude	Adj.	Crude	Adj.	
DTP											
≥ 4 doses	78.9	79.5	73.9	77.0	67.8	72.8	83.0	84.8	79.8	79.9	76.4
Hepatitis A											
≥ 1 dose	65.8	66.4	68.1	69.9	61.4	64.2	77.0	77.2	68.8	68.9	72.6
≥ 2 dose	26.0	26.4	20.3	19.6	18.1	20.5	33.3	31.8	22.2	22.2	27.4
Hepatitis B											
3 doses	86.4	86.7	81.5	82.5	80.1	83.2	90.4	90.6	86.6	86.7	86.3
MMR											
≥ 1 dose	90.0	90.3	88.8	89.7	86.3	88.6	93.7	93.9	90.7	90.8	90.4
Polio											
≥ 3 doses	90.3	90.6	86.6	87.4	82.5	86.2	92.7	93.0	88.7	88.7	88.3
Varicella											
≥ 1 dose	82.3	82.7	79.7	81.6	80.8	82.8	87.3	87.8	84.0	84.0	84.1
Series											
4:3:1	76.0	76.6	70.7	73.5	65.5	70.4	80.7	82.3	76.8	76.9	74.0

Source: Nevada Behavioral Risk Factor Surveillance Survey (BRFSS), 2010
[1] Native American

all other racial/ethnic groups, Latinos report the highest consumption of fruits and vegetables on a daily basis.[12]

Infectious Diseases and Immunizations

Infectious diseases are those disorders caused by pathogenic microorganisms, such as bacteria, fungi, viruses, or parasites. Infectious diseases can be spread from one individual to another, either through direct or indirect contact. Although sexually transmitted diseases and infections are considered communicable and infectious diseases, this section focuses specifically on vaccine-preventable infectious diseases.

The prevalence of vaccine-preventable diseases is at an historic low. And yet, Nevada ranks forty-ninth among the states for the percentage of children who have not received the standard vaccination protocol for toddlers by their third birthday. The implications of this statistic suggest that both Nevada's adult and adolescent populations are under-immunized, which means Nevada is at high risk for an infectious disease outbreak. However, in a study of vaccination rates of Nevada adolescents, researchers found that vaccination is highest among Latino adolescents compared to all other racial/ethnic groups (table 5.1).[13]

Even after accounting for socioeconomic status and income difference, the high rate of vaccination among Latinos appears to be consistent across the lifespan. The assertion has been made that cultural factors and access to targeted health information on the importance of vaccinations may explain why Hispanics/Latinos are the leading group for vaccinations. Among Nevadans ages 6 months and older, White non-Hispanics and Hispanic/Latinos have the highest influenza immunization rates compared to every other racial/ethnic group, with Latinos having the second-highest vaccination rate among groups.

HIV and AIDS

In 2016, an estimated 39,782 new cases of HIV were reported in the United States. Among Nevadans, an estimated 485 adults and adolescents were diagnosed as new cases in 2015. In 2017, the most recent year for which complete data are available, Nevada's HIV diagnosis rate was 16.5 per 100,000 population.[14] It is also important to note that HIV incidence rates both in Nevada and nationwide have consistently been on the decline since 2008. Despite the overall rate decline, the number of new cases among Latinos

FIGURE 5.7. Estimated HIV Incidence among Persons 13 years of Age and Older, by Race/Ethnicity, 2014–2018

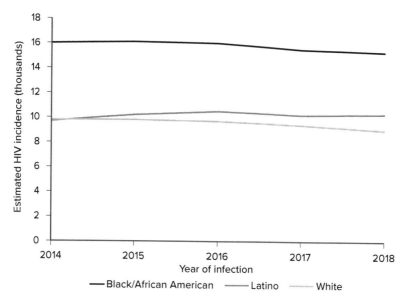

Source: Centers for Disease Control and Prevention. Estimated HIV Incidence and Prevalence in the United States 2014–2018

has been on the rise since 2014 (fig. 5.7). Nationwide, Latinos are disproportionately affected by HIV. In 2015, although Latinos represented approximately 16 percent of the US population, they accounted for almost 25 percent of all new HIV cases, and from 2014 to 2018, HIV diagnoses increased by 6.2 percent among Latinos. Among Hispanics/Latinos, men comprised 89 percent of all new HIV cases within this group in 2018, with the majority (87 percent) of these the result of unprotected sex with same-sex partners. The remaining 11 percent of infections were among Hispanic/ Latina women, and 83 percent of those new cases among Latinas were the result of heterosexual sex.

Latinos are at greater risk for delayed detection and diagnosis of HIV and AIDS when compared to all other racial/ethnic groups, with Latino males and foreign-born Latinos at the greatest risk.[15] The consequence of delayed diagnosis is increased mortality among those infected with HIV and AIDS. In Nevada, Latinos have had second-highest reported number

FIGURE 5.8. Estimated Adults and Adolescents Diagnosed with HIV, by Race/Ethnicity, Nevada, 2015

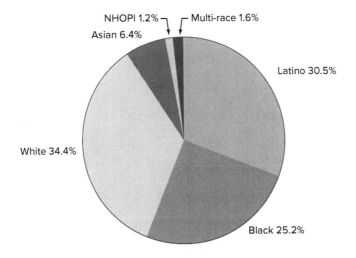

Source: Centers for Disease Control and Prevention. Nevada-State Health Profile, 2015

Note: NHOPI = Native Hawaiian/Other Pacific Islander

of new HIV cases in the state in the most recent year (fig. 5.8). According to health assessment data and the CDC, Hispanics, both in Nevada and nationwide, are at the highest risk of any other group for contracting the disease because of poverty, migration patterns, lower educational levels, and language barriers.

Mental Health and Suicide Deaths

Drawing on data from the US Institutes for Mental Health, the American Psychiatric Association found that in 2016, 18 percent of the adult population in the US presented with a diagnosable mental health disorder each year, and approximately 4 percent of the adult population probably experienced serious mental illness.[16] Further, mental health disorders are among the most expensive conditions for adults (ages 18 to 64) and a major contributor to disability. The seriousness of the mental health crisis in the United States is most evident when considering that fewer than half (43 percent) of those individuals diagnosed with a mental health disorder receive treatment or counseling, and this is not accounting for the

TABLE 5.2. Serious Psychological Distress among Adults 18 Years of Age and Older, by Percent of Poverty Level, 2013–2014

Poverty Level	Hispanic	Non-Hispanic White	Hispanic/Non-Hispanic White Ratio
Below 100%	8.2	10.7	0.8
100%–less than 200%	5.0	6.5	0.8
200%–less than 400%	3.2	2.7	1.2

Source: CDC, 2016; Health United States, 2015. Table 46. http://www.cdc.gov/nchs/data/hus/hus15.pdf

individuals suffering from an undiagnosed mental health condition.[17] This situation speaks largely to mental health disorder awareness and access to treatment. Disparities in health information and access disproportionately affect low-income individuals and minorities—including Latinos—in the US.

There is a clear relationship between measures of poverty and physical health indicators. This direct correlation is also salient for mental health status. According to the CDC, Hispanics/Latinos who live below the poverty level experience lower mental health and psychological distress compared to non-Hispanic Whites in poverty (table 5.2). However, at higher levels of poverty (i.e., 200 percent to 400 percent below the poverty line), this pattern is reversed, with Latinos experiencing higher rates of distress relative to non-Hispanic Whites. And we find that non-Hispanic Whites are two times more likely to receive mental health treatment than Hispanics, even when controlling for socioeconomic status (fig. 5.9). This suggests that disparities in access to mental health services remain a significant issue for the Latino community.

In 2016, Mental Health America published a comprehensive *The State of Mental Health in America*, where it reported on how well each state addressed mental health challenges. It employed data on state residents' access to mental health care and the percentage of individuals with diagnosed mental health disorders who were without mental health services or treatment. The report revealed that nationwide, Nevada is a low-ranked state for individuals with mental health challenges. The report found that the majority of adult residents with mental health disorders were not receiving treatment, in large part because of a shortage of health-care providers in Nevada.

FIGURE 5.9. Percentage of Adult Individuals Diagnosed with Mental Illness Receiving Mental Health Treatment Services, by Race/Ethnicity, 2015

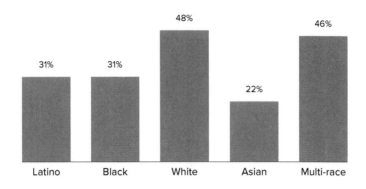

Source: Substance Abuse and Mental Health Services Administration, National Survey on Drug Use and Health

Data on mental health in Nevada broken down by race and ethnicity are gathered at the county level. Given that two-thirds of Nevada's population is concentrated in Clark County, we focus on the data for that county. In the 2012 Behavioral Risk Factor Surveillance System (BRFSS), Clark County Hispanic/Latino respondents reported fewer physically or mentally unhealthy days compared to all other racial/ethnic groups (table 5.3). The findings from the BRFSS self-report survey appear to be consistent with overall county data statistics on the rates of depression across racial and ethnic groups. The data in figure 5.10 reveal that when compared to all other groups, Hispanics had the lowest reported prevalence rates of depression in 2015.

Despite these data it is important to note three features regarding mental health in general with respect to racial and ethnic minorities in both Nevada and nationwide. First, while the rates of depression are lower in Blacks and Hispanics than in Whites, research suggests that depression among Blacks and Hispanics appears to be more persistent and ongoing across one's lifespan.[18] Second, minorities, and specifically Latinos, are more likely than any other racial/ethnic group to go undiagnosed, and then untreated for a mental illness when they are diagnosed. Thirdly, and this point is related to the second, because of cultural stigma, language barriers, low health insurance coverage rates, and low rates of mental health

TABLE 5.3. Mental Health by Race in Clark County, 2012

Physical and Mental Health	WNH	BNH	AEA[1]	API	Hispanic
Average number of physically unhealthy days in past month	4.1	4.4	5.8	2.5	1.8
Average number of days in past month when mental health was not good because of stress, depression, and emotional problems	3.7	4.3	5.1	2.1	2.4

Source: Nevada Behavioral Risk Factor Surveillance Survey (BRFSS), 2012
[1] American Indian/Eskimo/Aleut

FIGURE 5.10. Prevalence of Adult Depression by Race/Ethnicity, Clark County, 2015

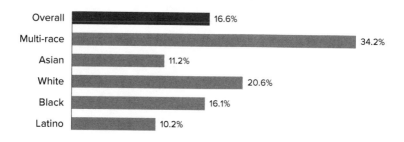

Overall 16.6%
Multi-race 34.2%
Asian 11.2%
White 20.6%
Black 16.1%
Latino 10.2%

Source: Nevada Behavioral Risk Factors Surveillance System (BRFSS), 2015

service penetration, these data may actually under-identify mental illness among Latinos in Nevada.

The relationship between suicide and mental health is both nuanced and multifaceted. The two conditions are inherently related because of the impact mental illness has on suicide deaths. Still, the majority of individuals diagnosed with a mental health disorder do not die by suicide. For example, 85–98 percent of individuals diagnosed with major depressive disorder do not die from suicide; likewise, 80–97 percent of individuals diagnosed with bipolar disorder, and 85–94 percent of individuals diagnosed with schizophrenia do not die from suicide.[19]

Suicide is not the leading cause of death among individuals diagnosed with mental illness, but those who suffer from a mental health disorder are at a higher risk of committing suicide than the general population. Also, the majority (90 percent) of those who die from suicide have been diagnosed with a mental illness.[20] In 2015, suicide was the seventh-leading cause of death among adult males and the fourteenth-leading cause of death among adult females. Among teenagers, suicide is the second-leading cause of death, surpassing homicide deaths, which dropped to third.[21] Among the teenage population, females are driving the higher overall suicide rate.

Nevada has consistently had one of the highest suicide rates in the United States for several decades. As Wray, Poladko, and Vaughan observe, "[i]n fact [Nevada] shares high suicide rates with eight other states in the Intermountain West, a region that has been called the 'American Suicide Belt'" (see appendix map 1).[22] Together with Alaska, the nine states in the Intermountain West region have consistently led the nation in the number of suicides per 100,000 persons each year.[23]

Several factors might explain Nevada's high rate of suicide. As previously mentioned, poor mental health access and treatment is a large factor in the high suicide rate among Nevadans. Many residents who require mental health services go untreated, which means they are either not diagnosed with a mental health condition, or they do not receive the requisite treatment to manage their mental health conditions. Compounding the problems associated with the mental health system, Nevadans engage in higher rates of addictive behaviors (e.g., gambling, substance abuse) compared to nationwide averages. Thus, the inadequacy of the mental health system in Nevada puts residents already at risk for mental health crises at a high risk for suicide death. Additionally, Nevadans reportedly experience high rates of social isolation, which is driven by the state's rapidly increasing population and demographic transformation. Lastly, the suicide death rate in Nevada has been attributed to higher-than-average gun ownership rates and liberal gun laws in Nevada (fig. 5.11).

When examining suicide rates across racial/ethnic groups, the figures for Nevada are consistent with nationwide trends. The suicide death rate among Whites is more than twice as high as the annual aggregate suicide death rate among all other racial/ethnic groups combined in Clark County (fig. 5.12). Further, there are no significant differences between the suicide death rate for Black non-Hispanics, Asian/Pacific Islanders, and Latinos. Also, when examining suicide death rates across racial/ethnic groups, Hispanic/Latinos have the lowest rate of suicide of any group (fig. 5.13). However, when compared to nationwide figures, suicide deaths are a significant problem among Nevada's Hispanic/Latino population. In 2016,

FIGURE 5.11. Percentages of Suicides by Method in Nevada, 2010

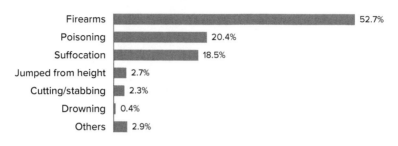

Source: Nevada State Health Division, 2010

FIGURE 5.12. Clark County Suicide Death Rate by Race/Ethnicity, 2008–2018

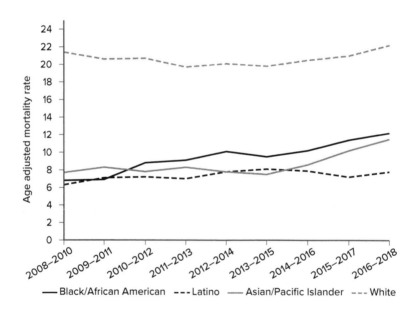

Source: Clark County Vital Records Mortality Data, 2004–2013

the suicide death rate among Hispanic/Latinos in the United States was 6.5 percent, compared to the suicide death rate among Hispanic/Latinos in Nevada, which was 9.4 percent. Thus, while suicide death is not a leading problem for Nevada's Hispanic/Latino population, it is still an area for concern given that the suicide death rate among Hispanic/Latino residents of Nevada far exceeds the national average for this group (fig. 5.14).

FIGURE 5.13. Clark County Age-Adjusted Suicide Death Rate by Race/
Ethnicity, 2014–2016

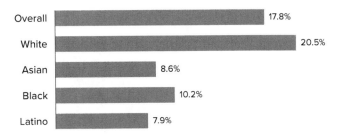

Source: Centers for Disease Control and Prevention

FIGURE 5.14. Suicide Death Rate in Nevada versus Nationwide by Race/
Ethnicity, 2016

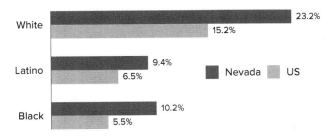

Source: 2016 America's Health Rankings, United Health Foundation

Smoking and Substance Abuse

An estimated one in three Americans engage in addictive substance use.
Addictive substance use refers to the use of a substance in a potentially
risky manner that could threaten an individual's overall health, safety,
and well-being. Although data are not comprehensive, this section offers
a snapshot of Nevadans' and specifically Latinos' use of tobacco products,
alcohol, illicit substances, and the misuse of prescription drugs.

In Nevada, alcohol abuse has consistently outpaced the national average among individuals 12 years and older (fig. 5.15); and with respect
to tobacco, about 18 percent of adults in Nevada use tobacco or smoke
cigarettes,[24] which is comparable to the national average of 17.5 percent.
Adjusting for race and ethnicity, Hispanic/Latinos report the lowest rate
of smoking and binge drinking compared to all other groups, while they
report comparable rates of heavy drinking compared to other groups

FIGURE 5.15. Alcohol Dependence or Abuse among Individuals Ages 12 or Older in Nevada and the United States, 2009–2013

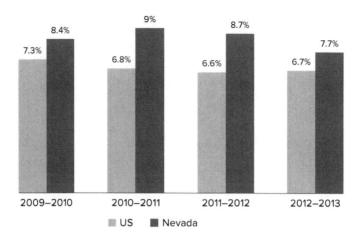

Source: SAMHSA, Center for Behavioral Health Statistics and Quality, National Survey on Drug Use and Health, 2009 to 2013

Note: These estimates are based on combined data from multiple years of the National Survey of Drug Use and Health (NSDUH), while estimates in the accompanying figure are from an estimation procedure that uses two consecutive years of NSDUH data plus other information from the state. The estimates from these two methods may differ.

FIGURE 5.16. Nevada Substance Use and Abuse Among Adults, by Race/Ethnicity, 2014

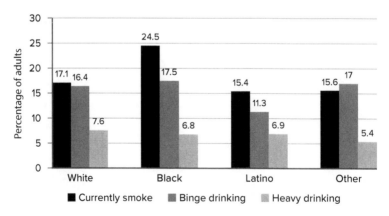

Source: Nevada Behavioral Risk Factor Surveillance Survey (BRFSS), 2014

Note: Binge drinking is defined as five or more drinks (men) or four or more drinks (women) in a single occasion within the past month. Heavy drinking is defined as more than two drinks (men) or having more than one drink (women) in a day.

FIGURE 5.17. Nevada Substance Use and Abuse among Adolescents by Race/Ethnicity, 2013

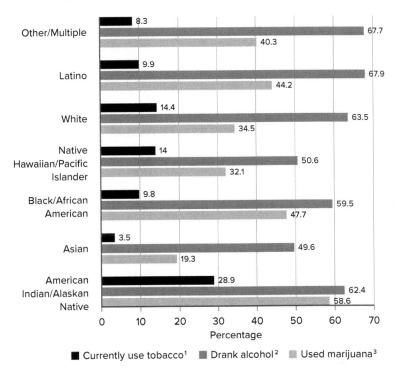

Source: Nevada Youth Risk Behavior Survey (YRBS), 2013

[1] Used cigarettes, smokeless tobacco, or cigars in the past month

[2] Had at least one drink of alcohol on at least one day during the past month

[3] Used one or more times in past month

(fig. 5.16). Substance use trends for Hispanic/Latino adults are also consistent among Hispanic/Latino adolescents, although alcohol use is relatively high (fig. 5.17).

The misuse and abuse of prescription drugs and illicit substances has become a serious health crisis in Nevada. The number of drug-related deaths in Nevada has nearly doubled in the past decade.[25] Among adult Nevadans, Hispanic/Latinos and Asian Americans are among the least likely to abuse prescription drugs or illicit substances; while Whites had the highest death rate (from prescription opioid poisonings and illicit drug-related overdoses), followed by American Indians/Alaska Natives,

FIGURE 5.18. Nevada Use of Prescription Drugs and Illicit Substances among Adolescents, by Race/Ethnicity, 2015

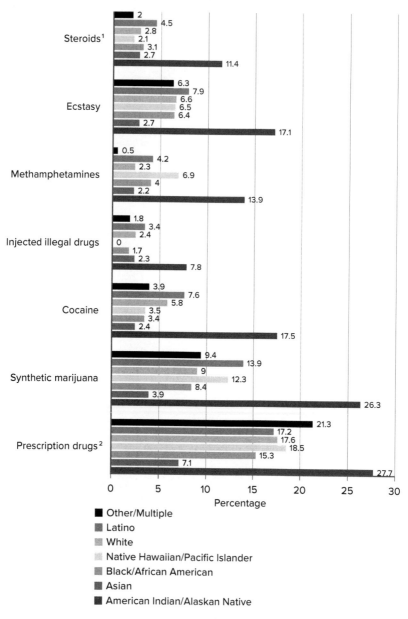

Other/Multiple
Latino
White
Native Hawaiian/Pacific Islander
Black/African American
Asian
American Indian/Alaskan Native

Source: Nevada Youth Risk Behavior Survey (YRBS), 2013

[1] Took steroid pills or shots without a doctor's prescription

[2] Took prescription drugs (e.g., Oxycontin, Percocet, Vicodin, Codeine, Adderall, Ritalin, or Xanax) without a doctor's prescription

[3] Ever used one or more times in their life

and then African Americans.[26] On the other hand, among Nevada adolescents, after American Indians/Alaska Natives, Hispanic/Latino youth had the second-highest use rate of synthetic marijuana, ecstasy, and cocaine in 2015 (fig. 5.18).

Latinos in Nevada's Health-Care Workforce

Up to this point in the chapter, the discussion has centered on the wellness outcomes across a number of health indicators for Nevada's Latino population. We have emphasized that a major impediment to healthy outcomes for this group is the lack of access to standard health care. While lack of insurance, poor health literacy, and problems associated with health-care affordability have been cited as the most crucial barriers to quality health care, another important factor that is rarely discussed and not well understood is the composition of the health-care workforce.

When referring to a state's health-care workforce, one is simply focusing on the total number of personnel who are employed or eligible for employment in the health-care industry within a state. Traditionally, the lack of diversity in a state's health-care workforce has not been considered an obstacle to health care, but that has been a mistake. Studies based upon patient surveys have determined that when patients feel understood by their health-care practitioner, the patient will more likely trust and subsequently follow the recommendations of their practitioner, which has been shown to improve the health outcomes of the patient.[27] Further, this vein of research indicates that when a patient's health-care practitioner demonstrates a familiarity with a patient's culture,[28] the patient is more likely to consider their practitioner relatable and understand their concerns.[29] While it encourages trust between the patient and the practitioner, and thus, has an incidental impact on patient health, cultural competency is central to patient health outcomes. When a health practitioner is familiar with a patient's diet, racial/ethnic predisposition for disease, their traditions surrounding health and wellness, as well as their cultural beliefs regarding medical treatment and the health system, the practitioner is better prepared to address the individual needs of their patient.

With respect to the diversity of Nevada's health-care workforce, we first look at the number of health-care education graduates. A state's educational pipeline drives the diversity of any workforce; therefore, the composition of the graduating student body is a key predictor of the future diversity of the workforce. With respect to the racial and ethnic diversity among the 2015 graduating class compared to the general population, White and Asian students are overrepresented across all of the selected health-care industry degree programs. However, Hispanics in Nevada have comparable representation rates to those of their proportion of the population (Nevada) in the following professions: dental hygienist, social worker, and substance abuse/addiction counselor. The least diverse professions in Nevada (as measured by whether 65 percent or more of the profession is represented by one racial/ethnic group) are: physical therapists, allopathic (MD) physicians, and psychologists. (See appendix table 1 that shows the percentage of health-care graduates by race and ethnicity in Nevada in 2015.)

There have been limited studies and data produced on the diversity of Nevada's health-care workforce. Similarly, minimal effort has been made to assess the specific impact of health practitioner underrepresentation on the health outcomes of racial and ethnic groups in Nevada. However, because of the shortages in nursing nationwide, researchers have worked to investigate how this shortage of nurses has affected various groups in the United States.

Despite the transformation of Nevada's population in the past decade, few Latinos/Hispanics enter the nursing profession. In the most recent National Sample Survey of Registered Nurses (NSSRN), for which data are available (2013), it was reported that 3.7 percent of registered nurses in Nevada are Hispanic/Latino (fig. 5.19). This figure is slightly higher than the national statistic, which indicates 3.3 percent of the registered nurses in the US are Hispanic/Latino. However, compared to the total Hispanic/Latino population in Nevada, which is approximately 28 percent, Latinos are significantly underrepresented in the field of nursing in the state of Nevada.

A closer examination of the Latino nursing workforce reveals that Latino nurses are concentrated in specific regions. One of the most highly concentrated regions is the Mountain West, which includes Nevada; however, even in areas of high Hispanic concentration, the percentage of Hispanic/Latino nurses still remains low compared to the population they serve. For example, 84.2 percent of nurses in the Mountain West are White, non-Hispanic. This statistic is not disaggregated by racial and ethnic minority group, but 15.5 percent of nurses in the Mountain West region

FIGURE 5.19. Percent of the Registered Nurse Population by Race and Ethnicity in Nevada, 2013

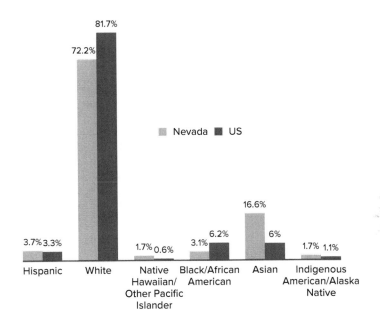

Source: Tabor Griswold, PhD, Laima Etchegoyhen, MPH, and John Packham, PhD (2014). "Registered Nurse Workforce in Nevada Findings from the 2013 National Workforce Survey of Registered Nurses, May 2014." *University of Nevada (Reno)-School of Medicine Report*

report that they belong to a member of a racial/ethnic minority group, which is consistent with the overall nationwide and statewide trends in which the nursing workforce lacks racial and ethnic diversity.

It has already been noted why a culturally diverse health-care workforce is essential, and this is particularly salient for the nursing field because nurses are generally the first contact person for a patient. With that in mind, it is important to better understand the entry barriers for Hispanics/Latinos in the field of nursing.

Several factors have been identified that serve as significant barriers for Hispanic/Latino entry into nursing, and we will discuss them in greater detail here. These factors include socioeconomic challenges, education barriers, home environment challenges, and cultural stereotypes surrounding the nursing field.

As previously discussed in earlier sections, Latino families in Nevada are at significant risk of living below the poverty line. Given the economic challenges facing Nevada's Latinos, and that socioeconomic indicators are highly correlated with educational outcomes, this implies that those Latinos who are eligible to pursue a college education are more likely to find full-time employment after high school rather than seek admission into an institution of higher education.

In addition to socioeconomic challenges, several aspects of the educational system create barriers for Hispanic entry into the Nevada health-care workforce. Comparisons across racial and ethnic groups reveal that Latinos have one of the highest high school dropout rates of all groups. In addition to high dropout rates, the traditional lack of recruitment efforts by career counselors served as a barrier for entry. In a study of minority high school students, 96 percent reported they aspired to obtain under-graduate, graduate, or professional degrees, but the college enrollment for Latinos was only 9 percent.[30] Beyond poor recruitment efforts, there is evidence that Latino students graduate from high school with academic deficiencies, largely because of differential treatment by teachers and counselors based upon stereotypes.[31] Furthermore, the lack of Latino mentors and role models in industries such as the health-care and medical fields has also discouraged this group's entry into the health-care workforce. In recent years, however, school counselors, health-care faculty, and professionals have tried to address recruitment issues by initiating mentoring programs for Latinos (including Deferred Action for Childhood Arrivals, or DACA, recipients) and other underrepresented groups in Clark County and in Reno.[32]

Research has also revealed disparities between the home environments of minority students and those of nonminority students. As Zalaya et al. noted in their study of Nevada, "It is reported that many Hispanic, African American, Caribbean, and ethnic minority students have parents who work in nontraditional jobs with extended hours."[33] As a result, minority students are expected to assume a number of responsibilities at home, such as caring for younger siblings, and functioning as a caregiver for elderly or infirm family members. From an early age, Latino students (particularly girls) may receive the message that family is to be prioritized. As recently as 2014, survey data suggest that two-thirds of Latinos who entered the private workforce or the military directly out of high school instead of enrolling in higher education listed familial support as the reason.[34] In this sense, then, Latino youth may not have always received familial support for pursuing higher education for nursing and health-care careers.[35] In recent years, however, these norms have changed, and many Latino parents emphasize the value of attending college or professional schools, including nursing schools.[36]

Another significant barrier into the nursing field is that of norms and perceptions. Culturally, Latinos may view nursing not as a profession but as a vocational trade. Historically, it was also considered a female profession,[37] and these gender stereotypes may have created a barrier for Latino men to enter the nursing field. Among men, nursing may have been viewed as maternalistic, with nurses perceived as nurturing, supportive, and feminine, which is incompatible with some norms of masculinity of Latino culture. Consequently, because nursing stands in contrast to gender roles, there have been fewer male Hispanic nurses in the United States. In 2013, for example, Hispanic male nurses accounted for less than a quarter of 1 percent of all nurses in the US.[38] However, particularly among younger Latinos, gender norms are changing. For this reason, one has reason to expect that more male Latinos may enter the profession in the future.

Discussion

The ranking of Nevada in the bottom half for overall health reflects the reality that Nevadans lack health insurance and access to primary care physicians, and engage in unhealthy behaviors that put them at a greater risk for worse health outcomes. Nevada has among the lowest rates of health insurance coverage in comparison to nationwide rates and even those of other states in the Intermountain West. To illustrate, in 2017, the American Community Survey indicated that 14 percent of residents (all ages) in Nevada were uninsured, which was the sixth highest rate of insured population across all US states.[39] By comparison, in that same year, the national average for uninsured individuals was 10.5 percent. As noted, Nevada also has a low physician-to-population ratio compared to other states in the US. For example, in 2015, there were 257 physicians per 100,000 population.[40] While this is an improvement over trends in the 2000s, the figure remains below the recommended population ratio. The health professional shortage is even more severe for mental health care. At the last recording of data in 2014, the US Department of Health and

FIGURE 5.20. Percentage of Nonelderly Uninsured in the United States, by Race/Ethnicity, 2012

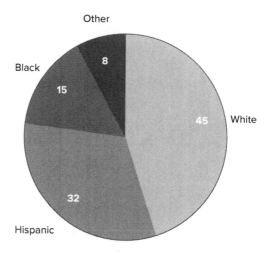

Total uninsured: 47.9 million

Source: U.S. Census-Current Population Survey, Annual Social and Economic Supplement, 2012

Note: "Other" includes Asian/Pacific Islander, American Indian/Alaska Native, and two or more races.

Human Services determined that 53 percent of Nevada's population, or 1.4 million people, live in an area designated as a Mental Health Professional Shortage Area (Mental HPSA) by the federal Health Resources and Services Administration.[41] These areas have a shortage of mental health providers, which includes psychiatrists, clinical psychologists, clinical social workers, and psychiatric nurse specialists.[42] Finally, beyond health-care workforce shortages, Nevada generally is a site of poor health outcomes because of poor health choices among residents. For example, Nevadans, but particularly Southern Nevadans, "are less likely to be physically active and more likely to have chronic diseases and risk factors attributed to physical inactivity such as coronary artery disease, obesity and diabetes."[43]

Nevada's low rankings for overall health indicators and health outcomes have important consequences for its Hispanic population. Nationwide, in 2012, Latinos represent the largest proportion of uninsured people of color, making up nearly one in three (32 percent) of the total uninsured population (fig. 5.20). Between 2010 and 2016, the effects of the Patient

FIGURE 5.21. Percentage of Nevada and US Population Without Health Insurance, by Race/Ethnicity, 2016

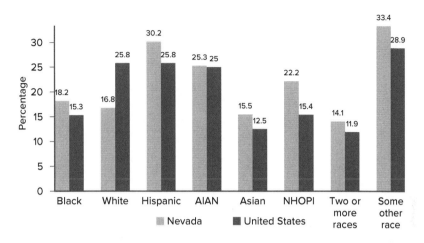

Source: 2011–2015 5-Year American Community Survey (ACS), which became available on December 8, 2016

Note: American Indian and Alaska Native are represented as AIAN, and Native Hawaiian and Other are represented as NHOPI.

Protection and Affordable Care Act ("Obamacare") had resulted in a 13 percentage point reduction in the rate of uninsured Latinos nationally,[44] but the disparities in coverage between Latinos and other groups have persisted. Similarly, in Nevada, Latinos are the single largest racial/ethnic group without health insurance (fig. 5.21). Partly because of the Healthy Immigrant Effect—in which, on average, immigrants are healthier than the native-born population and their native-born racial/ethnic counterparts—the primarily foreign-born Latino population in Nevada score generally well across the examined health indicators. For example, Hispanics have low rates of chronic disease; are physically active; maintain a generally healthy diet; have high rates of vaccination against infectious diseases; report low rates of depression and mental health disorders; have among the lowest rates of suicide death; and report low rates of smoking and tobacco use, illicit drug use, and prescription drug abuse. Consequently, the low rates of health insurance among Nevada's Latino population may not be considered an obvious or even immediate health need for this group; however, the overall health of Nevada's Latino population is more complex than statistics would suggest.

Nevada's Latino population report high obesity rates, high rates of alcohol abuse, and are at the highest risk for new HIV infections. The lack of health insurance and access to a primary care physician mean that Latinos in Nevada go without critical health information regarding obesity prevention, weight reduction and weight management; they go without treatment for alcohol abuse; and they do not receive adequate HIV/AIDS and STI screenings to prevent the spread of HIV/AIDS and sexually transmitted diseases, which is at the heart of why Hispanics are at the greatest risk for new HIV infections. Further, the lack of diversity in Nevada's health-care workforce only compounds the health-care challenges for Nevada's Latinos. The greater the cultural awareness a health-care practitioner possesses with regard to their patient population, the better the health outcomes are for their patients.

Thus, while the Healthy Immigrant Effect is salient across several health indicators for Nevada's Latino population, tackling the problems associated with high uninsured rates, the lack of health access and service penetration, and low levels of health-care workforce diversity is critically important to ensuring that the health needs of Nevada's growing Latino population are being adequately addressed.

CHAPTER 6

Educational Access and Outcomes

The incremental increase of Latino students in postsecondary/tertiary institutions in Nevada over the last decade has demonstrated a promising pattern, displaying consistent development between demographic growth and enrollment in higher education. Closely associated with this trend has been the performance of Latino high school students. High school dropout rates among Latinos, on average, have declined, or in specific years remained constant, and high school graduation rates among Latinos have consistently increased. With an increased number of students graduating high school, this has translated to healthy enrollment numbers in tertiary institutions, contributing to some of these institutions achieving Hispanic-Serving Institution (HSI) status with the US Department of Education. On the reverse side of these trends, however, have been two important limitations: 1) while high school graduation rates have increased, thus contributing to higher enrollment in tertiary institutions, Latinos still lag behind Whites and Asians with respect to postsecondary enrollment as a percentage of total high school graduates; and 2) increased enrollment in higher education, especially in four-year institutions, has not translated to increased graduation rates; rather, graduation rates from four-year institutions have actually witnessed concerning patterns of decline among Latino students in Nevada.

The High School Dropout Rate

Observable quantitative improvements to dropout rates among Latino high school students (ninth–twelfth grade) have naturally correlated with improved graduation rates, providing for a positive pattern from 2007 to 2017.[1] As table 6.1 displays, in the 2007–2008 school year, the average dropout rate for Latino high school students was 6.2 percent, double the rate for White students (3.6 percent) and Asian students (3.2 percent), respectively,

TABLE 6.1. High School Dropout Rates by Race/Ethnicity, 2007–2017

	2007/08	2008/09	2009/10	2010/11	2011/12	2012/13	2013/14	2014/15	2015/16	2016/17
All Students	4.7%	4.4%	4.2%	4.1%	3.9%	4.7%	N/A	3.5%	3.6%	3.2%
American Indian	5.5%	6.1%	4.4%	4.4%	4.3%	6.0%	N/A	4.4%	4.7%	3.6%
Asian	3.2%	3.0%	3.0%	3.0%	1.8%	2.2%	N/A	1.6%	1.7%	1.6%
Latino	6.2%	5.4%	5.1%	4.9%	4.4%	5.4%	N/A	3.7%	3.9%	3.4%
Black	6.4%	5.2%	6.1%	6.3%	5.8%	8.4%	N/A	5.8%	5.4%	5.7%
White	3.6%	3.6%	3.2%	3.2%	3.3%	3.6%	N/A	2.9%	3.1%	N/A
Pacific Islander	N/A	N/A	N/A	N/A	4.2%	4.8%	N/A	3.8%	3.4%	2.7%
Two or more	N/A	N/A	N/A	N/A	3.1%	4.3%	N/A	3.3%	3.6%	3.2%

Source: Nevada Accountability Portal. http://www.nevadareportcard.com/DI/nv

TABLE 6.2. Twelfth-Grade Dropout Rates, 2014–2017

	2014/2015	2015/2016	2016/2017
All Students	6.7%	7.9%	4%
American Indian	9.1%	10.3%	5.6%
Black	10.7%	9.6%	7%
Latino	8%	9.7%	4.7%
White	5.2%	6.3%	N/A
Asian	3.3%	4.4%	1.4%
Two or more races	5.5%	7.3%	2.8%
Asian	5.5%	7.9%	4.1%

Source: Nevada Accountability Portal. http://www.nevadareportcard.com/DI/nv

while only second to Black students (6.4 percent) for the highest ethnic dropout rate. In subsequent years, however, an incremental drop is observable for each year until 2012, with the year 2012–2013 being an exception, while the school years from 2014 to 2017 held steady at 3.7 percent, 3.9 percent, and 3.4 percent, respectively.

Contextually, within a decade, the dropout rate among Latino high school students showed an exponential improvement, as dropout rates went from 6.2 percent in 2007 to 3.4 percent by 2017, cutting dropout rates by more than 50 percent. The improved dropout rate of Latino high school students is part of a general observable pattern throughout Nevada's high schools: there has been a collective decline, on average, of the overall dropout rates in the last decade. Whereas the average dropout rate in 2007–2008 was 4.7 percent for the entire state, by 2011 it had declined to 3.9 percent, and fell further to 3.2 percent by the 2016–2017 school year.

While the average dropout rates for ninth through twelfth grades indicate strong improvement, the disaggregation of the data does display some concerns. As table 6.2 shows, dropout rates for specifically twelfth graders remain quite high among Latinos. For the 2014–2015 school year, 8 percent of Latino twelfth graders dropped out; a more telling statistic than the average dropout rate for the entire span of the high school years. For school year 2015–2016, the dropout rate for Latino twelfth graders rose to 9.7 percent, only to see a healthy drop to 4.7 percent 2016–2017. Thus, while recent developments are encouraging, the pattern of very high dropout rates for twelfth graders does appear to be problematic.

Although twelfth-grade dropout rates, on average, are naturally higher than the lower high school grades, thus providing for a skewed overall average for the high school years, the numbers are still not very favorable for Latino high school seniors: their dropout rates remain higher than Whites, Asians, and Pacific Islanders. Granted, the average twelfth-grade dropout rate for all students is also exponentially higher than the ninth–twelfth-grade dropout rate for all students. In comparative terms, ninth–twelfth-grade dropout rates for all students for 2014–2015 is 3.5 percent, while the twelfth-grade dropout rate is 6.7 percent; for 2015–2016, it is 3.6 percent to 7.9 percent; while for 2016–2017, it is 3.2 percent to 4 percent. These overall dropout rates are quite similar to the Latino rates with respect to the differences between the two averages: for ninth–twelfth grade, the Latino dropout rate is 3.7 percent for 2014–2015, while the twelfth-grade rate is 8 percent; for 2015–2016, it is 3.9 percent to 9.7 percent; and for 2016–2017, it is 3.4 percent to 4.7 percent, respectively. As we can see, the disparity in dropout rates for all students from ninth to twelfth grade and the dropout rates for twelfth grade were quite large from 2014 to 2016, only to narrow by 2017. This pattern is consistent with the disparity in dropout rates for Latinos as well, as the disparities between the two averages remained high from 2014 to 2016, only to see the gap close to a difference of 1.3 percentage points by 2017.

The causes of trends in high school dropout rates among Latino students in Nevada are complex and multifaceted. To be sure, dropping out of high school may be influenced by contextual factors and dynamics within students' families. However, recent studies of Latino students in Nevada also suggest that social structural and institutional factors also play a role, because these variables shape the opportunities for student achievement. With regard to structural factors, it is important to recall that the majority of Latino students are concentrated in the Clark County School District (CCSD) in the Las Vegas metropolitan area. The CCSD is the fifth-largest metropolitan school district in the United States. Most students in the district attend neighborhood "zoned" schools, which are prone to segregation, because many residential areas in the metropolitan area are segregated on the basis of race, ethnicity, and income. Looking at panel data (2007–2013) in the CCSD, Welsh found that Latino students in the district were likely to be enrolled in segregated schools (as measured by a standard dissimilarity index).[2] During the study period, Welsh also demonstrated that Latino students were less likely to change schools either between years or midyear, and they were at risk for being in schools that exhibit low proficiency and poverty, with attendant consequences for dropout rates. This suggests that policies to address school segregation in Nevada may yield benefits for reducing the risk of Latino dropout.

In addition, it is important to consider the role that institutional factors play in high school exit. First, despite some improvement, the state has struggled to provide sufficient services and resources to address the growth of English-language learner students, including Latino ELL students, and particularly in the CCSD. The data suggest that ELL students remain at higher risk of dropping out of high school.[3] Second, the number of Latino students with disabilities has increased in Nevada. Among Latino students (ages 6–17) in the state, the number with disabilities increased by

115 percent from 2007 to 2012. A notable increase occurred in the Clark County School District, where the number of Latino children (ages 6 to 17) with autism and speech and language impairment increased by 265 percent and 133 percent, respectively, during this period.[4] Because of budget constraints, there is often a delay in providing services (or adequate services) to children with disabilities in Nevada. Employing data from the US Department of Education, McFarland et al. found that in 2015–16, students with disabilities in Nevada were at very high risk for not completing high school compared to their nondisabled peers.[5]

High School Graduation Rates

While the dropout rates provide some magnitude in gauging retention rates for Latino high school students, the graduation rates provide a more robust indicator of qualitative improvements for the last decade, as well as a conceptual framework in analyzing the increased number of Latino students enrolling in tertiary institutions. The general trend over the last decade is both positive and promising, and when analyzed through a comparative lens, Latino graduation rates appear to be the most improved in relation to any other minority/ethnic group. As table 6.3 displays, Latino graduation rates in 2007–2008 were extremely low, with only 57 percent of Nevada's Latino students graduating high school, only second from last, while lagging behind the overall graduation average by almost 12 percentage points. Although the Latino graduation average slightly increased and remained constant for the next three school years, it did undergo a severe drop in the 2011–2012 school year, declining by 5 percentage points. Very closely related to the economic fallout after the Great Recession (chapter 3), this reduction in graduation rates was not unique to Latinos; rates dropped across the board in the entire state. From 2010 to 2012, graduation rates declined by an overall average of 7 percentage points, only to bounce back and stabilize by the 2012–2013 school year. This stabilization was accompanied by increased improvement by Latino graduates, as graduation rates reached 69.75 percent by the 2016–2017 school year.[6]

In comparative terms, when observing the ten-year trend of Latino graduation rates, the outcome is encouraging, as indicated in table 6.4. From 2007 to 2017, the graduation rate for Latino students increased from 57 percent to 69.75 percent, an improvement of 12.75 percentage points. Latinos by far demonstrate the most improved graduation rates.

TABLE 6.3. Graduation Rates, by Race/Ethnicity, 2007–2016

	2007/08	2008/09	2009/10	2010/11	2011/12	2012/13	2013/14	2014/15	2015/16
All Students	68.7%	71.3%	70.3%	68.8%	63.1%	70.7%	70%	70.8%	73.55%
American Indian	58%	64.4%	64.1%	57.6%	53.9%	58.7%	52.3%	52.33%	64.7%
Asian	80.7%	82%	81.3%	75.8%	74.8%	82%	84.3%	84.7%	87.9%
Latino	57%	60.5%	60.3%	60%	54.9%	64.4%	64.6%	66.7%	69.75%
Black	54.5%	57.7%	57.6%	50%	48.3%	56.7%	53.9%	55.5%	56.5%
White	76.8%	79.2%	78.4%	77.7%	72.4%	77.2%	76.9%	78%	79.9%
Pacific Islander	N/A	N/A	N/A	N/A	72.2%	74.8%	73.9%	71%	75.9%
Two or more	N/A	N/A	N/A	N/A	77.7%	80.1%	75.7%	75.6%	76.8%

Source: Nevada Accountability Portal. http://www.nevadareportcard.com/DI/nv

TABLE 6.4. Improvement in Graduation Rates by Ethnicity, 2007/2008 and 2016/2017

	2007/2008	2016/2017	Total Improvement
All Students	68.7%	73.55%	4.85
White	76.8%	79.9%	3.1
Black	54.5%	56.5%	2
Latino	57%	69.75%	12.75
Asian	80.7%	87.9%	7.2
Native American	58%	64.7%	6.7

Source: Nevada Accountability Portal. http://www.nevadareportcard.com/DI/nv

In relation to White and Asian students, Latinos did have far more room for improvement, but their numbers still remain impressive in relation to the improvement rates of Native American, Black, and White students. On closer examination of this general progression, the percentage point improvement in Latino graduation rates in this period was approximately three times higher than the overall improvement average for the state. Furthermore, Latino rates lagged behind the overall average by 12.7 percentage points in 2007; this gap has been largely diminished by 2017 to 3.8 percentage points.

Latino Enrollment in Postsecondary Institutions

Demographic trends in Nevada, coupled with a developing labor market that is diversifying and becoming more knowledge-based, have raised important issues concerning Nevada's future workforce and the role of Latino workers. The analytical scope then becomes quite straightforward: postsecondary education, and access for Latino students to such education, are inherently intertwined in developing Nevada's future workforce. According to the 2010 US Census, Latinos comprised 27 percent of Nevada's population,[7] and considering that healthy growth has continued, the Latino population is very likely to surpass 30 percent by the 2020 Census. Latinos are concentrated in the under-30 population, a large number of whom are currently either in postsecondary institutions or in the job market. As these trends continue, and considering the relative youth of the Latino population, their insertion into the future job market and their effectiveness to both Nevada's economy and workforce remain heavily contingent upon their success in attaining postsecondary education.

An overview of Latino enrollment rates in Nevada's postsecondary institutions reveals a positive trend, showing a continuous and incremental increase from 2009 to 2014. As figure 6.1 displays, Latino enrollment numbers in tertiary institutions increased from 2,504 in 2009 to 4,108 in 2014. These enrollment rates, of course, are correlated with the increased number of Latino students graduating high school. This is shown in figure 6.2, in which the increased graduation numbers for every year consistently translate to an increase in Latino enrollment in tertiary institutions. In sheer numbers, Latinos account for the second-largest number of enrollments in postsecondary institutions in Nevada, second only to White students. While 2,504 Latino students enrolled in tertiary institutions in 2009, White student enrollment was 6,912; in 2010, there were 3,058 Latinos and

FIGURE 6.1. Latino Post-Secondary Enrollments, 2009–2014

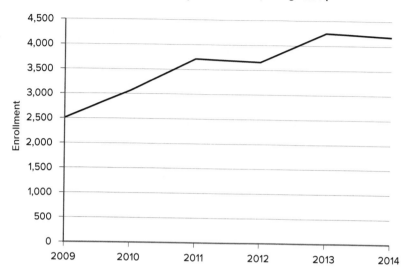

Source: Nevada Department of Education

FIGURE 6.2. Latino High School Graduation Trends, 2009–2014

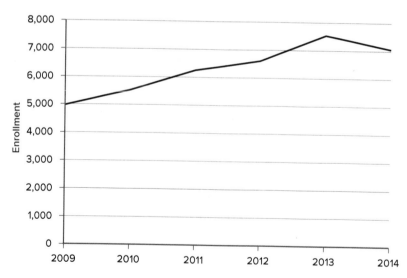

Source: Nevada Department of Education

7,091 White students; in 2011, the numbers were 3,713 and 6,792, respectively; in 2012, 3,687 and 5,961; in 2013, 4,250 and 6,518; and in 2014, 4,180 and 6,026. Collectively, as the number of Latino graduates has increased, we have slowly seen a narrowing of the college enrollment gap, which is an important indicator of the continued access of Latino students to postsecondary education.

While these trends have been positive, a more nuanced look at the numbers, however, suggests both room for improvement and slight concerns for the disparity between the number of Latino high school graduates and those graduates actually enrolling in tertiary institutions. Simply put, while the overall numbers show incremental growth, the proportional representation of Latinos in tertiary institutions remains low. Table 6.5 provides the percentile breakdown for high school graduates who enrolled in postsecondary institutions across racial/ethnic groups.

As table 6.5 shows, the percentage of Latino high school graduates enrolling in tertiary institutions is comparatively low compared to Black students, Asian students, and White students. In 2009, for example, only half of Latino high school graduates enrolled in postsecondary institutions, the lowest among all other ethnic groups. While a slight increase is observed in 2010 and 2011, the enrollment numbers held steady in 2012 and 2013, only to show a healthy improvement in 2014 at 59.4 percent. Collectively, however, four observations must be noted. First, Latino enrollment rates remain just shy of 60 percent, indicating that more than 40 percent of Latino high school graduates enter the workforce without having had any access to higher education. Second, Latino enrollment rates consistently lag behind the overall average, although the gap narrowed in 2014, with total graduation rates at 66.1 percent and Latino rates at 59.2 percent. Third, higher graduation rates do not translate to higher enrollment rates as percentage of population size. Because more Latinos are graduating high school, overall, more Latinos are enrolling in postsecondary institutions; but this increase is a by-product of population growth and not a qualitative increase in percentage rates. And fourth, Latinos still lag behind all other ethnic groups in college enrollment rates, having been surpassed by Pacific Islanders and Native Americans in 2014.

The above data note enrollment in all postsecondary institutions, both in-state and out-of-state, for students graduating from Nevada high schools. When considering the enrollment rates for in-state tertiary

TABLE 6.5. Percentage of High School Graduates Enrolling in Postsecondary Institutions

	2009			2010			2011			2012			2013			2014		
	HSG[1]	PSE[2]	%	HSG	PSE	%	HSG	PSE	%	HSG	PSE	%	HSG	PSE	%	HSG	PSE	%
All Students	19,605	12,188	62.2	20,208	13,241	65.5	21,015	13,754	65.4	20,884	12,993	62.2	22,996	14,334	62.3	20,584	13,610	66.1
Native American	246	125	50.8	257	160	62.3	232	130	56	191	106	55.5	226	117	51.8	180	111	61.7
Asian	2,038	1,433	70.3	2,167	1,560	72	1,562	1,161	74.3	1,545	1,151	74.5	1,735	1,279	73.7	1,588	1,269	79.9
Latino	4,967	2,504	50.4	5,514	3,058	55.5	6,251	3,713	59.4	6,605	3,687	55.8	7,538	4,250	56.4	7,062	4,180	59.2
Black	1,849	1,199	64.8	1,980	1,368	69.1	1,697	1,182	69.7	1,847	1,174	63.6	1,870	1,166	62.4	1,548	1,048	67.7
White	10,454	6,912	66.1	10,281	7,091	69	10,072	6,792	67.4	9,239	5,961	64.5	9,999	6,518	65.2	8,755	6,026	68.8
Pacific Islander	n/a	n/a	n/a	n/a	n/a	n/a	289	176	60.9	313	189	60.4	329	182	55.3	277	171	61.7

Source: Nevada Accountability Portal. http://www.nevadareportcard.com/DI/nv

[1] High School Graduates

[2] Postsecondary Enrollment

institutions alone, the data are problematic regarding the extent to which Latino high school graduates are being educated in state tertiary institutions, as they are expected to comprise a substantial proportion of Nevada's future workforce.

Every year Nevada loses approximately 8 percent of its Latino high school graduates to out-of-state postsecondary institutions.[8] This context suggests that there is a decrease in the number of Latino students enrolling in Nevada's tertiary institutions upon graduating from high school. In 2010, for example, Nevada had 5,514 Latino students who graduated high school, of which 3,058 (55.5 percent) went on to enroll in a postsecondary institution. Of those 3,058 students, however, 2,654, or 87 percent, enrolled in one of Nevada's postsecondary institutions. By 2014, 4,180 high school graduates enrolled in a postsecondary institution; of this figure, 3,586 remained in Nevada. As such, when controlling for the students who leave the state for tertiary education, the in-state levels for Latino Nevadans collectively drops. While data are not exactly available on the 8 percent who leave the state and the extent to which they return and join Nevada's future workforce, conservative analysis leans toward excluding a large portion of these individuals from returning to Nevada's workforce upon graduation. As a result, the percentage of Latino high school graduates specifically attending Nevada postsecondary institutions remains in the range of the 50th percentile.

Enrollment of Latino Students in Nevada's Postsecondary Institutions: Two-Year Programs

Latino students in Nevada's higher education system are disproportionately enrolled in two-year institutions, and in general, this is actually consistent with disproportionate Latino enrollment in US higher education.[9] In relation to all other ethnic groups, Latinos are the most likely to enroll in community colleges. This trend, however, has seen an impressive alteration in the last decade, as more Latino students in Nevada have begun enrolling in four-year institutions. Despite this, enrollment in two-year programs appears to have been the norm for Latino students, as it is perceived as a gateway to four-year programs. The problem, however, as studies have shown, is that attending community colleges may actually have an adverse effect on graduation, completion, and transfer rates.[10] The reasons for this adverse effect are threefold: First, students who enroll in two-year programs are generally disadvantaged socioeconomically; second, there

TABLE 6.6. Number of Latino Students Enrolled in NSHE Two-Year
Programs, 2005–2015

Year	Latino Student Population	Students in Two-Year Programs	Proportion of Latino Student Population
2005/2006	12,366	8,406	68.4%
2006/2007	13,797	9,670	70%
2007/2008	15,056	10,617	70.5%
2008/2009	16,767	11,975	71.4%
2009/2010	20,269	14,260	70.3%
2010/2011	21,467	15,120	70.4%
2011/2012	18,882	12,167	64.4%
2012/2013	20,698	13,023	63%
2013/2014	21,935	13,358	60.8%
2014/2015	24,028	14,263	59%
2015/2016	24,604	14,219	57.8%

Source: Nevada System of Higher Education. https://www.nevada.edu/ir/

are fundamental limitations in academic preparedness for community college students; and third, community colleges, in general, suffer from funding and resource shortages.[11] Thus, research indicates that enrollment in two-year programs does not necessarily translate into access to four-year programs, even though the initial intent of Latino students enrolling in community colleges may be precisely that. The 2005–2012 data indicate the disproportional enrollment of Latino students in two-year programs; however, from 2013 on, the data are far more promising and show a robust growth in four-year program enrollments (tables 6.6–6.8).

Table 6.6 displays the number of Latino students enrolled in one of the Nevada System of Higher Education's (NSHE) two-year programs,[12] and the percentage of the community college enrollment as a proportion of the overall enrollment of Latino students in all NSHE institutions.

As can be seen, the percentage of Latino students enrolling in two-year programs is quite high from 2006 through 2010, with approximately 70 percent, on average for each year, of all Latino students enrolling in a two-year program. The years 2008 and 2010 stand out. In 2008, out of 16,767 Latino students who enrolled in NSHE institutions, 11,975 enrolled in community colleges; and in 2010, out of 21,467 Latino NSHE enrollments, 15,120 enrolled in two-year programs. Considering the lack of acceptance criteria for two-year programs, the relative low funding of these institutions, and the general lack of academic preparation in relation to four-year programs, an extraordinarily large portion of the Latino student population remains vulnerable to the adverse effects of two-year programs. A relatively positive outlook, however, develops after 2010, when a 6-percentage point drop in community college enrollment is observed within the Latino student population (2011); and there is a continuous and incremental decrease for every subsequent year, with 2015 standing at 57.8 percent, which is a more than 10 percentage point decrease over a ten-year period. Consequently, this decline suggests an increase in four-year program enrollments among Nevada's Latino student population.

Enrollment of Latino Students in Nevada's Postsecondary Institutions: Four-Year Programs

While trends in two-year program enrollments have been encouraging, thus hinting at the positive growth in enrollments for four-year programs, Latinos suffer from two important limitations with respect to pursuing a four-year undergraduate degree. First, in relation to other racial/ethnic groups, Latino enrollment in four-year programs remains low. Second, graduation rates and/or degree attainment from four-year institutions is also low among Latino students. These assessments, however, do not suggest that improvements are not being observed; more specifically, proportional increases in the enrollment of Latinos in four-year institutions have been consistent in the last decade, although they continue to lag significantly behind White and Asian students. Tables 6.7 and 6.8 illustrate these trends.

In 2005, for example, while Latinos had the third-highest enrollment in raw numbers, they actually ranked last in proportion to their student population size. Of the total number of Latinos enrolling in NSHE institutions, only 31.7 percent enrolled in four-year institutions; this lagged behind Black students at 38.4 percent, White students at 45.4 percent, and Asian students at 46 percent. These numbers continue along a downward trajectory for the next four years. While overall enrollment numbers in four-year institutions increased, again because of the overall growth of the Latino population, these numbers however remained heavily disproportionate. In 2006, only 30 percent of Latino students enrolled in Nevada's four-year institutions, a drop of 1 percentage point from the previous year, to finally bottom out in 2010 at 29.5 percent. Granted, drops in enrollment rates were not only specific to Latino students; relative decreases were also observed among Black students and White students, which likely can

TABLE 6.7. Enrollment in NSHE Four-Year Institutions, by Race/Ethnicity, 2005–2015

	2005/ 2006	2006/ 2007	2007/ 2008	2008/ 2009	2009/ 2010	2010/ 2011	2011/ 2012	2012/ 2013	2013/ 2014	2014/ 2015	2015/ 2016
Asian	4,557	4,898	5,237	5,661	5,140	5,062	5,142	5,146	5,400	5,396	5,505
Black	2,462	2,543	2,628	2,699	2,696	2,705	2,639	2,688	2,655	2,813	2,837
Latino	3,926	4,127	4,439	4,792	6,009	6,346	6,715	7,675	8,577	9,765	10,385
White	26,088	25,428	24,823	25,072	26,361	26,084	24,873	24,040	23,720	23,692	23,489

Source: Nevada System of Higher Education. https://www.nevada.edu/ir/

TABLE 6.8. Percentage of Enrollment in NSHE Four-Year Institutions, by Race/Ethnicity, 2005–2015

	2005/ 2006	2006/ 2007	2007/ 2008	2008/ 2009	2009/ 2010	2010/ 2011	2011/ 2012	2012/ 2013	2013/ 2014	2014/ 2015	2015/ 2016
Asian	46%	46%	48.4%	47.8%	51.6%	50.3%	53.2%	53%	55.3%	54.4%	55.2%
Black	38.4%	39%	37.3%	36.5%	33.4%	32.6%	33%	35.8%	36.9%	36%	38.6%
Latino	31.7%	30%	29.4%	28.5%	29.6%	29.5%	35.5%	37%	39.1%	40.6%	42.2%
White	45.4%	44.6%	43.6%	43.3%	43%	42.7%	46%	46.2%	47.4%	47.7%	49.3%

Source: Nevada System of Higher Education. https://www.nevada.edu/ir/

be attributed to dynamics related to the Great Recession, as discussed in chapter 4. Consequently, Asian students were the only group that maintained a continuous growth trajectory during this period. By 2011, however, Latino enrollments rebounded to 35.5 percent, surpassing the rate for Black students, yet still lagging by healthy margins behind White and Asian enrollments.

When data are disaggregated to the institutional level, three general observations become clear. First, Latino enrollment at the University of Nevada, Reno (UNR), has shown a healthy growth from 1,068 in 2005 to 3,576 in 2015. This growth, however, has not greatly reduced the large gap in relation to White enrollment. In 2005, White enrollment exceeded Latino enrollment by 10,342 students; by 2015, while a slight change is observed, the gap has not closed much: in a decade, the gap has only narrowed to 9,018.

Second, the University of Nevada, Las Vegas (UNLV), has shown substantial improvement in both Latino enrollment and in closing the enrollment gap. In 2005 Latino enrollment stood at 2,858, only to grow to 6,809 by 2015. UNLV displays an advantage in raw numbers, consistent with the much larger Latino population in Southern Nevada, but UNR displays a more impressive proportional growth. In terms of the enrollment gap, however, UNLV appears to have made far greater progress. In 2005, the enrollment gap stood at 11,820 (White). By 2015, this gap was narrowed to 4,086 (White).

Third, as the percentage of total enrollment, Latinos made up 6 percent of UNR students in 2005, only to grow to 17 percent of UNR's student body, an improvement of 11 percentage points. Similarly, at UNLV, Latinos made up 10 percent of the total enrollment in 2005, only to grow to 23.8 percent by 2015—an improvement of 12.8 percentage points.

Graduation Rates of Latino Students
from Nevada's Four-Year Institutions

The improvements in enrollment rates and the overall numbers for Latinos at four-year institutions, while promising, have not translated to graduation rates. At both of Nevada's two major universities (UNLV and UNR), the graduation rate for Latino students ranks below the national average, without much improvement over the last decade. This development is quite significant, considering that freshmen retention rates for Latino students

TABLE 6.9. UNR Graduation Rates, by Race/Ethnicity, 2005–2015

	2005/ 2006	2006/ 2007	2007/ 2008	2008/ 2009	2009/ 2010	2010/ 2011	2011/ 2012	2012/ 2013	2013/ 2014	2014/ 2015
Asian	53%	60%	59%	No data	No data	58%	68%	50%	57%	71%
Black	36%	33%	48%	41%	40%	51%	39%	43%	37%	45%
Latino	41%	41%	39%	42%	42%	49%	44%	47%	47%	49%
White	50%	47%	49%	48%	51%	52%	56%	52%	57%	60%
Total	49%	46%	48%	46%	49%	51%	54%	51%	55%	59%

Source: Nevada System of Higher Education. https://www.nevada.edu/ir/

TABLE 6.10. UNLV Graduation Rates by Race/Ethnicity, 2005–2015

	2005/ 2006	2006/ 2007	2007/ 2008	2008/ 2009	2009/ 2010	2010/ 2011	2011/ 2012	2012/ 2013	2013/ 2014	2014/ 2015
Asian	44%	46%	43%	No data	No data	40%	48%	49%	41%	47%
Black	29%	32%	32%	34%	33%	32%	29%	34%	34%	26%
Latino	40%	36%	38%	36%	35%	38%	39%	38%	35%	35%
White	39%	42%	41%	40%	42%	40%	41%	42%	40%	43%
Total	39%	41%	41%	39%	40%	39%	41%	43%	39%	40%

Source: Nevada System of Higher Education. https://www.nevada.edu/ir/

are quite high, and as such, it is not a scenario where high enrollments are offset by high dropout rates in the first year of college. Within this context, the freshman retention rates for Latino students in Nevada's universities were 83.7 percent in school year 2011–2012, 81.8 percent in 2012–2013, 82.4 percent in 2013–2014, 81.6 percent in 2014–2015, and 83 percent in 2015–2016.[13] The strong retention rates, coupled with increased enrollment rates, are incommensurate with the low graduation rates. Latino graduation rates lag behind both Asian and White graduates, while also lagging behind the overall average. More specifically, while graduation rates for both White and Asian students consistently surpass the fifty percentile, Latino graduation rates have not broken this barrier, either at UNR or UNLV, as of 2015. Further, when the data are disaggregated to the institutional level, an important observation stands out: UNR graduation rates for Latinos are much higher than the Latino graduation rates at UNLV, even though Latino enrollment is much higher at UNLV.

Table 6.9 displays the graduation rates by ethnicity for UNR, which indicate a positive trend for Latino graduation rates. However, as the data show, Latino graduation rates consistently lag behind Asian and White students, and are consistently below the overall average. In the timespan covered by the data, Latino graduation rates improved by 8 percentage points, growing from 41 percent in 2005 to 49 percent by 2015. However, even with an improvement of 8 percentage points over the decade, Latino graduation rates in 2015 lagged behind White student graduation rates by 11 percentage points, and Asian student graduation rates by 12 percentage points. In this sense, the Latino graduation rates at UNR, while undergoing modest growth, have actually not kept pace with the improved rates of White or Asian students, nor stayed on par with the overall average.

In relative terms, Latino performance with regard to graduation rates is even lower, and more problematic at UNLV, indicating two troubling trends. First, unlike UNR, where incremental growth, albeit controlling for fluctuation, is observed over the last decade, at UNLV, the graduation rates for Latino students have experienced a negative trajectory. And second, while the overall graduation averages are much lower for UNLV in relation to UNR, Latino graduation rates at UNLV have also failed to at least meet the overall average. These nuanced observations aside, the trends at UNLV appear to be similar to those of UNR: Latino graduation rates consistently lag behind Asian and White graduation rates. The data in table 6.10 reflect these trends, specifically the negative trajectory of the Latino graduation rates for students at UNLV from 2005 to 2015.

In the timespan reported in table 6.10, 2005–2015, the net effect of graduation rates are as follows: Asian, up 3 percentage points; Black, down 3 percentage points; Latino, down 5 percentage points; and White, up 4 percentage points. And when the figures from table 6.10 and table 6.9 are compared, the numbers become more telling. In the same timespan, the net effect of graduation rates for UNR is: Asian, up 18 percentage points; Black, up 9 percentage points; Latino, up 8 percentage points; and White, up 10 percentage points. Three observations at this point become quite evident. First, while the net effect for all ethnic groups is positive for UNR, this is not the case for UNLV, as both Black and Latino net effects are negative. Second, for both data sets and relative to all racial/ethnic groups, the Latino net effect for graduation rates is the lowest. And third, while the increased Latino enrollment rates at UNR are commensurate with a modest increase in graduation rates, this is actually the opposite for UNLV— while the enrollments for Latino students have exponentially increased in the last decade, the graduation rates have actually decreased.

Discussion

Two general considerations are proposed in addressing both the increasing number of Latino students in postsecondary institutions as well as evaluating the performance of such students to produce better outcomes: funding and a more conducive academic environment. The discourse on funding focuses primarily on Hispanic-Serving Institutions (HSIs), while studies on the academic and campus environment for Latino students address several models, ranging from the academic culture, curriculum structure, and policies and practices that facilitate academic-preparedness. The overarching objective of both approaches is to improve graduation rates, degree efficiency, and the knowledge-based skills to allow for success in the chosen career paths of Latino students.

HSIs are classified as postsecondary institutions that encompass Hispanic full-time enrollment (or its equivalent) that is at least 25 percent, while emerging HSIs are qualified accordingly if the Latino student population encompasses from 15 percent to 24.9 percent of the student body.[14] HSI designation is granted by the US Department of Education, and institutions that qualify for HSI designation receive funding to improve academic performance, programs and curriculum development, institutional management, and fiscal stability.[15] Postsecondary institutions that are emerging HSIS, but have not attained full HSI designation, may also apply for funds, but these are competitive grants for which these institutions may apply under the Title III and Title V programs of the US Department of Education. UNLV achieved HSI status in 2015,[16] while Nevada's other six institutions have an emerging HSI status, including UNR.[17] As emerging HSIS, Nevada's postsecondary institutions have been applying for competitive grants, such as the Developing Hispanic-Serving Institutions Program, Hispanic-Serving Institutions STEM and Articulation Program, and the Promoting Post-baccalaureate Opportunities for Hispanics Program (PPOHA).[18]

Competitive funding under Title III and Title V programs, however, in of itself, is not sufficient to improve the performance and degree-attainment rates for Latino students. With increased funding comes the expectation that institutions will implement policies, programs, and curriculum to accommodate and support the growing population of Latino students. The scholarly consensus suggests a holistic approach that includes student performance-enhancement, instructional methods, curriculum development, and intervention.[19] Identifying struggling students at high risk of eventually dropping out and intervening during their freshman and sophomore years may prove instrumental to stem the relative decline in Latino graduation rates at UNLV. Additional funding is required to offer better advising programs, tutorial assistance, and more robust intervention that increase the performance of at-risk students, modestly helping them stay in school longer.

The second school of thought considers the academic environment when evaluating the outcomes of Latino students, and for this analysis, paying specific attention to institutional factors that contribute to the experiences and performances of Latino students in predominantly White institutions. Collectively, Latino students continue to struggle with racial inequities in higher education: Latino students "are substantially less likely than their White peers to matriculate into a four-year institution, attend a selective college or university, enroll in college full-time, and complete a bachelor's degree."[20] With respect to academic environment, multiple factors contribute to the performance of Latino students in tertiary institutions: degree of academic-preparedness, culturally exclusive curriculum, financial difficulties,[21] and the combination of campus racial cultures and campus racial climates.[22] These complications become even more detrimental as they contribute to perceived sentiments of marginalization, stress, low class participation and attendance, and overall, lower levels of degree completion among Latino students.[23]

From the lens of pedagogy and curriculum development, the lack of culturally inclusive educational models leads to negative outcomes for Latino students.[24] Incongruity of cultural values and belief systems inherently place Latino students at a disadvantage, producing a sense of apathy within the college environment that negatively affects academic performance. While discourse on multiculturalism and diversity does important work in bridging this incongruity in cultural values and belief systems of Latino students, supplementing this with an array of more culturally engaging programs can alleviate the sense of marginalization among Latino students that impedes performance and, in turn, graduation rates. Simply put, if students are not able to develop a degree of belonging in their academic environment, their performance levels will not be commensurate with the expected course-completion requirements necessary for graduation.

Nevada's postsecondary institutions have demonstrated a concerted effort to provide a more culturally inclusive campus environment, implementing policies and programs that promote diversity and multiculturalism. While it would be premature to suggest campus racial climates and campus racial cultures have been fully alleviated, it is safe, however, to assert that a great deal of progress has been made in implementing diversity initiatives and promoting a campus culture of inclusiveness. UNR's Office of Diversity and Inclusion initiatives, for example, seeks to "sustain a diverse, inclusive and welcoming environment for all University members, including students, faculty, staff and alumni."[25] UNR's programs use such campus structures as the Cultural Diversity Committee and the Diversity Council. The Cultural Diversity Committee is comprised of academic and administrative faculty, along with staff and students who seek to advance equity and diversity on campus. The Cultural Diversity Committee is comprised of the Diversity Summit Committee (responsible for organizing the annual Northern Nevada Diversity Summit) and the Equity and Inclusion Committee (which develops action items that can be institutionally implemented). The Diversity Council, on the other hand, engages in planning and program development for a diverse learning community, establishing such things as standardized operating procedures, training and educational programs, with the goals of improving the campus climate, enhancing recruitment and retention, strengthening inclusive curricular and co-curricular programs, and strengthening communication among diversity advocates.[26]

UNLV possesses perhaps the most developed and advanced diversity and multicultural policies and programs of any of the institutions of higher education in the state. UNLV's Office of Diversity Initiatives recognizes academic achievement to be "intertwined with a commitment to diversity in all aspects of university life."[27] As such, initiatives seek to cultivate and institutionalize diversity as a fundamental and transformative force at the university.[28] From 2010, UNLV has implemented many initiatives to accommodate the growing number of minority students, especially Latinos, who make up the largest proportion. In 2010–2011, UNLV conducted the Campus Climate Survey, and the Faculty Senate approved recommendations requesting the university's president to form a "committee to work with the Office of Diversity Initiatives to develop a diversity planning process to provide structure, accountability, and stability."[29] In 2012, UNLV established the Leadership Development Academy and the Committee on Full Participation, Diversity, and Engagement. By 2015 it was determined that the newly appointed chief diversity officer would annually administer the Campus Climate Survey. And in 2017, the Strategic Diversity Project Implementation was revealed. It included the following: initiating a diversity branding campaign (UNLV is the second-most diverse campus nationally); improving diversity fundraising; organizing annual campus diversity celebrations; creating annual diversity reporting structures; examining low-pass-rate courses for disproportionate impact along racial/ethnic/gender dimensions; assessing the Faculty Diversity Hiring Program; and exploring the adequacy of the current diversity curriculum.[30]

Collectively, institutional diversity efforts by NSHE's postsecondary institutions indicate a positive trend toward enhancing a campus culture and a learning environment that accommodates minority students, and more specifically, Latino students. In sum, as Nevada's Latino student population continues to grow, along with student enrollments in four-year institutions, the success of many of these diversity initiatives will be better evaluated by observing improvements in the university graduation rates of Latino students and their preparedness to join Nevada's workforce.

CHAPTER 7

Conclusion—The Future

Although the majority of the Latino population in Nevada only began to arrive in the 1960s, the historical contributions Latinos have made to the state's mining, railroad, farming, ranching, and tourism industries have been well documented. Their impact on Nevada's development has been substantial and enduring, and with the steady growth of the Hispanic population, Nevada's Latinos will continue to influence all aspects of society in Nevada. This book provides only a snapshot of Nevada's Latino population as it has stood in the past and stands today. And yet, this study informs us on the central role Nevada's Latino population will play in the evolution of the state.

The Latino Community

The Latino community in Nevada is vibrant and thriving. It is also a diverse, multinational group with unique interests (table 7.1). It is a common belief that the Latino community is monolithic. However, many immigrants view themselves as having a distinct cultural identity. As one Guatemalan civic leader in Las Vegas noted, "Although I consider the Hispanic community a very large family joined together by language and history...when we say Hispanic, it's not all Mexicans...The Guatemalan community has its own identity, and it's important to recognize the richness and wealth of each community."[1] Moreover, in Nevada, and especially in Clark County, there have been periods of discord and disunity among Latinos of differing national origins. The divisiveness among Latinos was largely attributed to class, political, and ethnic/national origin differences. Mexican Americans have always been the largest Hispanic-origin group in Nevada. However, following the Cuban Revolution (1958), a large exodus of upper- and middle-class Cubans moved to the United States in the 1960s, and a sizeable proportion migrated to Nevada. Several more waves of Cuban migration followed. Cultural differences and class tensions were especially salient between Mexican and Cuban Americans. During the 1970s, Cuban Americans in Nevada tended to be middle and upper class, and they frequently spurned Mexican Americans who were more economically disadvantaged. In turn, Mexicans and Puerto Ricans in Nevada viewed Cubans as socially and politically ignorant because they had not experienced discrimination and social exclusion in the United States, and they could not empathize with their experience. Tensions were exacerbated as more Cubans opened businesses or gained employment in highly paid positions in the gaming and tourism sectors, while other Hispanic groups, but particularly Mexican Americans, tended to occupy hourly positions in hospitality, residential construction, and low-skilled trades.[2] Consequently, while Latino organizations and interest groups have made some progress, which will be discussed toward the end of this chapter, intra-ethnic conflict has been a significant barrier to initiatives and programs that would benefit the entire Hispanic/Latino community in Nevada.

Latinos and Linguistic, Intra-Ethnic, and Religious Diversity

The state's growing Latino population and its sociocultural diversity are evident by the number of programs and agencies that have increased in response to this group's specific needs, particularly its language needs (table 7.2). For example, the Clark County and Washoe County School Districts continue to develop dual-language education programs, which have been introduced in a number of schools in each district.[3] Similarly, the Las Vegas–Clark County Library District offers patrons access to Spanish language movies and television. Additionally, the district prints library guides and cards in Spanish. As of 2020, there are at least thirteen Spanish-language radio stations across Nevada, and until 2014 when the license of KNVV-LP, the affiliate of UniMas that served Reno, was canceled, there were seven Spanish-language television stations in Nevada. At the present time, six television stations remain in the state. The increasing number of Spanish-language advertisements and commercials reveal that the burgeoning Latino population is significant to the social fabric and economy of the entire state.

Research on the diversity of the Latino population in the United States, and particularly in Nevada, remains scant; still, scholars are recognizing that the Latin American identity is not monolithic. This diversity, however,

TABLE 7.1. Latino Population in Nevada, by Country of Origin, 2010

Country of Origin	Number	Percent
Hispanic or Latino	2,700,551	100
Hispanic or Latino (of any race)	716,501	26.5
Not Hispanic or Latino	1,984,050	73.5
Hispanic or Latino by origin country		
Hispanic or Latino (of any race)	716,501	26.5
Mexican	540,978	20
Puerto Rican	20,664	0.8
Cuban	21,459	0.8
Dominican (Dominican Republic)	2,446	0.1
Central American (excludes Mexican)	55,937	2.1
Costa Rican	1,433	0.1
Guatemalan	13,407	0.5
Honduran	4,481	0.2
Nicaraguan	4,475	0.2
Panamanian	1,615	0.1
Salvadoran	30,043	1.1
Other Central American	483	0
South American	19,056	0.7
Argentinean	3,419	0.7
Bolivian	481	0
Chilean	1,683	0.1
Colombian	5,230	0.2
Ecuadorian	2,045	0.1
Paraguayan	116	0
Peruvian	4,581	0.2
Uruguayan	407	0
Venezuelan	878	0
Other South American	216	0
Other Hispanic or Latino	55,961	2.1
Spaniard	10,980	0.4
Spanish	8,024	0.3
Spanish American	523	0
All Other Hispanic or Latino	36,434	1.3

Source: US Census, 2010

TABLE 7.2. Languages Spoken in Nevada, 2016

Language	Population	Percent
English	1,940,748	76.21
Spanish	517,935	20.34
Chinese	17,580	0.69
German	7,945	0.31
French	7,940	0.31
Amharic	7,075	0.28
Cantonese	4,495	0.18
Mandarin	4,375	0.17
Samoan	2,985	0.12
Portuguese	2,755	0.11

Source: 2016 American Community Survey 1-Year Survey

is most often discussed within the context of the regional variation of the Latino population across US states, and frequently overlooks other dimensions of intra-ethnic diversity, particularly among the foreign-born Latino population.

In Portes and Rumbaut's study of second-generation immigrants living in the United States, for example, the authors found that "there was an obvious convergence of race and ethnicity in the way they [second-generation immigrants] define their [own] identities."[4] Of those second-generation immigrants who identified ethnically as Asian, 92 percent identified Asian as their race; of those second-generation immigrants who ethnically identified as Black, 85 percent identified Black as their race; and of those second-generation immigrants who ethnically identified as Hispanic or Latino, 58 identified Hispanic or Latino as their race.[5] Their findings highlight a significant dynamic that has hampered racial and ethnic classification and reporting in the United States, including at the level of the US Census: the construction of ethnicity and race as synonymous identities, which has led to the explicit racialization of the Hispanic-Latino category. To illustrate, the 2010 US Census establishes a racial category for Asians, but an ethnic category for Hispanics, despite that both categories define a group of people according to the geographic origins of themselves or their ancestors. As a consequence of conflating race and ethnicity, the racial diversity of the Latino population is often obscured.

FIGURE 7.1. Nevada's Hispanic Population by Race, 2010

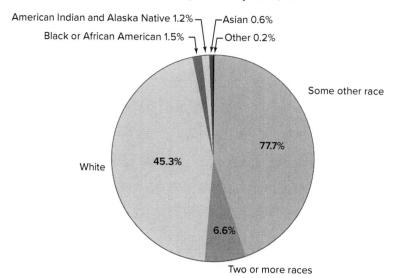

American Indian and Alaska Native 1.2%
Asian 0.6%
Black or African American 1.5%
Other 0.2%

Some other race

77.7%

White

45.3%

6.6%

Two or more races

Source: US Census Bureau, 2010 Census, Summary File 2, PCT 1 & 43

FIGURE 7.2. Nevada's Hispanic Population by Origin Region, 2010

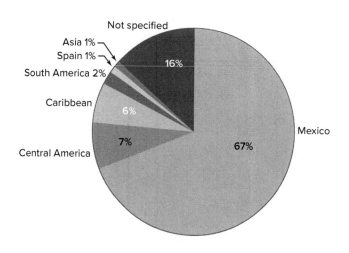

Not specified
Asia 1%
Spain 1%
South America 2%

16%

Caribbean

6%

Mexico

Central America

7%

67%

Source: US Census Bureau, 2010 Census, Summary File 2, PCT 1 & 43

Following the distribution of the 2010 Census, the US Census Bureau published a supplemental brief that provided greater detail on the intra-ethnic diversity of Nevada's Latino population. The findings of the supplemental study indicated that for Nevada's Latino population, the most prevalent racial identifications were "white alone" (45.3 percent) and "some other race" (44.7 percent).[6] The third most common racial identification for Nevada's Latino population was "two or more races" (6.6 percent). The other racial categories each accounted for less than 2 percent of Nevada's Latino population. Additionally, while the Mexican-origin group represents the largest and most prevalent foreign-born Latino group in Nevada, six other origin groups comprise at least 1 percent of Nevada's population, with individuals from El Salvador, Guatemala, and Cuba having relatively higher numbers (table 7.1 and fig. 7.2).

The intra-ethnic diversity of the foreign-born Latino population is mirrored by the growing religious diversity of the Latino community. Surveys carried out by the Pew Research Center found that in 2013, 55 percent of Latinos in the US identified themselves as Roman Catholic, while 22 percent identified as Protestant, with Evangelicals the majority. Although the predominance of Roman Catholicism among Latinos distinguished them as an ethnic group historically, the religious landscape appears to be changing. The Pew data suggest that from 2010 to 2013, the share of Protestant adherents among Latinos in the US grew rapidly, and came largely at the expense of affiliation with the Catholic Church, which experienced a decline of 12 percentage points in affiliation among Latinos during this period.[7] Moreover, two further distinctions can be observed when considering country of origin and nativity. For example, in 2013, 60 percent of the foreign-born Latino adult population identified as Catholic compared to 40 percent of the native-born. In addition, the percentage of Catholics among the foreign-born population from Mexico and the Dominican Republic is higher than for individuals from Puerto Rico, Cuba, or El Salvador.[8]

Very little has been written on the recent religious life of Latinos in Nevada. This is largely because historically, the majority of Latinos in Nevada were Roman Catholic, while the Church of Jesus Christ of Latter-day Saints (LDS, or Mormon) remained the predominant religion in the state. The salience of the Mormon tradition continues today. What little research that exists on the religiosity of Latinos in Nevada is fragmented and focused primarily on the Las Vegas valley. Still, some tendencies can be discerned. The Catholic Church continues to be an important part of the social fabric of the Latino community, and particularly among immigrants from Mexico. By 2020, for example, the Roman Catholic Diocese of Las Vegas was celebrating Mass in Spanish at no fewer than thirteen Catholic churches in the metropolitan area, which represented a substantial increase over the number in the 2000s.[9] Consistent with national trends, a growing number of immigrants from El Salvador, Guatemala, and Mexico have also started attending evangelical churches in the Las Vegas metropolitan area, including the Iglesia Cristiana Evangélica, the Iglesia Baustista Monte Horeb, and the Iglesia Bautisa El Refugio. Services in these evangelical churches are conducted in Spanish, but in the Iglesia Cristiana Evangélica, the pastor and members also speak in Otomi, an indigenous language from central Mexico.[10] Prior research also found that Guatemalans in Las Vegas use Kanjobal words occasionally in evangelical services, and some of their religious traditions in the household involve syncretism, a mix of practices of Roman Catholic and Maya origin.[11] Beyond these tendencies, we know very little about the religious composition of Latinos in Nevada, which is a key area for further study.

Latino Civic Organizations and Interest Groups

Latinos are also actively involved in a number of civic organizations and groups in Nevada. These groups comprise business and labor interests, sociocultural groups and associations, and other advocacy organizations. Latino membership in labor and business groups comes from a cross-section of the population, and these groups have sustained their activities over several decades. Civic organizations representing immigrants from Mexico and other Latin American countries have also grown, although levels of engagement vary across these groups.

Within the labor movement, the Culinary Workers Union Local 226 is the largest and most visible private sector union in Nevada.[12] First organized in 1935, the union's membership increased from 1987 to 2010, but then stabilized. In early 2020, the union estimated that it had approximately 60,000 members, of which about 45 percent (or more) are Latino.[13] There are no reliable estimates of the number of immigrant members in the union, but leaders suggest that a significant share of their Latino members are from Mexico, El Salvador, Guatemala, and other Central American countries. As noted in chapter 2, the current leader of the Culinary Union, Geoconda Arguëllo-Kline, is an immigrant from Nicaragua.

The Culinary Union is a model of social movement unionism. In addition to providing collective bargaining and workforce training,[14] the Culinary Union has also played a significant role in several policy areas. For example, since 2001, the union has partnered with several other civic organizations to support the Citizenship Project, a nonprofit association that provides free services to individuals who are seeking to become naturalized citizens. These services have become critical during the past few years, as the Trump administration has increased application fees for citizenship applications while implementing complex new rules (e.g., the "public charge rule") intended to make it more difficult for legal permanent residents to naturalize.[15] In addition, the union has been on the forefront of advocacy for immigration reform. In 2006, the Culinary Union was central to the mobilization of the May 1 immigration protest and rally on the Las Vegas Strip. Union members have staged a number of rallies to protest health care, immigration, asylum, and travel ban policies associated with the Trump administration, while the union has mobilized the vote. In March 2020, after Nevada governor Steve Sisolak shuttered casinos, restaurants, and bars in response to the COVID-19 pandemic, the Culinary Union negotiated with MGM Resorts International and Caesars Entertainment for the maintenance of pay and health benefits for many of its members affected by layoffs, and it organized other support services.[16]

Latinos are also active in other unions in Nevada. The Laborers Union Local 872, which represents workers in the commercial and skilled construction trades sector, has many Latino members.[17] Officials estimated that in 2008, at the onset of the Great Recession, the Laborers Union had about 5,600 members, of which about 65 percent were Latino. The majority of members were from Mexico, and, to a lesser extent, from Guatemala and El Salvador.[18] More recent membership data are not available, but the recovery of commercial construction since 2015 appears to have had a beneficial effect on the union's overall size. Compared to the Culinary Union, the Laborers Union is less active politically, although it does provide workers with apprenticeship and training programs that help to upgrade skill levels.[19]

During the late 1990s, Latinos joined unions in other segments of the construction trades. The International Brotherhood of Electrical Workers, in cooperation with the Southern Nevada Building and Construction Trades Council, unionized day laborers, carpenters, cement masons, and roofers who worked in residential and light commercial construction. At its peak, the unionization campaign employed forty organizers (including organizers who were fluent in Spanish) and employed prayer vigils, civil disobedience, corporate campaigns, and protest.[20] The results of the effort were impressive: the campaign unionized about 3,000 new members, including many Latinos.[21] Partly because of these efforts, unionized Latino workers continue to have a presence in the residential construction industry.

Beyond the labor movement, Latinos have also formed business interest groups. Created in the 1970s, the Latin Chamber of Commerce (LCC) promotes business opportunities for Latino-owned businesses. The (LCC) has also focused on the inadequacy of provision of grants for education and other social services for Latinos in Clark County.[22] Cuban Americans initially assumed prominent leadership positions in the group, and, as noted, the dominance of Cubans led to tensions occasionally with Mexican American business owners. Nonetheless, over time, business owners from a variety of different backgrounds joined its ranks. The (LCC) has claimed a membership of about 1,500 in recent years,[23] and at present, it provides financial support for workforce training, internships, and other programming to benefit Latino students. The group continues to advocate for the interests of minority-owned businesses, while strongly supporting the need to improve education and reform immigration policy.[24] The latter issue has gained salience for some members as the Trump administration has imposed more restrictions on immigration. As with the Culinary Union, members of the (LCC) have expressed interest in federal relief to mitigate the economic crisis associated with the COVID-19 emergency.

Finally, Latin American immigrants in Nevada have formed immigrant clubs and organizations. To varying degrees, immigrant associations support charitable projects in the "home" country, while sponsoring local events and promoting cultural cohesion. For example, one civic leader commented: "the Chihuahua association participated as a community liaison with the Las Vegas Fair held in Freedom Park. The proceeds earned by the association from the event were donated in their entirety to Emmanuel Children's Home in Juárez, México, a self-sustained orphanage and free-of-charge childcare facility."[25] They have also coordinated their activities with government officials to help people register to vote.

By most accounts, the number of immigrant groups per country varies. Because of the lack of state registry data, it is difficult to estimate the number in Nevada. However, based upon information obtained from Mexican authorities, there are a number of Mexican associations in Nevada, and, as in other parts of the United States, immigrants tend to form clubs based on their home state in Mexico. In recent years, at least nine Mexican associations were organized from individuals from Michoacán, Colima, Hidalgo, Guadalajara, Jalisco, Puebla, Durango, Chihuahua, and Zacatecas.[26]

Central American countries immigrants have also formed civic associations. Created in 2002, El Comité de Unidad Guatemalteco (COMUGUA—Guatemalan Unity Committee) represents Guatemalans. Like many Mexican hometown associations, COMUGUA sponsors festivals, produces a radio program, and helps immigrants obtain important services from the Guatemalan government. In contrast to the organizations founded by Mexicans and Guatemalans in Nevada, individuals from the Salvadoran community have found it difficult to sustain civic associations. One recent association, the Fundación Salvadoreña, has sought to assist members with voter registration and other services, but it apparently has a low level of visibility in the local community.[27]

Latino Spending Power

Beyond the contribution of Latinos to a number of economic and labor industries, this group wields tremendous consumer power nationwide and in Nevada. The economic contribution of Latinos to the United States has been considerable. In 2015, it was estimated that Latinos had an after-tax income of more than $687.8 billion.[28] In other words, almost one out of every ten US dollars of disposable income is held by Latinos in the United States, and foreign-born Latinos account for almost half of that figure. It is estimated that in the same year, the spending power of foreign-born Latinos totaled $322.1 billion. Latino families also contributed almost $215 billion to US tax revenues in 2015, including almost $76 billion in state and local tax revenue; while foreign-born Latinos contributed nearly $97 billion in tax revenue nationwide, which represented $36 billion in state and local taxes and more than $61 billion in federal tax revenue.[29]

Consistent with national figures, Latinos account for a substantial proportion of spending power and tax revenue in Nevada. The earnings of Latino households, after taxes, accounted for more than one-sixth of the spending power in the state. To break these figures down further, in 2015

Latino families in Nevada paid $2.6 billion in federal taxes and $1.6 billion in state and local taxes (including more than $500 million in sales taxes), while the spending power of Latinos in Nevada is more than $14 billion. This suggests that Latinos have an important contribution to the state's overall growth and total gross state product.

Policies, Problems, and Prospects for the Future

Despite the advances and progress made by Latinos in Nevada, many problems remain. Nevada's Latino families are twice as likely as White families to be at risk for poverty and, in 2015, they had the second-lowest median household earnings among racial and ethnic groups (~$43,800); and estimates for 2013 to 2017 reported that 19 percent of Latino children in Nevada lived in low-income neighborhoods where poverty is 30 percent or higher.[30] The 2020 economic crisis is just emerging, but it will probably worsen poverty in the state. As noted in chapter 4, preliminary estimates suggest that 206,000 employees in Nevada's gaming sector have been temporarily laid off. In addition, a forecast from the Economic Policy Institute—which took into consideration preliminary information on the federal emergency stimulus—suggests that Nevada may see a loss of 65,000 jobs, or 5.4 percent of private sector employment, in the near-term.[31] In this context, poverty in Latino families might increase because Latinos are concentrated in gaming and hospitality, which places them at higher risk for unemployment. However, if the federal government expands income support and provides supplemental unemployment funding, these policies might mitigate the growth of poverty among Latinos and other groups.

Latino students in Nevada are the least likely to complete high school or the equivalent. As noted in chapter 6, despite some gains, Latino children in Nevada are also least likely to complete college, with only 8.4 percent of Nevada's Latino students graduating from college, compared to 16.8 percent of African Americans, 26.2 percent of Whites, and 37 percent of Asian Americans. Of equal significance is the astounding lack of data on Latinos in the criminal justice system. In an analysis of state criminal justice data, 40 states reported race (e.g., "white," "black," "other") in their arrest records, while only 15 states reported ethnicity.[32] Beyond arrest data, only 39 percent of states reported data on two or more of the five measures of the population under the control of the criminal justice system (e.g., prison population, prison population by offense, arrests, probation population, and parole population) based upon ethnicity. Nevada does report data on Latinos, but only for arrests. The failure of Nevada to collect and report comprehensive data on the criminal justice system has implications for not only Latinos, but for the criminal justice system as a whole. The reporting of offenders as either "black" or "white" means Latinos are most often classified as "white," which results in the artificial inflation of the "white" racial category, thereby obscuring the significant racial disparities that exist across the criminal justice system. It also makes it impossible for Nevada to assess how the criminal justice system affects Latinos in the state.

The aforementioned factors—low income, lack of educational attainment, and interaction with the criminal justice system—are all intertwined, and poor indicators across these measures function to impede the socioeconomic mobility and advancement of Nevada's Latino population. Yet, in spite of these challenges, Latinos in the state recognize the importance of political mobilization and how crucial it is to achieving societal progress.

Latinos in Nevada demonstrate a high level of political engagement. Nevada's Latinos account for a growing share of the electorate, and, as noted in chapter 3, their turnout has been important in recent elections. At the same time, however, although almost one-third of Nevada's population is Latino, they are grossly underrepresented with respect to elected officials. As of the 2018 midterm elections, 8 percent of Nevada's elected officials are Hispanic/Latino.[33] Experts note that the lack of Latino political representation in Nevada is not so much because of a lack of desire, motivation, or enthusiasm—traits exhibited by voter turnout. The problem has more to do with a history of a lack of party engagement of potential candidates, a lack of information regarding the candidacy process, and the belief that campaigns are resource intensive. This is evident by the challenges of recruiting Latino candidates to run in Nevada's Fourth Congressional District, despite it being approximately 27 percent Hispanic. Elected in 2016, Rubén Kihuen, an immigrant from Mexico, served as the House representative in the Fourth Congressional District until 2019. Because of allegations of sexual misconduct, however, he did not seek reelection. Despite this setback, grassroots organizations (e.g., the Las Vegas–based group, Hispanics in Politics) are working to recruit and support potential

Latino candidates and channel the political activism of Nevada's Latino population into political representation.

The political engagement and representation of Latinos in Nevada are especially significant, given the current political climate and increasing rise of anti-immigrant legislation. Almost 75 percent of Nevada's Latino population is comprised of persons of Mexican descent (table 7.1)—the Latino origin group most affected by immigration policy. In the 2018 *Latino Decisions* Election Eve Poll for Nevada, 34 percent of Latinos surveyed indicated that improving the economy "is the most important issue facing the Latino community that politicians should address."[34] Nonetheless, health care and immigration/DACA ranked as second- and third-most important issues, at 26 and 24 percent, respectively.[35] One of the main reasons why immigration remains a major political issue for Latinos in Nevada, and to many citizens across the United States, is because of more targeted anti-immigration legislation.

Beginning in 1986, the Immigration Reform and Control Act (IRCA) permitted the initiation of removal proceedings for any immigrant convicted of a "deportable offense," which included some misdemeanor infractions under state law. The federal government has since enacted a series of punitive laws, which now criminalizes nonviolent immigration offenses. This legislation was followed by the Illegal Immigration Reform and Immigrant Responsibility Act (IIRIRA) and the Anti-Terrorism and Effective Death Penalty Act (AEDPA), which strengthened the Immigration and Naturalization Service (INS) by expanding its authority to arrest, detain, and deport noncitizens, even if the individual has native-born children, is a longtime settled resident, and is not a violent crime or felony offender. After the September 11, 2001, terrorist attacks, the US Patriot Act transformed the policy frame of unauthorized immigration from that of a criminal offense to a threat to national security. This heightened level of scrutiny was further sanctioned by the joint US Department of Homeland Security (DHS) and US Department of Justice (DOJ) initiative, Operation Streamline, which while passed in 2005, was not fully implemented until 2010, under President Barack Obama. This initiative prompted much of the criticism that Obama was the so-called "Deporter-in-Chief," because a record number of unauthorized immigrants were deported under his administration (fig. 7.3).

FIGURE 7.3. ICE Removals under Obama and Trump Administrations, 2015–2019

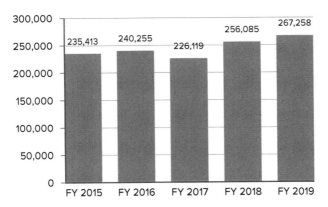

Source: US Immigration and Customs Enforcement
Note: This includes individuals arrested by ICE in the interior of the country and individuals apprehended by immigration officials at the border and turned over to ICE for removal.

Under President Donald Trump, figures released by the DHS indicate that the total number of deportations initially declined in FY 2016 and FY 2017—to the lowest level seen since 2006—but increased in the following two fiscal years. However, deportation has become less selective since Trump took office in January 2017. Despite the overall decline in removals, more longtime settled residents in the United States were deported in FY 2019 compared to 2016 (fig. 7.4). With Trump's demand for a border wall between Mexico and the US, the as-yet-undetermined fate of the DACA program—whose cancellation is being challenged in federal courts—has placed thousands of "Dreamers" in jeopardy and legal limbo. Ruling in June 2020, the US Supreme Court held that the Trump administration did not terminate the DACA program lawfully, but noted that the administration could still end the program by following the required administrative procedures. As a result, Dreamers remain in a precarious legal position. The uncertain status of Dreamers resonates with the broader community in Nevada. An analysis of microdata from the American Community Survey indicates that 12,280 Latinos in Nevada had received DACA protection by 2017, and many have ties to extended family, educational institutions,

FIGURE 7.4. ICE Interior Removals under Obama and Trump Administrations, 2015–2019

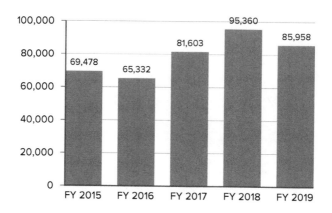

Source: US Immigration and Customs Enforcement
Note: This includes the deportation of people who have already lived in the United States and excludes deportations of people detained at the border.

and business in the state.[36] At the same time, with talk of broader immigration reforms, such as ending the US Immigration and Customs Enforcement (ICE) "catch and release" program as well as the diversity visa lottery, immigration to the United States is poised to remain a salient issue at the heart of a national debate.

Immigration also remains central and controversial at the regional and state level. In 2005, the governors of Arizona and New Mexico declared border emergencies and demanded increased federal help to secure their borders. In a controversial and highly publicized move, an organization of volunteers called the Minutemen Project joined the US Border Patrol to dramatize the situation and to help apprehend undocumented border crossers.

In response to the increasingly anti-immigrant rhetoric in US politics, Latinos and Latin American immigrants in Las Vegas and other cities mobilized major protests in 2006, and in 2007, and demanded immigration reform. More recently, "restrictive" immigration legislation (e.g., SB 1070) was adopted in Arizona, and other states have generated political debate and legal challenges in federal courts. Similarly, in Nevada, the Nevada Prevent Sanctuary Cities Initiative,[37] a citizen-proposed constitutional amendment for the November 2020 election, failed to qualify for the ballot. The Nevada Prevent Sanctuary Cities Initiative was designed to effectively prevent the enactment of laws by the state legislature, county commissioners, and city councils that would make Nevada a sanctuary state, as well as any city or county in Nevada.

As the statewide and national debate continues, immigration policy will continue to be an important issue to Latinos in Nevada. Beyond immigration policy, the issues of education, health care, and the economy are salient to Latinos in the state. Ultimately, however, with the sustained growth of Nevada's Latino population, there is a significant opportunity for Latinos in Nevada to translate their considerable political and consumer purchasing power into tangible socioeconomic gains in the near future and beyond.

Appendix

A. Data Sources

Analysis presented in chapters 2, 3, and 4 employs data from several sources, allowing us to capture dimensions of Latino political behavior over time and at different levels. Many of these sources raise methodological issues, however, because of concerns about their ability to measure the behavior of a representative cross-section of Nevada's Latino population. In particular, evidence from 2012 in Nevada and nationally for prior cycles reveals that attempts to assess the preferences of Latino voters consistently under-sample segments of the Latino population that are the most Democratic leaning (e.g., young and first-time voters and less educated and poorer Latinos). In what follows, we detail some of the specific issues surrounding the data sources used in our analysis.

1. Exit Polls

To estimate the Latino share of the Nevada electorate in chapter 3 we use data from the Voter News Service (2000 and 2002) and National Election Pool (NEP) exit polls (2004–2012) for Nevada. The main concern with these data is their ability to estimate the vote preferences of the Latino electorate. However, because we use these data to assess the share of the Nevada electorate that was Latino, as opposed to the vote choice of Latino voters, this issue has less bearing on our analysis. A more significant concern is that exit polling does not survey voters who cast their ballots early, an increasingly common practice in Nevada. Thus, the degree to which the demographic characteristics of early voters differ from Election Day voters could be a source of error in estimating the racial and ethnic composition of the Nevada electorate.

2. Current Population Survey (CPS)

The CPS is a monthly national survey conducted by the US Census Bureau that yields a sample of 50,000 occupied households. The survey employs in-person and telephone interviews. Each state sample is conducted independently, and results are weighted to reflect updated census estimates. Because the CPS uses probability sampling to select respondents, the estimates it provides are subject to sampling variation. Unfortunately, the error margins for the CPS estimates can be quite large, particularly for minority groups. Thus, the data presented in figures 3.3 and 3.4 should be interpreted cautiously given the large confidence intervals for some of these estimates.

3. The impreMedia/Latino Decisions Election Eve Poll

Much of the analysis presented in chapter 3 uses data from a survey conducted in the days leading up to the 2012 election and includes responses from 400 Latino voters in Nevada who had either voted early or reported that they were certain to vote on Election Day. The poll's margin of error is 4.9 percent. Respondents were selected based upon three sources of information: Latino surnames gleaned from voter registration data; US Census data capturing the geography of Nevada's Latino population; and consumer information such as magazine subscriptions. Surveys were conducted in both English and Spanish using cell phones and landlines. The result is that the survey contains a representative cross-section of Nevada's Latino population, including subgroups of Latino voters (e.g., first-time voters and lower socioeconomic Latinos) who are often under-sampled in election polling conducted in Nevada.

4. Latino Voter Turnout in Clark County

The voter turnout data provided by the Clark County Election Department consist of a Latino surname search of registered voters who voted in the November 2012 election. Because these data are available only for Clark County, we are unable to analyze Latino turnout in the rest of the state. The major limitation associated with these data is they rely on surnames to identify Latino voters. Because roughly 80 percent of Latinos can be identified in this manner, these data are likely to underestimate Latino turnout.

B. Figures

APPENDIX MAP 1. Intermountain West Region—The Suicide Belt (2000–2006)

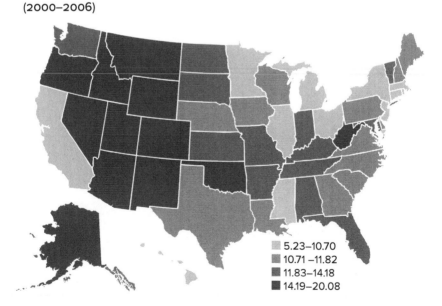

5.23–10.70
10.71 –11.82
11.83–14.18
14.19–20.08

Source: US Suicide Rate, 2000–2006. Age-adjusted death rates per 100,000 population

APPENDIX MAP 2. Percent of US Population that is Foreign-Born, 2010

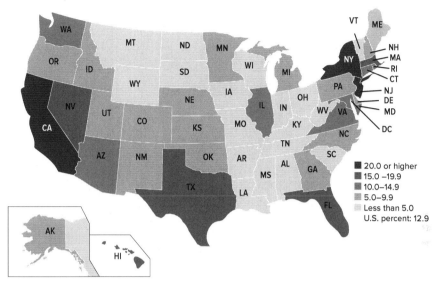

Source: US Census Bureau, American Community Survey, 2010

APPENDIX FIGURE 1. US Population Projection, 1990–2050 (in Percentages)

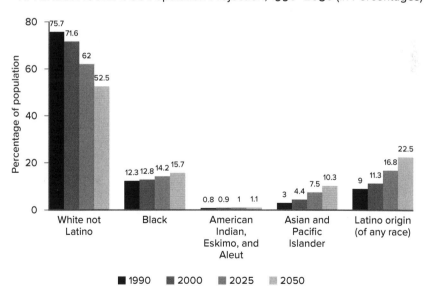

Source: US Census Bureau, Population Division

APPENDIX MAP 3. Net Domestic Migration Per 1,000 Residents, July 1, 2016–July 1, 2017

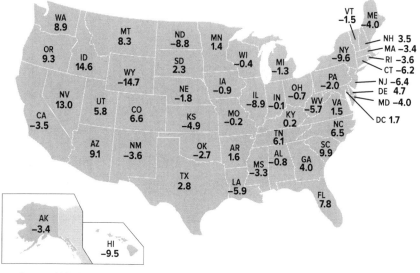

Source: U.S. Census Bureau, Population Division

Note: Net migration is measured by inflows minus outflows in the specified period. A negative sign means that there was a net outflow per 1,000 residents.

APPENDIX TABLE 1. Percentage of Health-Care Graduates in Nevada, by Race and Ethnicity, 2015

Occupation/ Degree Program	Total Completions AY 2014–2015	White	Black	Hispanic	Asian	Other
Physicians						
Doctor's Program-Allopathic (MD)	70	65.7	2.9	7.1	15.7	8.6
Doctor's Program-Osteopathic (DO)	129	52.7	1.6	5.4	39.5	0.8
Physician Assistants						
Master's Programs	57	59.6	5.3	10.5	21.1	2.3
Registered Nurses						
Associate's Programs	512	60.4	5.3	15	12.7	6.6
Bachelor's Programs	539	52.7	3.5	10.4	21.5	11.9
Nurse Practitioners						
Master's Programs	26	65.4	3.8	3.8	11.5	15.4
Dentists						
Doctor's Programs	76	59.2	0.0	6.6	23.7	10.5
Dental Hygienists						
Bachelor's and Associate's Programs	52	51.9	7.7	21.2	7.7	11.5
Pharmacists						
Doctor's Programs	260	54.6	3.5	3.1	29.6	9.2
Psychologists						
Doctor's Programs	26	69.2	0.0	3.8	3.8	23.1
Social Workers						
Master's Programs	98	48	14.3	23.5	3.1	11.2
Marriage and Family Therapists						
Master's Programs	0	0.0	0.0	0.0	0.0	0.0
Substance Abuse/Addiction Counselors						
Associate's Programs	5	60	0.0	20.0	20.0	0.0
Physical Therapy						
Doctor's Programs	64	73.4	1.6	9.4	9.4	6.3
Public Health Professionals						
Master's Programs	64	42.2	7.8	6.3	7.8	7.8

Source: Griswold, Tabor, John Packham, Christopher Marchand, Laima Etchegoyhen, and Troy Jorgensen (2017). "Health Workforce Supply in Nevada-2017 Edition." University of Nevada (Reno)-School of Medicine Report. Available at: file:///Users/tiffiany howard/Downloads/HWIN_Supply_Report_2017_FINAL2%20(3).pdf

Notes

Chapter 1: Introduction—A History

1. See Brian Gratton and Emily Klancher Merchant, "An Immigrant's Tale."
2. At the time, the territory of Nevada formed part of the Mexican province known as Alta California. Developed by Antonio Armijo, the Old Spanish Trail linked parts of contemporary Utah to Southern Nevada in the early nineteenth century. By some accounts, US Interstate 15 follows one of the original branches of the trail. See *Las Vegas Review-Journal*, "Retrace Nevada history along Old Spanish Trail," September 25, 2011, https://www.reviewjournal.com/entertainment /entertainment-columns/trip-of-the-week/retrace-nevada-history-along-old -spanish-trail/.
3. For a classic treatment of this period from a Mexican perspective, see Vázquez and Meyer, *México frente a Estados Unidos*, chaps. 2–3.
4. Scholars suggest that the term "Latino" emerged in the mid-nineteenth century, as a way for individuals in former colonies in Latin America, including Mexico and other countries, to distance themselves from Spain. It is derived from Amérique Latine, a French term that referred to areas of South America colonized by the "Latin" countries of southern Europe.
5. On the use of the patio process during Mexico's colonial period, see Elías Trabulse, "Aspectos de la tecnología minera en Nueva España a finales del siglo XVIII," *Historia Mexicana* 30, no. 3 (1981): 311–57. For a discussion of the arrastra mines and the process, see Grant H. Smith, *The History of the Comstock Lode, 1850–1920* (Reno: University of Nevada Press, 1943).
6. See the Nevada Bureau of Mines and Geology, "The Washoe Process," accessed February 29, 2020, http://www.nbmg.unr.edu/ScienceEducation/ScienceOfThe Comstock/Chemistry-Ore.html.
7. For details on the Spanish Ranch, see Miranda, *History of Hispanics*, 53–57; and Shawn Hall, *Connecting the West: Historic Railroad Stops and Stage Stations in Elko County, Nevada* (Reno: University of Nevada Press, 2002), 9, 86, 169–70, 189.
8. Richard J. Orsi, *Sunset Limited: The Southern Pacific Railroad and the Development of the American West, 1850–1930* (Berkeley: University of California Press, 2005), 114, 231–32, et passim.
9. Miranda, *History of Hispanics*, 76–78.
10. Miranda, 78.
11. Camille Guerin-Gonzales, *Mexican Workers and American Dreams: Immigration, Repatriation, and California Farm Labor, 1900–1939* (New Brunswick: Rutgers University Press, 1994), 8.

12. On the demise of the program and opposition from the AFL-CIO, see Richard B. Craig, *The Bracero Program: Interest Groups and Foreign Policy* (Austin: University of Texas Press, 1971), 28, 182, 187–90. For estimates on labor flows, see Barbara Driscoll, *The Tracks North: The Railroad Bracero Program of World War II* (Austin: University of Texas Press, 1999), 156–58.

13. D'Vera Cohn, "Future Immigration," http://www.pewresearch.org/fact-tank/2015/10/05/future-immigration-will-change-the-face-of-america-by-2065/.

14. Krogstad, "Reflecting a Racial Shift," https://www.pewresearch.org/fact-tank/2019/08/21/u-s-counties-majority-nonwhite/.

Chapter 2: Immigration

1. In this chapter and subsequent chapters, we follow the convention and use "Latino" and "Hispanic" interchangeably. See Wright, Tuman, and Stevenson, "Immigration and Ethnic Diversity," in *Social Health of Nevada*, ed. Dmitri N. Shalin, accessed May 28, 2013, http://digitalscholarship.unlv.edu/social_health_nevada_reports/44.

2. Throughout this report, we use the following data files. For the 2000 and 2010 Census, we draw upon: US Census Bureau, 2000 Census. File DP-1. "Profile of General Demographic Characteristic: Census 2000 Summary File (SF1), Nevada"; "2000 Census. QT-P9. Hispanic or Latino by Type: 2000 Census. Geographic Area, Clark County"; 2010 Census File DP-1; "Profile of General Population and Housing Characteristics: 2010 Demographic Profile Data, Nevada"; 2010 Census File DP-1; "Profile of General Population and Housing Characteristics: 2010 Demographic Profile Data. Geography: Clark County." For one-year estimates from 2011, we use the American Community Survey: US Census Bureau, "2011 American Community Survey, 1-year Estimates. File S0506, Selected Characteristics of the Foreign-Born Population by Region and Birth: Latin America. Geography: Nevada"; "2011 American Community Survey, 1-year Estimates. File B01001I; "Sex by Age (Hispanic or Latino). Geography: Nevada." Finally, for the 2018 1-year estimates, we use: "Hispanic or Latino, percent (Nevada)," Vintage 2018 Population Estimates Program."

3. For examples of theoretical work that discusses push and pull factors and local context, see Massey and Espinosa, "What's Driving Mexico-US," 939–99; Massey, and Riosmena, "Undocumented Migration from Latin America," 294–321; and Massey, Durand, and Malone, *Beyond Smoke and Mirrors*.

4. According to data from the American Community Survey (ACS), in 2011, Latinos accounted for 27.1 percent of Nevada's population. It should be noted that when we discuss trends over time, we generally make use of the decennial census data to avoid problems with the comparability between different census figures and estimates reported by the ACS. According to the US Census Bureau, it is not advisable to compare data on the "Hispanic origin" population from the 2011 ACS to data from the 2000 Census: "The ACS question on Hispanic origin was revised in 2008 to make it consistent with the Census 2010 Hispanic origin question.

Any change, compared with Census 2000, may be due to demographic changes, questionnaire changes, differences in ACS population controls, and/or methodological differences in the population estimates." (US Census Bureau, "American Community Survey: Guide to Data Users, Hispanic Origin," accessed April 17, 2013, https://www.census.gov/programs-surveys/acs/guidance/comparing-acs -data/2011.html). For this reason, when we compare changes over time (before 2008), we employ data from the 2000 Census and 2010 Census. For one-year estimates for the most recent data available, we employ the ACS data.

5. In 2011, approximately 51.3 percent of the Latino population was male, while 48.7 percent was female. The proportion of men and women in the foreign-born population from Latin America in Nevada is the same. See US Census Bureau, "2011 American Community Survey, 1-year Estimates. File B010011. Sex by Age (Hispanic or Latino). Geography: Nevada."

6. Beginning with the 2010 Census, the US Census Bureau shifted some of the more detailed questions on Hispanics and the foreign-born population to the ACS (which is based on a large voluntary sample but not a complete population count). For this reason, we report the ACS data (from 2011) in this section because it provides the only estimate for this group. See US Census Bureau, "American Community Survey: History," accessed April 17, 2013, http://www .census.gov/history/www/programs/demographic/american_community_survey .html.

7. In the same year, immigrants from Mexico represented 32.5 percent of Nevada's total population.

8. See Wright and Moody, "The Salvadorans," 247–67; Tuman and Gearhart, "The Guatemalans," 210–30.

9. See Lindstrom, "Economic Opportunity in Mexico," 357–74; Massey and Espinosa, "What's Driving Mexico-US Migration," 939–99; Massey and Riosmena, "Undocumented Migration from Latin America," 294–321; Massey, Durand, and Malone, *Beyond Smoke and Mirrors*; Creighton and Riosmena, "Migration and the Gendered Origin," 79–99.

10. The percentages are calculated from data on age structure of the population in Mexico from the 1970–2010 Mexican census. See Instituto Nacional de Estadística y Geografía (INEGI), *Censo General de Población y Vivienda 1970* (Aguascalientes, Mexico: INEGI, 1970), https://www.inegi.org.mx/programas /ccpv/1970/; Instituto Nacional de Estadística y Geografía (INEGI), *Censo General de Población y Vivienda 1980* (Aguascalientes, Mexico: INEGI, 1980), https:// www.inegi.org.mx/programas/ccpv/1980/; Instituto Nacional de Estadística y Geografía (INEGI), *Censo General de Población y Vivienda 1990* (Aguascalientes, Mexico: INEGI, 1990), https://www.inegi.org.mx/programas/ccpv/1990/; Instituto Nacional de Estadística y Geografía (INEGI), *Censo General de Población y Vivienda 2000* (Aguascalientes, Mexico: INEGI, 2000), https://www.inegi.org.mx /programas/ccpv/2000/; Instituto Nacional de Estadística y Geografía (INEGI), 2010, *Censo General de Población y Vivienda 2000* (Aguascalientes, Mexico:

INEGI, 2010), https://www.inegi.org.mx/programas/ccpv/2010/. All INEGI files accessed April 5, 2013.

11. On the longer-term trends, see Tuman, "Labor Markets and Economic Reform," 173–87; and Tuman, *Reshaping the North American Automobile*. The term "formal sector" refers to work that is counted and measured in government employment surveys and in reporting for government social security contributions and national income accounts.

12. Sanchez and Pacheco, "Rural Population Trends in Mexico," 155–68.

13. The under-14-years-old age share of the population in Mexico and El Salvador has declined recently, which will eventually reduce pressure on labor markets as more people move into retirement. In Guatemala, the reduction in the 0–14 age share has been slight (indeed, fully 43 percent of the population in 2011 was still in the 0–14 age range). For comparison purposes, it should be noted that only 20 percent of the US population was 15 and under in 2010. Estimates are obtained from the World Bank, 2013. *World Development Indicators*. Data Series: "Fertility rate, total (births per woman)." Online statistical database, accessed February 24, 2013, http://databank.worldbank.org/.

14. Fox and Haight, "Mexican Agricultural Policy," 9–50.

15. From 1999 to 2008, some of the volatility in manufacturing employment in the Mexican maquila sector was exacerbated by industrial relocation of low-wage export assembly from northern Mexico to China. The recent rise in fuel, shipping, and unit labor costs in China has reversed some of this trend.

16. Miguel Flores et al., "NAFTA, Industrial Concentration, Employment," 155–72.

17. Tuman and Gearhart, "The Guatemalans"; Wright and Moody, "The Salvadorans." As noted, Latinos born in Cuba also constitute one of the top five Latino groups in Nevada. Although some Cubans who have come to Nevada are political refugees, the vast majority of recent immigrants appear to be motivated by economic considerations.

18. Transcript of interview with Geoconda Arguëllo-Kline by Claytee D. White, September 18, 2014, Latinx Voices of Southern Nevada, UNLV Library Special Collections, https://cdm17304. contentdm.oclc.org/digital/collection/ohi/id/338 /rec/1.

19. Anonymous interview #2, Las Vegas, Nevada, 2007. (This interview was conducted as part of the research project for Tuman and Gearhart, "The Guatemalans.")

20. The stagnation in real wages has been observed in the dynamic sectors of Mexican manufacturing as well, including the Mexican automobile industry (see Tuman, *Reshaping the North American Automobile*). It is interesting to note that wage returns for lower-skilled labor improved in the early 2010s (see Lustig, Lopez-Calva, and Ortiz-Juarez, "Decline in Inequality in Latin America," accessed May 29, 2013, https://papers.ssrn.com/sol3/papers.cfm?abstract_id =2113476).

21. Several studies have noted the negative relationship between labor productivity and real wage settlements in Mexico. For a review, see Cypher and Delgado Wise,

"Restructuring Mexico, Realigning Dependency"; Tuman, *Reshaping the North American Automobile*.

22. Lustig, Ortiz-Juarez, and Lopez-Calva "Decline in Inequality."

23. Lindstrom, "Economic Opportunity in Mexico"; Massey and Espinosa, "What's Driving Mexico-US"; and Sanchez and Pacheco, "Rural Population Trends."

24. Tuman and Gearhart, "The Guatemalans."

25. Lindstrom, "Economic Opportunity in Mexico"; Massey, Durand, and Malone, *Beyond Smoke and Mirrors*.

26. Tuman and Gearhart, "The Guatemalans."

27. Wright, Tuman, and Stevenson, "Immigration and Ethnic Diversity."

28. Authors' tabulation and analysis of Question K19 in the LNS, "Have you lived in another state in the US previously?" and (if yes), "Which state was that?" The analysis adjusted for only those Mexican-born respondents who were residing in Nevada at the time of the survey (Mexican-born in Nevada = 262; see table 2.2). A limitation of the data is that the survey item does not allow us to sort out which states in which respondents resided immediately before living in Nevada. An additional limitation is that respondents could select more than one state; still, given that almost three-fourths reported California, this is a minor limitation.

29. Tuman and Gearhart, "The Guatemalans." Although comparable data for El Salvador and Guatemala are not available, other studies have pointed to a large wage gap between each of these two countries and the US.

30. Data for this comparison are taken from Nevada Department of Employment, Training and Rehabilitation, 2012; "Nevada Occupational Employment and Wages" (2012), "Statewide Occupational Wage Estimates All Industries–SOC 472061," http://www.nevadaworkforce.com/admin/uploadedPublications/2857 _OES_WAGE_Statewide_2012. Xls; and Secretaría del Trabajo y Previsión Social, "Salario de Cotización al IMSS por Sector de Actividad Económica—Pesos por día—Construcción," accessed April 5, 2013, http://www.stps.gob.mx/bp /secciones/conoce/areas_atencion/areas_atencion/web/menu_infsector.html. Of course, this is a broad average that does not adjust for specific occupations within construction.

31. Tuman, *Latin American Migrants*.

32. Transcript of interview with Geoconda Arguëllo-Kline by Claytee D. White, September 18, 2014, at section 8, Latinx Voices of Southern Nevada, UNLV Library Special Collections, https://cdm17304.contentdm.oclc.org/digital/collection/ohi /id/338/rec/1.

33. Waddoups and Eade, "Hotels and Casinos."

34. Tuman, *Latin American Migrants*.

35. Tuman and Gearhart, "The Guatemalans."

36. Prior studies have not found that membership in an immigrant association from Latin America creates a barrier to assimilation or naturalization among immigrants in Nevada and the US. For statistical evidence and analysis, see Fernandez, Tuman, and Stevenson, "Transnational Ties and Political Behavior."

37. We thank Dr. Jaewon Lim, associate professor of public policy and leadership at UNLV, for assistance with tabulation of the 1-percent PUMS data on interstate migration.

38. See Passel and Cohn, "US Unauthorized Immigration Flows." Certainly, this finding is consistent with our calculations from the ACS data. From 2007 to 2010, the number of people born in Mexico and residing in Nevada fell. We will elaborate more on state-to-state and international migration trends in a separate report. It should be noted that our results are preliminary and only for the Mexican population, without any adjustments for immigration status, while Passel and Cohn examine the unauthorized population in the entire state, without adjustments for the country of origin of the immigrant.

39. See Passel, Cohn, and Gonzalez-Barrera, "Net Migration from Mexico Falls."

Chapter 3: Political Profile

1. See, for example, Frey, "Hispanics, Race and the Changing Political Landscape," 82–106. For studies of the political influence of Latinos in the US., see Abrajano and Alvarez, *New Faces, New Voice*; De la Garza and Jang, "Why the Giant Sleeps," 895–916; Fraga et al., "Su casa es nuestra casa," 515–21; and Leal et al., "Latinos, Immigration, and the 2006," 309–17.

2. For an extended discussion, see Damore, "The 2001 Nevada Redistricting," 149–68.

3. See Damore, "Swimming against the Tide," 67–86.

4. With the expulsion of Steven Brooks from the Nevada Legislature on March 28, 2013, the number of Latinos serving in the Assembly was reduced by one.

5. Assembly District 27 in Washoe County, which has a Latino voting-age population of 19 percent, is represented by Democrat Teresa Benitez-Thompson.

6. See the appendix for methodological limitations associated with the data used in this section.

7. See Tuman, *Latin American Migrants*, 14–15; Tuman and Gearhart, "The Guatemalans," 213–30; Bada et al., *Context Matters*, 57–59; and Barreto et al., "Mobilization, Participation and Solidaridad," 376–764.

8. Note that 20 percent of the sample either did not know or refused to report their household income.

9. Calculated from the US Census Bureau, 2011 American Community Survey (ACS), 1-year Estimates. File S0506. "Selected Characteristics of the Foreign-Born Population by Region and Birth: Latin America. Geography: Nevada," and File B010011, "Sex by Age (Hispanic or Latino). Geography: Nevada." Note that although the ACS data do include data for the Latino population ages 29 and younger, they do not include an estimate of the foreign-born Latino population 25–29 (they report foreign-born Latinos 25–44). As a result, we use the 24-and-under data here because it allows us to adjust for immigration.

10. Note that for these questions, the sample was split in half so that 200 respondents were asked the Obama DHS question and 200 respondents were asked the Romney "self-deport" question.

11. Although dated, the 2006 Latino National Survey, which included a representative sample of immigrants in the US and in Nevada, remains one of the best sources for immigrant attitudes. See Luis Fraga et al., Latino National Survey (2006), ICPSR machine-readable data set. While attitudes toward abortion and other social issues remain conservative in Latin America, other attitudes are changing. For some discussion on Mexico and other Latin American countries, see Tuman, Roth-Johnson, and Jelen, "Conscience and Context," 100–112; and Jelen, Roth-Johnson, and Tuman, "Culture Wars in Latin America," 1–7.

12. *Latino Decisions* estimates that without taking into consideration the Latino vote, President Obama trailed Mitt Romney by four points in Nevada (see Barreto, "Comprehensive Immigration Reform," accessed March 18, 2012, http://www .latinodecisions.com/files/2813/6250/5298/Immigration_refom_March5_Final .pdf).

13. See Barreto, "Proving the Exit Polls Prong, *The Latino Decisions* (blog), accessed March 18, 2013, https://latinodecisions.com/blog/proving-the-exit-polls-wrong -harry-reid-did-win-over-90-of-the-latino-vote/; Damore "Reid vs. Angle," 32–53.

14. Ella Nilsen, "Nevada's Entrance Polls Look Good for Bernie Sanders," *Vox*, February 22, 2020, https://www.vox.com/2020/2/22/21148770/nevada-caucuses -entrance-polls-2020-bernie-sanders; and Nicole Narea, "Latinos Were Bernie Sanders' Key to Victory in Nevada," *Vox*, February 22, 2020, https://www.vox .com/policy-and-politics/2020/2/22/21121694/nevada-caucuses-bernie-sanders -latino-vote-2020.

Chapter 4: The Great Recession, Labor Market Conditions, and Employment

1. Jorge Durand, Douglas S. Massey, and Karen A. Pren, "Double Disadvantage: Unauthorized Mexicans in the US Labor Market," *The Annals of the American Academy of Political and Social Science* 666, no. 1 (2016): 78–90; Esther Yoona Cho, "Revisiting Ethnic Niches: A Comparative Analysis of the Labor Market Experiences of Asian and Latino Undocumented Young Adults," *RSF: The Russell Sage Foundation Journal of the Social Sciences* 3, no. 4 (2017): 97–115; Tuman, Damore, and Ágreda, "The Impact of the Great Recession," 1–14, https://digital scholarship.unlv.edu/brookings_pubs/28/.

2. See Nevada Department of Employment, Training and Rehabilitation, "Nevada Labor Market Overview," September 2016, 1–28.

3. Bureau of Labor Statistics, *Geographical Profile of Employment and Unemployment* reports, Washington, DC, Bureau of Labor Statistics, Local Area Unemployment Statistics Program (LAUSP), US Department of Labor. The BLS data are annual estimates and are derived from the Current Population Survey (CPS), which samples approximately 60,000 households in the US. The BLS also develops model-based estimates using other state data, including claims on unemployment. The state-level data on labor force participation, unemployment, and employment (with adjustment for race, ethnicity, and gender) may be reliably compared over time. When the Census Bureau provides new weights

or controls, or revisions in claims on state unemployment programs occur, the LAUSP may revise prior estimates. For a discussion, see Bureau of Labor Statistics, "Local Area Unemployment Statistics—Overview," at http://www.bls.gov /lau/lauov.htm. In this study, the data in figures 4.1 through 4.6 were obtained from the BLS-LAUSP *Geographical Profile of Employment and Unemployment* reports.

4. Flood et al., Integrated Public Use Microdata.

5. Tuman, Damore, and Ágreda, "Impact of the Great Recession," http://www.unlv .edu/sites/default/files/19/ImpactofGreatRecession-120113.pdf, 1–14.

6. Aaronson et al., "Labor Force Participation," http://www.federalreserve.gov/pubs /feds/2014/201464/201464pap.pdf; and Flippen and Tienda, "Pathways to Retirement," s14–s27.

7. The data on net migration from Nevada to other US states among Latinos (and the foreign-born Latino population) is consistent with this supposition. See Lim, Tuman, and Damore, "Interstate Migration Among Latinos," http://digital scholarship.unlv.edu/brookings_pubs/26, 1–14. On the impact of failure among self-employed Latino small-business owners, see US Department of Labor, "The Latino Labor Force," https://ecommons.cornell.edu/handle/1813/78877.

8. The overall labor force participate rate data from the BLS go through 2014, while the data adjusted for gender are available through 2015.

9. Statistical analysis of the Current Population Survey's microdata (for the years 2006, 2009, and 2013) indicates that, controlling for age, education, and gender, Latino men in Nevada are more likely (in comparison to women) to have an occupation in construction ($p<0.01$). For details on the methods, see note 12.

10. See Blau, Kahn, and Papp, "Gender, Source Country Characteristics," 43–58.

11. See Tuman, "Labor Markets and Economic Reform," 173–87; and Gasparini et al., "Female Labor Force Participation," 1–32. Concerning the share of Mexicans in the foreign-born Latino population in Nevada, see Tuman, Damore, and Ágreda, "Immigration and the Contours," https://digitalscholarship.unlv.edu/cgi/view content.cgi?article=1021&context=brookings_pubs, 1–18.

12. The microdata are from the March ASEC of the Current Population Survey and were obtained from IPUMS. Because the ASEC has a larger sample and about twice the number of Hispanic households (compared to the CPS sample), it is appropriate for this project. Person-level weights (WRSUPP) for each year are employed in the analysis. Although the CPS-ASEC data can be linked for longitudinal analysis, doing so is challenging. For this reason, I have selected three years—before, during, and after the recession—for analysis. Initial diagnostics (power analysis, for logistic regression) suggested the subsample sizes were sufficient for modeling with logistic regression. (For additional discussion of the limitations and practice of analyzing subsamples, see Lee and Forthofer, *Analyzing Complex Survey Data*.) The IPUMS weight (WRSUPP) for the CPS ASEC, which cover all groups in the full sample, were employed in the analysis. The models were estimated through the survey regression option for logit, for subsamples, in

STATA, with linearized standard errors. Latina labor force participation (which is binary, 1 for labor for participation, 0 otherwise) and controls for education (high school or less; reference was some or completed higher education), age, and marriage were included in the estimation. A limitation of the model is that no covariates for real median hourly wages or proxies for household wealth were included (but these are highly collinear with education). Full results of each regression model are available from the author.

13. Hollander, *Sunburnt Cities*, xi, 50–52; Muro, *Unify, Regionalize, Diversify*.

14. Chinn and Frieden, *Lost Decades*, 28–30, 45.

15. Eadington, "Analyzing the Trends in Gaming," 37–50.

16. Austin, "Unemployment Rates Are Projected," accessed October 26, 2013, http://www.epi.org/files/2013/unemployment-rates-white.pdf; and Bureau of Labor Statistics, *The Latino Labor Force*, accessed September 3, 2013, https://ecommons.cornell.edu/handle/1813/78877.

17. The data in this report come from the Bureau of Labor Statistics, Local Area Unemployment Statistics Program (LAUS) and the Current Population Survey. The Current Population Survey is based on a sample size of approximately 60,000 households in the US. The CPS data may be disaggregated by race, ethnicity, gender, and geographical area. One of the drawbacks, however, is that the state-level CPS estimates from the LAUS Program do not allow one to differentiate between the US and foreign-born Latino population. The data in this report are drawn from tables for various years in the annual *Geographical Profile of Employment and Unemployment* reports, Washington, DC, Bureau of Labor Statistics, Local Area Unemployment Statistics Program, US Department of Labor, accessed March 13, 2013 and September 3, 2013, http://www.bls.gov/opub/gp/laugp.htm. Additional information is available at http://www.bls.gov/opub/gp/laugp.htm.

18. These figures refer to unemployment as a share of the Latino civilian labor force. The CPS and BLS define "unemployed person" as: "all persons who had no employment during the reference week, were available for work—except for temporary illness—and made specific efforts to find employment sometime during the 4-week period ending with the reference week," Bureau of Labor Statistics *Geographic Profile of Employment and Unemployment*. Appendix B: Concepts and Definitions for Data Derived from the Current Population Survey. In addition, because the CPS did not apply the 2000 Census weights to the state-level samples for 2000 and 2001, we exclude CPS data from those years in the analysis.

19. That is, the number of unemployed Latinos as a percent of the total number of Latinos in the labor force. This measure follows the convention used by the Bureau of Labor Statistics.

20. In 2011, the highest annual average Latino unemployment rate was in in Rhode Island (21.6 percent), followed by Connecticut (17.8 percent). Nevada's rate (14.5 percent) was higher than levels in Colorado, Arizona, Utah, New Mexico, and California. Only Washington registered a slightly higher rate in 2011

(14.8 percent). See Bureau of Labor Statistics, *The Latino Labor Force*, accessed September 3, 2013, https://ecommons.cornell.edu/handle/1813/78877.

21. See Tuman, Damore, and Ágreda, "Immigration and the Contours," 1–18. When the unemployment rate for the Las Vegas-Paradise MSA is included on figure 4.1 it mirrors the state rate.

22. Current Population Survey, "Glossary of Terms," accessed September 5, 2013, http://www.bls.gov/bls/glossary.htm.

23. Bureau of Labor Statistics, "Ranks of the Discouraged Workers." Nevada's "U–4" rate, which is an alternative measure that includes the unemployed *and* discouraged workers (as a percent of the total civilian labor force and discouraged workers), reached 15.2 percent in 2010, and then fell to 11.9 percent in 2012; Bureau of Labor Statistics, "Alternative Measures of Labor."

24. That is, Latinos employed or unemployed as a percentage of the total Latino civilian noninstitutional population (ages 16 years or older).

25. In 2008 and 2009, the Latino civilian labor force in Nevada declined by 18,000, while the Latino noninstitutional population (ages 16 and older) fell by only 4,000. This suggests that demographic factors alone are not the main factors affecting the participation rate.

26. Certainly, outmigration among foreign-born Latinos might influence these data as well.

27. Tuman, Damore, and Ágreda, "Impact of the Great Recession."

28. Calculated from Current Population Survey data for Nevada, adjusting for the Hispanic "Adult Civilian Population" in poverty in 2008 and 2012. The 2010 Census weights were employed in the estimation (accessed October 26, 2013, http://www.census.gov/cps/data/cpstablecreator.html).

29. This trend was also evident among female and male workers in different racial and ethnic groups in Nevada, including Whites and African Americans. The magnitude of the male-female unemployment rate gap was similar among Whites and African Americans (in some years) from 2009 to 2012, although the gap was small among Asians (note, too, that unemployment among Asian women also remained higher than for Asian men for some years after 2008).

30. From 2008 to 2012, Latina women's labor force participation rate in Nevada fell from 56.3 percent to 52.5 percent. During the same period, the participation rate for Latino men fell from 78.8 percent to 68.4 percent. Thus, while the rate was falling for both groups, it is clear that the rate for women remained below levels for men throughout the period.

31. In 2012, for example, 19.5 percent of all unemployed workers in Nevada were in construction, while only 9.1 percent of the state's unemployed were in hospitality. Of course, other factors may also be playing a role. We lack more complete data on whether women or men Latinos were more likely to become "discouraged workers" (i.e., unemployed and available for work, but not counted because they were not actively seeking work) and, if so, how this affected the unemployment rates that are adjusted for the sex and ethnicity (or race) of the worker.

32. Unfortunately, because of small sizes for certain population subsamples, the CPS did not provide data on the unemployment rate among 16–19 year old Latinos for other years, except for 2002 (the figure was 9.2 percent in 2002). There are no other data on comparable age groups (16–19) among African American and Asian workers. For White workers, the unemployment rate among individuals 16–19 was higher compared to other groups of White workers (women, men), but lower than the levels experienced by Latinos from 2009 to 2012.

33. Scarpetta, Sonnet, and Manfredi, "Rising Youth Unemployment," accessed November 11, 2013, https://ideas.repec.org/p/oec/elsaab/106-en.html.

34. Tuman, Damore, and Ágreda, "Immigration and the Contours."

35. The CPS data clearly demonstrate that unemployment levels were far higher among workers with some or completed high school (compared to workers with more formal education) from January 2008 to December 2010 (see Ryan and Siebens, "Education Attainment in the United States."

36. See Bureau of Labor Statistics, "Employment Status of the Foreign-Born," accessed September 3, 2013, http://www.dol.gov/news.release/forbrnt03.htm. As discussed in note 3, the BLS provides national-level estimates that adjust for the US and foreign-born Latino population. However, BLS staff indicated that the estimates are not available at the state level because of small subsample sizes.

37. Because the CPS merged some sectors (e.g., mining and logging) after 2002, we confine the analysis to the period of 2003 through 2012 to avoid problems of comparability.

38. It is important to recall that the labor force participation rate was declining during this period. If discouraged workers who left the labor force were heavily concentrated in one sector, such as construction, this would have affected the relative percentages of the remaining Latinos employed in different sectors. We remain hopeful that future research will attempt to address this hypothesis.

39. Bureau of Labor Statistics, "Employment Status of the Foreign-Born."

40. Interview with Linda Rivera, oral history by Layne Karafantis, October 2, 2009, Latinx Voices of Southern Nevada, UNLV Library, http://d.library.unlv.edu /digital/collection/ohi/id/168.

41. Tuman, Damore, and Ágreda, "Immigration and the Contours."

42. According to data from the US Department of Labor, in 2010 Nevada was allo- cated $263,888 from the Trade Adjustment Assistance (TAA) program to finance job training for an estimated total of sixty-three Nevada workers. In 2011, Nevada received no TAA allocation and in 2012 the state was allocated $873,106 to assist with job training for an estimated 570 displaced workers (accessed November 8, 2013, http://www.doleta.gov/tradeact/Stateoverview.cfm). Similarly, after two rounds of Trade Adjustment Assistance Community College Training (TAAC-CCT) grants, which fund partnerships between community colleges and local industries to retrain displaced workers, Nevada has failed to submit a qualifying application. As a consequence, the state has received the minimum guaran- teed awards totaling $5.2 million out of a total allocation of $1 billion (accessed November 8, 2013, http://www.doleta.gov/taaccct/grantawards.cfm).

43. On this point, see *Las Vegas Sun*, "Solar Jobs Benefit Nevada," http://lasvegassun
.com/news/2015/dec/09/solar-jobs-benefit-nevadas-hispanics/. Still, Latinos are
not well represented in solar and "green" jobs in other parts of the country. See
Brook and Holloman. "Empowering Energy Justice."

44. *Reno Gazette Journal*, "COVID-19 Fallout: 206,000 Casino Employees out of
Work, AGA Says," May 19, 2020, https://www.rgj.com/story/news/2020/03/19
/covid-19-fallout-206–000-nevada-casino-employees-out-work/2881729001/;
and *Las Vegas Review-Journal*, "Furloughs, layoffs hit MGM Resorts due to
coronavirus crisis," March 13, 2020, https://www.reviewjournal.com/business
/tourism/furloughs-layoffs-hit-mgm-resorts-due-to-coronavirus-crisis-1980266/.
See also John P. Tuman, "Impact of the COVID-19 Pandemic," 367–81.

45. US Department of Labor, Bureau of Labor Statistics, Western Information Office,
"Nevada—monthly unemployment rate (seasonally adjusted), 2020," https://
www.bls.gov/regions/west/nevada.htm#eag_nv.f.2.

Chapter 5: The Social Determinants of Health

1. Monnat, "Disease Prevalence and Behavioral Risk," https://digitalscholarship
.unlv.edu/cgi/viewcontent.cgi?article=1031&context=social_health_nevada
_reports.

2. Office of Disease Prevention and Health Promotion, *Social Determinants of
Health*, https://www.healthypeople.gov/2020/topics-objectives/topic/social
-determinants-of-health.

3. American Community Survey, "Poverty Status in the Past 12 Months, 2013–2015
5-Year Estimates, American Community Survey: Nevada," March 21, 2020, https://
factfinder.census.gov/faces/tableservices/jsf/pages/productview.xhtml?src=CF.

4. Tabulated by authors from 1-percent Integrated Public Use Microdata Series
(IPUMS) for the 2018 American Community Survey, adjusting for Nevada. Data
extracted from IPUMS on March 21, 2020.

5. Centers for Disease Control. *Chronic Diseases*.

6. Centers for Disease Control and Prevention, "Leading causes of death," table 19
https://www.cdc.gov/nchs/data/hus/hus15.pdf#019[PDF–13.4MB].

7. Dadsetan, "Chronic Disease and Associated Risk," http://www.healthysouthern
nevada.org/content/sites/snhd/chronic-disease-and-associated-risk-factor
-disparities-051717.pdf.

8. R.A. Goodman et al., "Defining and Measuring Chronic Conditions," E66,
http://doi.org/10.5888/pcd10.120239.

9. See Goodman et al., "Defining and Measuring Chronic Conditions."

10. See Nevada Wellness, *Social Determinants of Health*, 2015; P. Muennig et al.,
"Gender and the Burden of Disease," 1662–1668; A. Anandacoomarasamy et al.
"Influence of BMI," 2114–118.

11. Trust for America's Health, *The State of Obesity*, https://www.tfah.org/report
-details/the-state-of-obesity-2018/.

12. Nevada State Health Needs Assessment, 2015, http://dpbh.nv.gov/uploadedFiles

/dpbhnvgov/content/Programs/OPHIE/Docs/Part%20I_FV_final%20Nov%20
2015.pdf.

13. Southern Nevada Health District, *Clark County Community Health Status Assessment*, 2012.

14. Centers for Disease Control and Prevention, *Diagnoses of HIV Infection in the United States and Dependent Areas 2017*, table 26, p. 114, https://www.cdc.gov/hiv /pdf/library/reports/surveillance/cdc-hiv-surveillance-report-2017-vol-29.pdf.

15. Chen, Gallant, and Page, "Systematic Review of HIV/AIDS," 65–81. doi: 10.1007 /s10903-011-9497-y.

16. American Psychiatric Association, "Mental Health Disparities: Diverse Populations," 2017, https://www.psychiatry.org/psychiatrists/cultural-competency/edu cation/mental-health-facts.

17. American Psychiatric Association, "Mental Health Disparities: Diverse Populations," 2017.

18. Budhwani, Hearld, and Chavez-Yenter, "Depression in Racial and Ethnic Minorities," 34–42. For a broader discussion of Latino immigrants, see Torres, and Wallace, "Migration Circumstances, Psychological Distress," 1619–1627; and Torres, "Predicting Levels of Latino Depression," 256; and Grey and Hall-Clark, *Cultural Considerations in Latino American*.

19. Centers for Disease Control and Prevention (CDC) Data and Statistics Fatal Injury Report for 2016.

20. Centers for Disease Control and Prevention (CDC) Data and Statistics Fatal Injury, p. 8.

21. Centers for Disease Control and Prevention (CDC) Data and Statistics Fatal Injury, p. 8.

22. Wray, Poladko, and Vaughan, "Suicide Trends and Prevention in Nevada," 1–2, http://digitalscholarship.unlv.edu/social_health_nevada_reports/30/.

23. Arizona, Colorado, Idaho, Montana, Nevada, New Mexico, Utah, Oregon, and Wyoming. Wray, Poladko, and Vaughan, "Suicide Trends and Prevention in Nevada," http://digitalscholarship.unlv.edu/social_health_nevada_reports/30/.

24. Tobacco Use in Nevada, 2015. Available at: https://truthinitiative.org/tobacco -use-nevada.

25. Southern Nevada Health District, *Southern Nevada: Community Health Assessment*, 2016, p. 32, http://www.healthysouthernnevada.org/content/sites/snhd /southern-nevada-cha-081716-wa.pdf; and Southern Nevada Health District, *Health Trends Bulletins: Drug Poisonings in Southern Nevada, 2001–2012*, http:// www.southernnevadahealthdistrict.org/stats-reports/index.php. For a general discussion for Latino youth in the US, see King and Vidourek, "Psychosocial Factors Associated with Recent Alcohol," 470–85.

26. Southern Nevada Health District, *Southern Nevada: Community Health Assessment*, 2016, 32–33; and Southern Nevada Health District, *Health Trends Bulletins*.

27. Awosogba et al., "Prioritizing Health Disparities," 17–30; Phillips and Malone, "Increasing Racial/Ethnic Diversity," 45–50.

28. Although we recognize that culture is a complex concept, we operationalize it here to include knowledge of customs and traditions, fluency in a patient's native language, and/or shared religious affiliation, racial/ethnic background, or national origin heritage. For a discussion in the context of health care, see Zalaya et al., "Need for Hispanic Nurses," 329–35.

29. Awosogba et al., "Prioritizing Health Disparities"; Phillips and Malone, "Increasing Racial/Ethnic Diversity," 45–50.

30. Hobson-Horton and Owens, "From Freshman to Graduate," 86–107.

31. McGlynn, "Hispanic Girls Most Likely," 30.

32. We are grateful to one of the anonymous reviewers for this observation.

33. See Zalaya et al., "Need for Hispanic Nurses"; Delgado, *Social Work with Latinos*.

34. See data in Pew Hispanic Center, "5 Facts about Latinos and Education," July 18, 2016, https://www.pewresearch.org/fact-tank/2016/07/28/5-facts-about-latinos -and-education/.

35. Villarruel, Canales, and Torres, "Bridges and Barriers," 245–51.

36. Pew Hispanic Center, "5 Facts about Latinos."

37. Dardón et al., "Diferencias entre hombres y mujeres," 204–28. Scholars have also noted that historically, Latinas were socialized to assume roles as wife and mother, as opposed to that of a professional working in an occupation outside the home. Although there is evidence of this practice historically, Latinas in the US work outside of the household, and we caution against generalizing this point.

38. *Minority Nurse*, "Hispanic Men in Nursing," May 30, 2013, https://minoritynurse .com/hispanic-men-in-nursing/.

39. American Community Survey 5-Year Estimates, for 2017, as reported and analyzed in Kenny Guinn Center for Policy Priorities, "Nevada's Uninsured Population," 2019, 5–6.

40. Nevada Health Workforce Taskforce, *Physician Workforce in Nevada*, University of Nevada, Reno, School of Medicine, 2018, 1, 5.

41. US Department of Health and Human Services, Health Resources and Services Administration. "Find Shortage Areas." Data as of August 29, 2014, http:// hpsafind.hrsa.gov/HPSASearch.aspx; US Census, American Community Survey 2012, 5-year estimate, table B01003. See also "Nevada's Mental Health Workforce: Shortages and Opportunities," 2014, Kenny Guinn Center for Policy Priorities, https://guinncenter.org/wp-content/uploads/2014/10/Guinn-Center-Policy-Brief _Mental-Health-Workforce-Final.pdf.

42. US Department of Health and Human Services, Health Resources and Services Administration. "Find Shortage Areas."

43. Pharr, Coughenour, and Gerstenberger, "Healthcare Access and Health Outcomes," 14, https://digitalscholarship.unlv.edu/cgi/viewcontent.cgi?article=1043 &context=njph.

44. See E. P. Zammitti, R. A. Cohen and M. E. Martinez, *Health Insurance Coverage: Early Release of Estimates from the National Health Interview Survey,*

January–June 2016 (Washington, DC: National Center for Health Statistics, Nov. 2016), https://www.cdc.gov/nchs/data/nhis/earlyrelease/insur201611.pdf. The figures for 2016 in this report refer to January to June. The change from 2010 to 2015 represented a 11-percentage point reduction in the uninsured Latino population.

Chapter 6: Educational Access and Outcomes

1. Data provided by Nevada Department of Education, Nevada Report Card, http://nevadareportcard.com/di/.

2. Richard O. Welsh, "Student Mobility, Segregation, and Achievement Gaps: Evidence from Clark County, Nevada." *Urban Education* 53, no. 1 (2018): 55–85. See in particular the regression coefficients for Latino students in table 1 of Welsh's paper, and his discussion on pp. 76–79. For a broader discussion in other parts of the US, see Hondo, Gardiner, and Sapien, *Latino Dropouts in Rural America;* Rodriguez, *Time Is Now*; Salas and Portes, *US Latinization.*

3. McFarland et al., *Trends in High School Dropout*, 1–44.

4. These figures (which are not normalized to Latino school enrollment) are calculated from unpublished data provided by the Nevada State Department of Education to the authors (Tuman and Damore) in 2014. For growth curve results on normalized autism and other disability rates in Nevada, see Tuman, Moonie, and Roth-Johnson, "Administrative Prevalence of Autism," 15–24.

5. McFarland et al., *Trends in High School Dropout*, op cit., pp. 44–45. Indeed, McFarland et al. found that in 2015–16, the completion rate for disabled students in Nevada was only 29 percent.

6. Nevada Report Card, op cit.

7. US Census Bureau, Current Population Survey, 2010.

8. https://www.nevada.edu/ir/page.php? p=diversity.

9. Santiago, Galdeano, and Taylor. *Factbook 2015: The Condition of Latinos in Education*, 10, https://ideas.repec.org/p/oec/elsaab/106-en.html. Also, NCES, Digest of Education Statistics, 2013 (table 306.20).

10. Magdalena Martinez, "Hispanic Students in Nevada Public," 3.

11. Martinez and Fernández, "Latinos at Community Colleges," 51–62.

12. The following NSHE institutions are qualified in this study as part of the two-year programs: College of Southern Nevada, Great Basin College, Truckee Meadows Community College, Western Nevada College, and Nevada State College. While Nevada State College is designated as a four-year program, for the sake of analytical consistency, NSC's size, curriculum structure, and the fact that it is a non-research institution, makes NSC more compatible in classifying it with NSHE's two-year programs, rather than classifying it with UNLV and UNR as a four-year institution. Further, NSC was not accredited until 2011, and as such, was operating under the accreditation of UNR. Considering the limited scope of programs and minors, along with an education structure more similar to NSHE's two-year program structures, and to control for this factor, NSC will not be classified with UNLV and UNR in this study.

13. See UNLV data provided by the Office of Decision Support, https://www.nevada.edu/ir/dashboard.php? d=persistence_rates.

14. Gasman and Turner, *Understanding Minority-Serving Institution.*

15. Martinez, "Hispanic Students in Nevada Public," 3.

16. See "UNLV Designated AANAPISI, HSI, and MSI Institution," https: //www.unlv.edu/diversityinitiatives/msi.

17. For UNR, see https: //www.unr.edu/diversity/groups/his; and for UNLV, see https://www.unlv.edu/diversityinitiatives/msi.

18. US Department of Education.

19. See Santiago, Galdeano, and Taylor, *Factbook 2015.* See also A. Nunez, S. Hurtado, and E. C. Galdeano, eds., *Hispanic-Serving Institutions*; and D. Solórzano and the University of California, *Latina Equity in Education.*

20. Kiyama, Museus, and Vega, "Cultivating Campus Environments."

21. Gloria, Castellanos, and Orozco. "Perceived Educational Barriers," 161–83.

22. For discussion of campus racial climates, defined as the overarching culture of racism in the given institution, see Solorzano, Ceja, and Yosso, "Critical Race Theory, Racial Microaggressions," 60–73. For a discussion of campus racial culture, defined as institutionally entrenched patterns of beliefs and structures that oppress minority populations, see Museus, Ravello, and Vega. "The Campus Racial Cultures," 28–45; G. Thompson, *Up Where We Belong.* See also Lowe et al., "Food for Thought," 569–600. This work addresses the extent to which campus racial climates become hostile and produce negative effects upon the college experience of Latino and minority students.

23. Castellanos and Gloria, "Research Consolidations and Theoretical Application," 378–96.

24. K. P. Gonzalez, "Campus Culture and the Experiences," 193–218.

25. See information at UNR, https: //www.unr.edu/diversity.

26. UNR diversity information, https://www.unr.edu/diversity. See also *Access for All: Expanding Opportunity and Programs to Support Successful Student Outcomes at University of Nevada, Reno*, ed. Melisa N. Choroszy and Theodor M. Meek (Reno: University of Nevada Press, 2019).

27. UNLV, About Diversity, https: //www.unlv.edu/diversityinitiatives/about.

28. UNLV, About Diversity.

29. UNLV, diversity information, at https://www.unlv.edu/diversityinitiatives/initiatives.

30. UNLV, updates on diversity initiatives, https://www.unlv.edu/sites/default/files/page_files/27/DiversityInitiatives-SDPUpdate-March2017.pdf.

Chapter 7: Conclusion—The Future

1 Aldo Aguirre, as quoted in Timothy Pratt, "More Guatemalans Move to the Valley," *Las Vegas Sun*, May 21, 2004, 8B.

2. Miranda, *A History of Hispanics.*

3. Clark County School District, "Master Plan for English Language Learner Success Overview," 2019, https://www.leg.state.nv.us/App/NELIS/REL/80th2019

/ExhibitDocument/OpenExhibitDocument?exhibitId=36105&fileDownload
Name=0214_CCSDm.pdf.

4. Portes and Rumbaut, *Legacies*, 177.

5. Portes and Rumbaut, 177.

6. Nevada's Hispanic Population-2010: A Supplement to the 2010 Census Brief.
   C2010BR–04.

7. Pew Research Center, "Shifting Religious Identity of Latinos," 9, 19, https://
   www.pewforum.org/2014/05/07/the-shifting-religious-identity-of-latinos-in-the
   -united-states/.

8. Pew Research Center, "Shifting Religious Identity of Latinos," 31–32. See Mulder,
   Ramos, and Marti, *Latino Protestants in America*; Espinosa, Elizondo, and
   Miranda, *Latino Religions and Civic Activism*.

9. The Roman Catholic Diocese of Las Vegas, Hispanic Ministry, "Misas en Español,"
   March 2020, https://dioceseoflasvegas.org/Misas% 20En% 20Espanol.shtml.
   For evidence on the 2000s, see Interview #12c (Tuman, Civic Engagement Study,
   2009), which noted that only one parish conducted mass in Spanish in 2008.

10. On the use of Otomi in religious services, see Interview 22a (Tuman, Civic
    Engagement Study, 2009). For trends in evangelical churches attended by Latin
    American immigrants, see Tuman, *Latin American Migrant*, 12–13, 32; and
    Tuman and Gearhart, "The Guatemalans," 213–30.

11. Tuman and Gearhart, "The Guatemalans."

12. Similar to many other unions, the Culinary Union (HERE) used a merger strategy
    to address declining national membership. In 2004, the national union merged
    with UNITE, another labor association with a significant Latino presence. In this
    book, we follow the local convention by referring to it as the "Culinary Union"
    (not "Culinary Workers Union").

13. In 2009, Pilar Weiss, the union's former political director, provided an estimate
    of 60,000 members (see Weiss's comments in roundtable discussions, in Tuman,
    Latin American Migrants, 30). In 2020, the union continued to provide an esti-
    mate of 60,000 members. See Culinary Workers Union, Local 226, "Our Union/
    History," March 19, 2020, https://www.culinaryunion226. org/union/history.

14. The Laborers Union has also made significant contributions to worker training
    for Latino workers (Interview 22, 2009).

15. From 1985 to 1999, there were 20,433 "Mexican Legal Permanent Residents" in
    Clark County; of this number, only 5,160 had become naturalized citizens (25.2
    percent naturalized; see US Department of Homeland Security 2007a, 2007b). In
    2005, 1,684 persons from Cuba, El Salvador, Guatemala, Mexico, and Peru who
    resided in Las Vegas became naturalized citizens (US Department of Homeland
    Security 2007a, 2007b). These data are for Las Vegas and represent top twenty
    countries by birthplace of the applicant.

16. See Culinary Workers Union Local 226, "Coronavirus update: Casinos Are
    Closed. Your Job and Health Benefits Are Protected," March 19, 2020, https://
    www.culinaryunion226; org/blog/coronavirus-update-casinos-are-closed
    -your-job-health-benefits-are-protected-20200318, *Las Vegas Review-Journal*;

"Culinary Union Seeks 'Bailout of American Worker' Following Closures,"
March 18, 2020, https://www.reviewjournal.com/business/casinos-gaming
/culinary-union-seeks-bailout-for-american-worker-following-closures-19845
97/; and Culinary Workers Union Local 226, "Culinary and Bartenders Unions
Conclude Historic COVID-19 Negotiations with MGM Resorts and Caesars Entertainment to Protect Workers," August 31, 2020, https://www.culinaryunion226
.org/blog/archive?month=march-2020.

17. Palladino notes that approximately 40 percent of the commercial and high-rise
construction sector in Las Vegas was unionized in this early 2000s. See Palladino,
Skilled Hands, Strong Spirits, 14.

18. Interview 22, 2009.

19. The Laborers Union tried to establish a binational health and safety training
program with the Confederation of Mexican Workers (Confederación de
Trabajadores de México), Mexico's largest "corporatist" labor association that
has a long history of little union democracy. This initiative stalled and was not
completed (Interview 22, 2008).

20. Palladino, *Skilled Hands, Strong Spirits*, 214–15.

21. Palladino, 215, 217.

22. For a detailed analysis of the history of the LCC, see Miranda, *History of Hispanics*, 160–67. During the 1970s, the LCC did not coordinate with other movements
that were arguing for improvements in welfare in Las Vegas. For a fascinating
study of activism among African American women (and others) during the 1970s,
see Orleck, *Storming Caesars Palace*.

23. See LCC, "Our History," https://lvlcc.starchapter.com/Our_History. This section
also draws on Tuman, *Latin American Migrants*.

24. For background, see Latin Chamber of Commerce (2007). Some information for
this section was also provided in previous communications from members.

25. Interview 16, 2008.

26. Tuman, *Latin American Migrants*, 19–20.

27. Wright and Moody, "The Salvadorans," 247–68.

28. New American Economy, "Power of the Purse: How Hispanics Contribute to
the US Economy," 2017, http://research.newamericaneconomy.org/wp-content
/uploads/sites/2/2017/12/Hispanic_V5.pdf.

29. New American Economy, 2017.

30. RCG Economics, Nevada by the Numbers, "Nevada's population is diversifying
rapidly; Hispanics lead growth %," May 12, 2016, https://rcg1.com/nevada-by
-the-numbers-blog/nevadas-population-is-diversifying-rapidly-hispanics-lead
-growth/; and *Nevada Current*, "NV childhood poverty rate drops overall, but
still high overall for children of color," September 24, 2019, https://www.nevada
current.com/blog/nv-childhood-poverty-rate-drops-overall-but-still-high-for
-children-of-color/.

31. See David Cooper and Julia Wolfe, "Every State Will Lose Jobs As a Result of
the Coronavirus," figure A: Estimated Job Losses by Summer 2020, Nevada,

Economic Policy Institute Working Economics, March 19, 2020, https: //www.epi
.org/blog/every-state-will-lose-jobs-as-a-result-of-the-coronavirus-policymakers
-must-take-action/.

32. Eppler-Epstein, Gurvis, and Ryan King, "Alarming Lack of Data on Latinos,
2016, http://apps.urban.org/features/latino-criminal-justice-data/.

33. Zapata, "Quest for Greater Hispanic Representation," https://thenevadaindepen
dent.com/article/quest-for-greater-hispanic-representation-in-nevadas-halls-of
-power-isnt-always-easy-candidates-say.

34. *Latino Decisions*, "2018 Election Eve Poll—Nevada," https://latinodecisions.com
/wp-content/uploads/2019/06/NV_2018_groups.pdf.

35. *Latino Decisions*, "2018 Election Eve Poll—Nevada."

36. Center for American Progress, "What we know about DACA recipients, by state,"
September 12, 2019, https://www.americanprogress.org/issues/immigration
/news/2019/09/12/474422/know-daca-recipients-state/. On the US Supreme
Court decision and DACA, see *Department of Homeland Security et al. v. Regents
of the University of California et al.*, No. 18–587, June 18, 2020, https://www
.supremecourt.gov/opinions/19pdf/18–587_5ifl.pdf.

37. Nevada Secretary of State, Initiative Petition—Constitutional Amendment, "Prevent Sanctuary Cities Initiative," filed October 30, 2017, https://www.nvsos.gov
/sos/home/showdocument? id=5127.

Bibliography

Aaronson, Stephanie, Tomaz Cajner, Bruce Fallick, Felix Galbis-Reig, Chistopher L. Smith, and William Wascher. "Labor Force Participation: Recent Developments and Future Prospects." *Federal Reserve Bank of Cleveland*, Paper 2014–64. http://www.federalreserve.gov/pubs/feds/2014/201464/201464pap.pdf.

Abalos, D. *The Latino Family and the Politics of Transformation*. Transformational Politics and Political Science. Westport, CT: Praeger, 1993.

Abrajano, Marisa, A. "Are Blacks and Latinos Responsible for the Passage of Proposition 8? Analyzing Voter Attitudes on California's Proposal to Ban Same-Sex Marriage in 2008." *Political Research Quarterly* 63, no. 4 (2010): 922–32.

Abrajano, Marisa A., and Michael Alvarez. *New Faces, New Voices. The Hispanic Electorate in America*. Princeton, NJ: Princeton University Press, 2010.

Abrajano, Marisa A., and Costas Panagopoulos. "Does Language Matter? The Impact of Spanish Versus English-Language GOTV Efforts on Latino Turnout." *American Politics Research* 39, no. 4 (2011): 643–63.

Abramson, Paul R., John H. Aldrich, Brad T. Gomez, and David W. Rohde. *Change and Continuity in the 2012 Elections*. Thousand Oaks, CA: CQ Press, Sage Publications, 2015.

Abrego, Leisy J., and Roberto G. Gonzales. "Blocked Paths, Uncertain Futures: The Postsecondary Education and Labor Market Prospects of Undocumented Latino Youth." *Journal of Education for Students Placed at Risk* 15, nos. 1–2 (2010): 144–57.

Acuña, Rodolfo. *Occupied America: The Chicano's Struggle Toward Liberation*. New York: Harper and Row, 1972.

———. *U.S. Latino Issues*. Westport, CT: Greenwood Press, 2003.

———. *Occupied America: A History of Chicanos*. 7th ed. Boston: Longman, 2011.

Adames, Hector, and Nayeli Y. Chavez-Dueñas. *Cultural Foundations and Interventions in Latino/a Mental Health: History, Theory, and Within-Group Differences*. Explorations in Mental Health. New York: Routledge, 2017.

Affigne, Tony, Evelyn Hu-DeHart, and Marion Orr. *Latino Politics en Ciencia Política: The Search for Latino Identity and Racial Consciousness*. New York: NYU Press, 2014.

Agency for Healthcare Research and Quality. *National Healthcare Quality and Disparities Reports*. Rockville, MD: Agency for Healthcare Research and Quality, 2009.

Agosto, Efraín, and Jacqueline M. Hidalgo. *Latinxs, the Bible, and Migration*. The Bible and Cultural Studies. Cham: Springer International Publishing, 2018.

Aguila, Jaime. "Mexican/US Immigration Policy Prior to the Great Depression." *Diplomatic History* 31, no. 2 (2007): 207–25.

Aguirre-Molina, Marilyn, Carlos W. Molina, and Ruth E. Zambrana. *Health Issues in the Latino Community*. Health Series. San Francisco: Jossey Bass, 2001.

Aguirre-Molina, Marilyn, Luisa N. Borrell, and William Vega. *Health Issues in Latino Males: A Social and Structural Approach*. Critical Issues in Health and Medicine. New Brunswick, NJ: Rutgers University Press, 2010.

Aizenman, N. C. "Economy, Not Immigration, a Top Worry of Latinos." *Washington Post*. 2009. http://www.washingtonpost.com/wpdyn/content/article/2009/01/15 /AR2009011502310.html.

Akers Chacón, Justin, and Mike Davis. *No One Is Illegal: Fighting Racism and State Violence on the US-Mexico Border*. Chicago: Haymarket Books, 2006.

Akhtar, Salman, and Solange Margery Bertoglia. *The American Latino: Psychodynamic Perspectives on Culture and Mental Health*. Lanham, MD: Rowman & Littlefield, 2015.

Alaniz, Maria L., and Chris Wilkes. "Reinterpreting Latino Culture in the Commodity Form: The Case of Alcohol Advertising in the Mexican American Community." *Hispanic Journal of Behavioral Sciences* 17, no. 4 (1995): 430–51.

Alba, Richard, and Nancy Foner. "Comparing Immigrant Integration in North America and Western Europe: How Much Do the Grand Narratives Tell Us?" *International Migration Review* 48 (2014): s263-s291.

Alba, Richard, and Tariqul Islam. "The Case of the Disappearing Mexican Americans: An Ethnic-Identity Mystery." *Population Research and Policy Review* 28, no. 2 (2009): 109–21.

Alegria, Margarita, David Takeuchi, Glorisa Canino, Naihua Duan, Patrick Shrout, Xiao-Li Meng, and William Vega. "Considering Context, Place and Culture: The National Latino and Asian American Study." *International Journal of Methods in Psychiatric Research* 13, no. 4 (2004): 208–20.

Aleinikoff, T. Alexander, and Douglas Klusmeyer. *Citizenship Policies for an Age of Migration*. Washington, DC: Carnegie Endowment for International Peace, 2002.

Allen, Walter Recharde, Erin Kimura-Walsh, and Kimberly A. Griffin. *Towards a Brighter Tomorrow: College Barriers, Hopes and Plans of Black, Latino/a and Asian American Students in California*. Research on African American Education. Charlotte, NC: IAP, Information Age Pub, 2009.

Altonji, Joseph, and David Card. "The Effects of Immigration on the Labor Market Outcomes of Less-Skilled Workers." In *Immigration, Trade and the Labor Market*, edited by John Abowd and Richard Freeman, 201–34. Chicago: University of Chicago Press, 1991.

Alvarado, Melissa, and Richard J. Ricard. "Developmental Assets and Ethnic Identity as Predictors of Thriving in Hispanic Adolescents." *Hispanic Journal of Behavioral Sciences* 35, no. 4 (2013): 510–23.

Álvarez, Inigo, and Ada Vargas, eds. *Latinos in the 21st Century: Their Voices and Lived Experiences*. Latin American Political, Economic, and Security Issues. New York: Nova Science, 2018.

Alvarez, R. *Delivery of Services for Latino Community Mental Health* (Educational Resources Information Center (US). ERIC documents; ED 118 673). Los Angeles: Spanish Speaking Mental Health Research and Development Program, University of California, 1975.

Alvarez, R. Michael, and Lisa García Bedolla. "The Foundations of Latino Voter Partisanship: Evidence from the 2000 Election." *The Journal of Politics* 65, no. 1 (2003): 31–49.

Alvarez, Sonya E., Claudia de Lima Copsta, Verónica Feliu, Rebecca J. Hester, Norma Klahn, and Millie Thayer, eds. *Translocalities/translocalidades: Feminist Politics of Translation in the Latin/a Américas*. Durham, NC: Duke University Press, 2014.

Amaro, Hortensia, and A. de la Torre. "Public Health Needs and Scientific Opportunities in Research on Latinas." *American Journal of Public Health* 92, no. 4 (2002): 525–29.

Amaro, Hortensia, Susan M. Blake, Pamela M. Schwartz, and Laura J. Flinchbaugh. "Developing Theory-Based Substance Abuse Prevention Programs for Young Adolescent Girls." *The Journal of Early Adolescence* 21, no. 3 (2001): 256–93.

Amberson, Mary M. McAllen. "'Better to Die on Our Feet, Than Live on Our Knees': United Farm Workers and Strikes in the Lower Rio Grande Valley, 1966–1967." *Journal of South Texas* 20, no. 1 (2007): 12–17.

Amos, Y. *Latina Bilingual Education Teachers: Examining Structural Racism in Schools*. Routledge Research in Education. New York: Routledge, 2018.

Amparano, J., and Penny Dann. *America's Latinos: Their Rich History, Culture, and Traditions*. Proud Heritage–The Hispanic Library. Chanhassen, MN: Child's World, 2003.

Anacker, Katrin B., James H. Carr, and Archana Pradhan. "Analyzing Foreclosures Among High-Income Black/African American and Hispanic/Latino Borrowers in Prince George's County, Maryland." *Housing and Society* 39, no. 1 (2012): 1–28.

Anandacoomarasamy, A., I. D. Caterson, S. Leibman, G. S. Smith, P. N. Sambrook, M. Fransen, and L. M. March. "Influence of BMI on Health-Related Quality of Life: Comparison Between an Obese Adult Cohort and Age-Matched Population Norms." *Obesity* (Silver Spring) 17, no. 11 (2009): 2114–118.

Andrews, J. O., G. Felton, M. E. Wewers, and J. Heath. "Use of Community Health Workers in Research with Ethnic Minority Women." *Journal of Nursing Scholarship* 36, no. 4 (2004): 358–65.

Antshel, Kevin M. "Integrating Culture As a Means of Improving Treatment Adherence in the Latino Population." *Psychology, Health & Medicine* 7, no. 4 (2002): 435–49.

Arenas, A., and E. Gómez. *Somos Latinas: Voices of Wisconsin Latina Activists*. Madison: The Wisconsin Historical Society Press, 2018.

Arkham, T. *Latino Americans and Their Jobs*. Hispanic Americans: Major Minority. Philadelphia: Mason Crest, 2013.

Arredondo, Patricia, Maritza Gallardo-Cooper, Edward A. Delgado-Romero, and Angela L. Zapata. *Culturally Responsive Counseling with Latinas/os*. Alexandria, VA: American Counseling Association, 2014.

Arteaga, L., C. Flagel, and G. Rodríguez. *The Latino Vote, 1998: The New Margin of Victory.* San Francisco: Latino Issues Forum, 1998.

Artico, C. *Latino Families Broken by Immigration: The Adolescents Perceptions* (New Americans (LFB Scholarly Publishing LLC). New York: LFB Scholarly Publ., 2003.

Arvizu, John R., and F. Chris Garcia. "Latino Voting Participation: Explaining and Differentiating Latino Voting Turnout." *Hispanic Journal of Behavioral Sciences* 18, no. 2 (1996): 104–28.

Asencio, M. *Latina/o Sexualities: Probing Powers, Passions, Practices, and Policies.* New Brunswick, NJ: Rutgers University Press, 2010.

Austin, Algernon. "Unemployment Rates Are Projected to Remain High for Whites, Latinos, and African Americans through 2013." *Economic Policy Institute, Issue Brief No. 350*, February 25, 2013. Washington, DC. Accessed October 26, 2013. http://www.epi.org/files/2013/ unemployment-rates-white.pdf.

Awosogba, Temitope, Joseph R. Betancourt, F. Garrett Conyers, Estela S. Estapé, Fritz Francois, Sabrina J. Gard, and Arthur Kaufman. "Prioritizing Health Disparities in Medical Education to Improve Care." *Annals of the New York Academy of Sciences* 1287, no. 1 (2013): 17–30.

Ayón, Cecilia. "Perceived Immigration Policy Effects Scale: Development and Validation of a Scale on the Impact of State-Level Immigration Policies on Latino Immigrant Families." *Hispanic Journal of Behavioral Sciences* 39, no. 1 (2017): 19–33.

Bada, Xóchitl, Jonathan Fox, Robert Donnelly, and Andrew Selee. *Context Matters: Latino Immigrant Civic and Political Participation in Nine US Cities.* Series on Latino Immigrant Civic Engagement. Washington, DC: Woodrow Wilson International Center for Scholars, 2010.

Bailey, Stanley, Aliya Saperstein, and Andrew Penner. "Race, Color, and Income Inequality Across the Americas." *Demographic Research* 31 (2014): 735–56.

Barrera, Mario. *Race and Class in the Southwest: A Theory of Racial Inequality.* South Bend, IN: University of Notre Dame Press, 1979.

Barreto, Matt. "Comprehensive Immigration Reform and Winning the Latino Vote." *The Latino Decisions* (blog). Accessed March 18, 2012. http://www.latino decisions.com/files/2813/6250/5298/Immigration_refom_March5_Final.pdf.

———. "Proving the Exit Polls Wrong—Harry Reid Did Win over 90% of the Latino vote." *The Latino Decisions* (blog). Accessed March 18, 2013. http://www .latinodecisions.com/blog/2010/11/15/proving-the-exit-pollswrong-harry-reid -did-win-over-90-of-the-latino-vote/.

Barreto, Matt A. *Ethnic Cues: The Role of Shared Ethnicity in Latino Political Participation.* Ann Arbor: University of Michigan Press, 2010.

———. *Glimpse Into Latino Policy and Voting Preferences.* Policy Brief. Claremont, CA: Tomás Rivera Policy Institute, 2002.

Barreto, Matt A., Luis R. Fraga, Sylvia Manzano, Valerie Martínez-Ebers, and Gary M. Segura. "Should They Dance with the One Who Brung 'Em?" Latinos and the 2008 Presidential Election. *PS*." *Political Science & Politics* 41, no. 4 (2008): 753–60.

Barreto, Matt A., Sylvia Manzano, Ricardo Ramírez, and Kathy Rim. "Mobilization, Participation and Solidaridad: Latino Participation in the 2006 Immigration Protest Rallies." *Urban Affairs Review* 44, no. 5 (2009): 376–764.

Barrett, Alice N., Gabriel P. Kuperminc, and Kelly M. Lewis. "Acculturative Stress and Gang Involvement among Latinos: US-Born Versus Immigrant Youth." *Hispanic Journal of Behavioral Sciences* 35, no. 3 (2013): 370–89.

Barrington, Clare, DeAnne K. Hilfinger Messias, and Lynn Weber. "Implications of Racial and Ethnic Relations for Health and Well-Being in New Latino Communities: A Case Study of West Columbia, South Carolina." *Latino Studies* 10, nos. 1–2 (2012): 155–78.

Bastian, Jean-Pierre. *Historia del protestantismo en México, Protestantismo y sociedad en México*. México, DF: Casa Unida de Publicaciones, 1983.

Bazan-Gonzalez, P., and S. Figueras. *The Hispanicization of the United States: The Latino Challenge to American Culture*. Lewiston, NY: The Edwin Mellen Press, 2017.

———. *Remaking the American Mainstream: Immigration*. Cambridge, MA: Harvard University Press, 2003.

Behnken, B. *Civil Rights and Beyond: African American and Latino/a Activism in the Twentieth-Century United States*. Athens: University of Georgia Press, 2016.

Bejarano, C. *The Latino Gender Gap in US Politics*. Routledge Research in American Politics and Governance. New York: Routledge, 2014.

Belgrave, Faye Z. "Latino Cultural Values: Their Role in Adjustment to Disability." *Social Behavior and Personality* 9, no. 5 (1994): 185–200.

Beltrán, Cristina. *The Trouble with Unity: Latino Politics and the Creation of Identity*. New York: Oxford University Press, 2010.

Bender, S. *Tierra y libertad: Land, Liberty, and Latino Housing*. Citizenship and Migration in the Americas. New York: New York University Press, 2010.

Bender, Steven, and William F. Arrocha. *Compassionate Migration and Regional Policy in the Americas*. London: Palgrave Macmillan, 2017.

Benitez, C. *Latinization: How Latino Culture Is Transforming the US*. Ithaca, NY: Paramount Marketing Pub., 2007.

Benton-Cohen, Katherine. *Borderline Americans: Racial Division and Labor War in the Arizona Borderlands*. Cambridge, MA: Harvard University Press, 2011.

Benuto, Lorraine T., Jena B. Casas, Caroline Cummings, and Rory Newlands. "Undocumented, to DACAmented, to DACAlimited: Narratives of Latino Students with DACA Status." *Hispanic Journal of Behavioral Sciences* 40, no. 3 (2018): 259–78.

Benuto, Lorraine T., and William T. O'Donohue. *Enhancing Behavioral Health in Latino Populations: Reducing Disparities Through Integrated Behavioral and Primary Care*. Switzerland: Springer International Publishing, 2016.

Berg, Gary A. *Low-Income Students and the Perpetuation of Inequality: Higher Education in America.* New York: Routledge, 2016.

Bergad, Laird W., and Herbert S. Klein. *Hispanics in the United States: A Demographic, Social, and Economic History, 1980–2005.* New York: Cambridge University Press, 2010.

Berliner, David. "Effects of Inequality and Poverty vs. Teachers and Schooling on America's Youth." *Teachers College Record* 115, no. 12 (2013): 1–26.

Bernal, Guillermo, and Yvette Flores-Ortiz. "Latino Families in Therapy: Engagement and Evaluation." *Journal of Marital and Family Therapy* 8, no. 3 (1982): 357–65.

Bjornstrom, Eileen. "To Live and Die in LA County: Neighborhood Economic and Social Context and Premature Age-Specific Mortality Rates Among Latinos." *Health and Place* 17, no. 1 (2011): 230–37.

Blackhawk, Ned. *Violence Over the Land: Indians and Empires in the Early American West.* Cambridge, MA: Harvard University Press, 2008.

Blau, Francine D., Lawrence M. Kahn, and Kerry L. Papps. "Gender, Source Country Characteristics, and Labor Market Assimilation Among Immigrants." *The Review of Economics and Statistics* 93, no. 1 (2011): 43–58.

Bleakley, Hoyt, and Aimee Chin. "Language Skills and Earnings: Evidence from Childhood Immigrants." *Review of Economics and Statistics* 86, no. 2 (2004): 481–96.

Bonilla, Frank. *Borderless Borders: US Latinos, Latin Americans, and the Paradox of Interdependence.* Philadelphia: Temple University Press, 2010.

Bordas, J. *The Power of Latino Leadership Culture, Inclusion, and Contribution.* BK Business. San Francisco: Berrett-Koehler, 2013.

Borjas, George J. "The Labor Demand Curve Is Downward Sloping: Reexamining the Impact of Immigration on the Labor Market." *Quarterly Journal of Economics* 118, no. 4 (2002): 1335–374.

———. "Welfare Reform and Immigrant Participation in Welfare Programs." *International Migration Review* 36, no. 4 (2002): 1093–123.

Bornstein, Marc H. "The Specificity Principle in Acculturation Science." *Perspectives on Psychological Science* 12, no. 1 (2017): 3–45.

Borrayo, E. A. "Where's Maria? A Video to Increase Awareness About Breast Cancer and Mammography Screening Among Low-Literacy Latinas." *American Journal of Preventive Medicine* 39, no. 1 (2004): 99–110.

Brabeck, Kalina, and Qingwen Xu. "The Impact of Detention and Deportation of Latino Immigrant Children and Families: A Quantitative Exploration." *Hispanic Journal of Behavioral Sciences* 32, no. 3 (2010): 341–61.

Brabeck, Kalina M., Erin Sibley, and M. Brinton Lykes. "Authorized and Unauthorized Immigrant Parents: The Impact of Legal Vulnerability on Family Contexts." *Hispanic Journal of Behavioral Sciences* 38, no. 1 (2016): 3–30.

Bracho, A. *Recruiting the Heart, Training the Brain: The Work of Latino Health Access.* Berkeley, CA; [Santa Ana, CA]: Hesperian Health Guides; Latino Health Access, 2016.

Branton, Regina. "Latino Attitudes Toward Various Areas of Public Policy: The Importance of Acculturation." *Political Research Quarterly* 60 (2007): 293–303.

Braveman, P. "Health Disparities and Health Equity: Concepts and Measurement." Review. *Annual Review of Public Health* 27 (2006): 167–94.

Brettell, Caroline B., and Faith G. Nibbs. "Immigrant Suburban Settlement and the 'Threat' to Middle Class Status and Identity: The Case of Farmers Branch, Texas." *International Migration* 49, no. 1 (2011): 1–30.

Brick, K., A. E. Challinor, and M. Rosenblum. *Mexican and Central American Immigrants in the United States.* Washington, DC: Migration Policy Institute, 2011.

Brodie, M., and Henry J. Kaiser Family Foundation. "What's the Diagnosis? Latinos, Media & Health: A Series of Three Reports from the Kaiser Family Foundation." Menlo Park, CA: Henry J. Kaiser Family Foundation, 1998.

Brook, Mary Finley, and Erica L. Holloman. "Empowering Energy Justice." *International Journal of Environmental Research and Public Health* 13, no. 9 (2016).

Brown, Tyson H. "Diverging Fortunes: Racial/Ethnic Inequality in Wealth Trajectories in Middle and Late Life." *Race and Social Problems* 8, no. 1 (2016): 29–41.

Budhwani H., K. Hearld, and D. Chavez-Yenter. "Depression in Racial and Ethnic Minorities: The Impact of Nativity and Discrimination." *Racial Ethnic Health Disparities* 2, no. 1 (2015): 34–42.

Buki, L., and L. Piedra. *Creating Infrastructures for Latino Mental Health.* New York: Springer, 2011.

Bureau of Labor Statistics. "Alternative Measures of Labor Underutilization, Nevada, 2012." Western Information Office, BLS, 2012.

———. "Employment Status of the Foreign-Born and Native-Born Population 25 Years and Over by Educational Attainment, Race, and Hispanic or Latino Ethnicity, 2011–2012." US Department of Labor, Bureau of Labor Statistics, May 22, 2013. Accessed September 3, 2013. http://www.dol.gov/news.release/forbrnt03.htm.

———. *Geographic Profile of Employment and Unemployment* reports. Washington, DC: US Department of Labor, 2016.

———. *The Latino Labor Force at a Glance.* Washington, DC: US Department of Labor, April 5, 2012. Accessed September 3, 2013. https://ecommons.cornell.edu/handle/1813/78877.

———. Local Area Unemployment Statistics Program (LAUSP). Washington, DC: US Department of Labor, 2016. http://www.bls.gov/lau/lauov.htm.

———. "Ranks of the Discouraged Workers and Others Marginally Attached to the Labor Force Rise During Recession." *Issues in Labor Statistics*, Summary 09-04, April 2009.

Buriel, Raymond, William Perez, Terri L. De Ment, David V. Chavez, and Virginia R. Moran. "The Relationship of Language Brokering to Academic Performance, Biculturalism, and Self-Efficacy Among Latino Adolescents." *Hispanic Journal of Behavioral Sciences* 30, no. 3 (1998): 283–97.

Burns, A. F. *Maya in Exile: Guatemalans in Florida.* Philadelphia: Temple University Press, 1999.

Burton, Linda M., Daniel T. Lichter, Regina S. Baker, and John M. Eason. "Inequality, Family Processes, and Health in the 'New' Rural America." *American Behavioral Scientist* 57, no. 6 (2013): 1128–151.

Bussert-Webb, K., M. Díaz, and K. Yanez. *Justice and Space Matter in a Strong, Unified Latino Community*. Critical Studies of Latinx in the Americas, vol. 3. New York: Bern; Frankfurt: Peter Lang 2017.

Caballero, A. Enrique. "Diabetes in the Hispanic or Latino Population: Genes, Environment, Culture, and More." *Current Diabetes Reports* 5, no. 3 (2005): 217–25.

Cabrera, Natasha J., Francisco A. Villarruel, and Hiram E. Fitzgerald. *Latina and Latino Children's Mental Health*. Child Psychology and Mental Health. Santa Barbara, CA: Praeger/ABC-CLIO, 2011.

———. "Understanding the Hispanic/Latino Patient." *The American Journal of Medicine* 124, no. 10 (2010): S10–S15.

Cain, B. E., D. R. Kiewiet, and C. J. Uhlaner. "The Acquisition of Partisanship by Latinos and Asian Americans." *American Journal of Political Science* 35 (1991): 390–422.

Camarillo, Albert. *Chicanos in California: A History of Mexican Americans in California*. San Francisco: Boyd & Fraser Publishing Company, 1984.

Cameron, Maxwell A., and Eric Hershberg, eds. *Latin America's Left Turns: Politics, Policies, and Trajectories of Change*. Boulder, CO: Lynne Rienner Publishers, 2010.

Campos, D., R. Delgado, and M. Huerta. *Reaching Out to Latino Families of English Language Learners*. Alexandria, VA: ASCD, 2011.

Cantú, Norma E., Cristina Herrera, and Larissa M. Mercado-López. *(Re)mapping the Latina/o Literary Landscape*. Literatures of the Americas. New York: Palgrave Macmillan, 2016.

Caravantes, E. *Clipping Their Own Wings: The Incompatibility Between Latino Culture and American Education*. Lanham, MD: Hamilton Books, 2006.

Card, David. "Immigrant Inflows, Native Outflows, and the Local Labor Market Impact of Higher Immigration." *Journal of Labor Economics* 19, no. 1 (2001): 22–64.

Cardenas, Gilberto. *La Causa: Civil Rights, Social Justice, and the Struggle for Equality in the Midwest*. Hispanic Civil Rights. Houston: Arte Público Press, 2004.

Cardoso, J. B., E. R. Hamilton, N. Rodriquez, K. Eschbach, and J. Hagan. "Deporting Fathers: Involuntary Transnational Families and Intent to Remigrate Among Salvadoran Deportees." *International Migration Review* 50, no. 1 (2014): 197–230.

Carling, J. "Migration in the Age of Involuntary Immobility: Theoretical Reflections and Cape Verdean Experiences." *Journal of Ethnic and Migration Studies* 28, no. 1 (2002): 5–42.

Carnoy, Martin, Raúl Andrés Hinojosa Ojeda, Hugh Daley, and Inter-University Program for Latino Research. *Latinos in a Changing US Economy: Comparative Perspectives on the Labor Market Since 1939*. New York, NY: Research Foundation of the City University of New York, 1990.

Carlo, Gustavo, Lisa J. Crockett, and Miguel A. Carranza. *Health Disparities in Youth and Families*. Nebraska Symposium on Motivation, vol. 57. New York: Springer, 2011.

Castañeda, D., B. Collins, and California Policy Seminar. "HIV/AIDS Education and Prevention Among Latinas and Latinos in California: The Role of Community Agencies." Working Paper. Latina/Latino Policy Research Program. Berkeley, CA: University of California Latina/Latino Policy Research Program, California Policy Seminar, 1994.

Castañeda, M., and J. Krupczynski. *Civic Engagement in Diverse Latinx Communities: Learning from Social Justice Partnerships in Action*. Critical Studies of Latinos/as in the Americas, vol. 17. New York: Peter Lang, 2018.

Castellanos, J., and A. M. Gloria. "Research Consolidations and Theoretical Application for Best Practices in Higher Education: Latinas and Latinos Achieving Success." *Journal of Hispanic Higher Education* 6, no. 4 (2007): 378–96.

Castellanos, J., and L. Jones. *The Majority in the Minority: Expanding the Representation of Latina/o faculty, Administrators, and Students in Higher Education*. 1st ed. Sterling, VA: Stylus Pub., 2003.

Castillo-Speed, Lillian. *Latina: Women's Voices from the Borderlands*. New York: Simon & Schuster, 1995.

Castro, Yessenia, Christine Vinci, Whitney L. Heppner, Miguel Ángel Cano, Virmarie Correa-Fernández, and David W. Wetter. "Revisiting the Relationship Between Acculturation and Smoking Cessation Among Mexican Americans." *Annals of Behavioral Medicine* 53, no. 3 (2018): 211–22.

Center, Pew Hispanic. *Statistical Portrait of Hispanics in the United States, 2010*. Washington, DC: Pew Hispanic Center, 2010. https://www.immigrationresearch.org/report/pew-hispanic-center/statistical-portrait-hispanics-united-states-2010.

Centers for Disease Control. *Chronic Diseases: The Leading Causes of Death and Disability in the United States*. 2017.

Centers for Disease Control and Prevention. "Leading causes of death and numbers of deaths, by sex, race, and Hispanic origin: United States, 1980 and 2014" (table 19). 2015. https://www.cdc.gov/nchs/data/hus/hus15.pdf#019[PDF – 13.4 MB].

Chandra, Kanchan. "What Is an Ethnic Party?" *Party Politics* 17, no. 2 (2011): 151–69.

Chang, Edward T., and Russell Charles Leong, eds. *Los Angeles—Struggles Toward Multiethnic Community: Asian American, African American, and Latino Perspectives*. Seattle: University of Washington Press, 2017.

Chang, P., L. Magaña, Tomás Rivera Center, and Tomás Rivera Policy Institute. *Latinos and Health Care Insurance Participation*. Claremont, CA: The Center, 1992.

Chapa, Jorge, and Emmanuel Garcia. "The Impact of Redistricting on Latino Education Policy: A Texas Case Study." *Journal of Hispanic Higher Education* 12, no. 2 (2013): 138–52.

Chapa, Jorge, and Richard R. Valencia. "Latino Population Growth, Demographic Characteristics, and Educational Stagnation: An Examination of Recent Trends." *Hispanic Journal of Behavioral Sciences* 15, no. 2 (1993): 165–87.

Chavez, L., and University of California. Latina/Latino Policy Research Program. "Comparative Views of Breast and Cervical Cancer Risk Factors Among Latinas, Anglo Women, and Physicians in Northern Orange County." Report to the California Policy Seminar, University of California, Latina/Latino Policy Research Program. Irvine, CA: L. R. Chavez, 1994.

Chavez, L. R. *The Latino Threat: Constructing Immigrants, Citizens, and the Nation.* Stanford, CA: Stanford University Press, 2008.

Chávez, M. *Everyday Injustice: Latino Professionals and Racism.* Lanham, MD: Rowman & Littlefield, 2011.

Chen, N. E., J. E. Gallant, and K. R. Page. "A Systematic Review of HIV/AIDS Survival and Delayed Diagnosis Among Hispanics in the United States." *Journal of Immigrant and Minority Health* 14, no. 1 (2012): 65–81.

Cheung, B. Y., M. Chudek, and S. J. Heine. "Evidence for a Sensitive Period for Acculturation: Younger Immigrants Report Acculturating at a Faster Rate." *Psychological Science* 21 (2010): 60–99.

Chinchilla, N. S., and N. Hamilton. *Seeking Community in a Global City: Guatemalans and Salvadorans in Los Angeles.* Philadelphia: Temple University Press, 2001.

Chinn, Menzie D., and Jeffry A. Frieden. *Lost Decades: The Making of America's Debt Crisis and the Long Recovery.* New York: W. W. Norton Press, 2011.

Choi, Kate, Arthur Sakamoto, and Daniel Powers. "Who is Hispanic? Hispanic Identity Among African Americans, Asian Americans, Others, and Whites." *Sociological Inquiry* 78, no. 3 (2008): 335–71.

Chong, N. *The Latino Patient: A Cultural Guide for Health Care Providers.* Yarmouth, ME: Intercultural Press, 2002.

Chong, N., and F. Baez. *Latino Culture: A Dynamic Force in the Changing American Workplace.* 1st ed. Yarmouth, ME: Intercultural Press, 2005.

Choroszy, Melisa N., and Theodor M. Meek, eds. *Access for All: Expanding Opportunity and Programs to Support Successful Student Outcomes at University of Nevada, Reno.* Reno: University of Nevada Press, 2019.

Chuang, Susan S., and Catherine S. Tamis-LeMonda. *Gender Roles in Immigrant Families.* Advances in Immigrant Family Research. New York: Springer, 2013.

Claassen, Ryan L. "Political Opinion and Distinctiveness: The Case of Hispanic Ethnicity." *Political Research Quarterly* 57, no. 4 (2004): 609–20.

Clark, Paul, and Anne Frost, eds. *Collective Bargaining Under Duress: Case Studies of Major US Industries.* Urbana: Labor and Employment Relations Association, 2013.

Clark County School District. "Master Plan for English Language Learner Success Overview." 2019. https://www.leg.state.nv.us/App/<NELIS/REL/80th2019/ExhibitDocument/OpenExhibitDocument?exhibitId=36105&fileDownload Name=0214_CCSDm.pdf.

Cobas, J. *Latino Peoples in the New America: Racialization and Resistance.* New Critical Viewpoints on Society. New York: Routledge, 2019.

Cobas, J., J. Duany, and J. Feagin. *How the United States Racializes Latinos: White Hegemony and Its Consequences.* Boulder, CO: Paradigm, 2009.

Cockcroft, J. *Latinos in the Making of the United States*. Hispanic Experience in the Americas. New York: F. Watts, 1995.

Coffin, Malcolm. "The Latino Vote: Shaping America's Political Future." *The Political Quarterly* 74, no. 2 (2003): 214–22.

Cohen, L. *Culture, Disease, and Stress Among Latino Immigrants*. RIIES Special Study. Washington, DC: Research Institute on Immigration and Ethnic Studies, Smithsonian Institution, 1979.

Cohn, D'Vera. "Future Immigration Will Change the Face of America by 2065." Pew Research Center, October 5, 2015.

Concannon, Kevin, Francisco A. Lomelí, and Marc Priewe. *Imagined Transnationalism: US Latino/a Literature, Culture, and Identity*. New York: Palgrave Macmillan, 2009.

Concha, Maritza, Mariana Sanchez, Mario de la Rosa, and María Elena Villar. "A Longitudinal Study of Social Capital and Acculturation-Related Stress Among Recent Latino Immigrants in South Florida." *Hispanic Journal of Behavioral Sciences* 35, no. 4 (2013): 469–85.

Cordova, C. *The Heart of the Mission*. Philadelphia: University of Pennsylvania Press, 2017.

Cortés, Carlos E. *Protestantism and Latinos in the United States*. Hispanics in the United States. New York: Arno Press, 1980.

Cortes, Patricia. "The Effect of Low-Skilled Immigration on US Prices: Evidence from CPI Data." *Journal of Political Economy* 116, no. 3 (2008): 381–422.

Costanzo, Joe, Cynthia Davis, Caribert Irazi, Daniel Goodkind, and Roberto Ramirez. "Evaluating Components of International Migration: The Residual Foreign Born." *Working Paper Series No. 61*, Population Division, US Bureau of the Census, 2001.

Creighton, Mathew J., and Fernando Riosmena. "Migration and the Gendered Origin of Migrant Networks Among Couples in Mexico." *Social Science Quarterly* 94, no. 1 (2013): 79–99.

Cresswell, T. *On the Move: Mobility in the Modern Western World*. London and New York: Routledge, 2006.

Crowder, Kyle, and Liam Downey. "Inter-Neighborhood Migration, Race, and Environmental Hazards: Modeling Micro-Level Processes of Environmental Inequality." *American Journal of Sociology* 115, no. 4 (2010): 1110–149.

Crowley, Martha, Daniel T. Lichter, and Richard N. Turner. "Diverging Fortunes? Economic Well-Being of Latinos and African Americans in New Rural Destinations." *Social Science Research* 51 (2015): 77–92.

Cuevas, Carlos A., Chiara Sabina, Anjuli Fahlberg, and Maria Espinola. "The Role of Cultural Factors on Dating Aggression and Delinquency Among Latino Youth." *Journal of Interpersonal Violence* (February 15, 2018).

Current Population Survey. "Glossary of terms–discouraged workers." Accessed September 5, 2013. http://www.bls.gov/bls/glossary.htm.

Currie, Janet, and Hannes Schwandt. "Mortality Inequality: The Good News from a County-Level Approach." *Journal of Economic Perspectives* 30, no. 2 (2016): 29–52.

Cypher, James, and Raúl Delgado Wise. "Restructuring Mexico, Realigning Dependency: Harnessing Mexican Labor Power in the NAFTA Era." In *Globalization and Beyond: New Examinations of Global Power and Its Alternatives*, edited by Jon Shefner and Maria Patricia Fernández-Kelly, 90–120. State College: Pennsylvania State University Press, 2011.

Dadsetan, Malia. "Chronic Disease and Associated Risk Factor Disparities Among Populations in Clark County, Nevada. *Southern Nevada Health District.* 2017. http://www.healthysouthernnevada.org/content/sites/snhd/chronic-disease -and-associated-risk-factor-disparities-051717.pdf.

Damore, David F. "The Impact of Density and Diversity on Reapportionment and Redistricting in the Mountain West." *Brookings Institution: Issues in Governance Studies* 43 (January 2012).

———. "Reid vs. Angle in Nevada's Senate Race: Harry Houdini Escapes the Wave." In *Cases in Congressional Campaigns: Storming the Hill*, 2nd ed., edited by David Dulio and Randall Adkins, 32-53. New York: Routledge, 2011.

———. "Swimming against the Tide: Partisan Gridlock and the 2011 Nevada Redistricting." In *The Political Battle over Congressional Redistricting*, edited by William J. Miller and Jeremy D. Walling, 67–86. Lanham, MD: Lexington Books, 2013.

———. "The 2001 Nevada Redistricting and Perpetuation of the Status Quo." *American Review of Politics* 27 (2006): 149–68.

Dancygier, R., and E. N. Saunders. "A New Electorate? Comparing Preferences and Partisanship Between Immigrants and Natives." *American Journal of Political Science* 50 (2006): 962–81.

Darder, A., Y. Rodríguez Ingle, Barbara G. Cox, Tomás Rivera Center, and Tomás Rivera Policy Institute. *The Policies and the Promise: The Public Schooling of Latino Children.* Claremont, CA: Tomás Rivera Center, 1993.

Darder, Antonia. *Culture and Power in the Classroom: Educational Foundations for the Schooling of Bicultural Students.* Boulder, CO: Paradigm Publishers, 2012.

Darder, Antonia, and Rodolfo Torres. "Latina/o Formations in the United States: Laboring Classes, Migration, and Identities." *Ethnicities* 15, no. 2 (2015): 157–64.

———. *The Latino Studies Reader: Culture, Economy, and Society.* Malden, MA: Blackwell, 1998.

Dardón, María Sandra C., Elizabeth V. Flota, Georgina G. Hernández, Silvia T. González, Guadalupe D. Sánchez, and Luis O. Hernández. "Diferencias entre hombres y mujeres respecto a la elección de carreras relacionadas con atención a la salud." *La Ventana: Revista de Estudios de Género* 3, no. 24 (2006): 204–28.

Darity, William, Jr., Darrick Hamilton, and Jason Dietrich. "Passing on Blackness: Latinos, Race, and Earnings in the USA." *Applied Economics Letters* 9, no. 13 (2002): 847–53.

Darling, C. M., C. P. Nelson, and R. S. Fife. "Improving Breast Health Education for Hispanic Women." *Journal of the American Medical Women's Association* 59, no. 3 (2004): 228–29.

Dávila, A. *Latino Spin: Public Image and the Whitewashing of Race.* New York: New York University Press, 2008.

Dávila, B., and University of California, Santa Barbara. Educational Leadership. *Negotiating "Special" Identities: Latina/o Student Experiences in Special Education.* Santa Barbara: University of California, Santa Barbara, 2011.

Day, F. *Latina and Latino Voices in Literature for Children and Teenagers.* Portsmouth, NH: Heinemann, 1997.

———. *Latina and Latino Voices in Literature: Lives and Works.* Updated and expanded. Westport, CN: Greenwood Press, 2003.

De Gaetano, Yvonne. "The Role of Culture in Engaging Latino Parents' Involvement in School." *Urban Education* 42, no. 2 (2007): 145–62.

De Genova, N. "The Deportation Regime: Sovereignty, Space and the Freedom of Movement." In *The Deportation Regime: Sovereignty, Space, and the Freedom of Movement,* edited by N. De Genova and N. Peutz, 33–65. Durham, NC: Duke University Press, 2010.

De Haymes, M., Keith Kilty, and Elizabeth Segal. *Latino Poverty in the New Century: Inequalities, Challenges and Barriers.* New York: Haworth Press, 2000.

De la Garza, Rodolfo O. "Dual Citizenship, Domestic Policies, and Naturalization Rates of Latino Immigrants in the US." *Tomas Rivera Center Policy Brief* (June 1996).

De la Garza, Rodolfo O., Angelo Falcon, and F. Chris Garcia. "Will the Real Americans Please Stand Up: Anglo and Mexican-American Support of Core American Political Values." *American Journal of Political Science* 40, no. 2 (1996): 335–51.

De la Garza, Rodolfo O., and Harry Pachon. *Latinos and US Foreign Policy: Representing the "Homeland"?* Lanham, MD: Rowman & Littlefield, 2000.

De la Garza, Rodolfo O., and Louis DeSipio. *Ethnic Ironies: Latino Politics in the 1992 Elections.* Boulder, CO: Westview Press, 1996.

De La Garza, Rodolfo O., and Seung-Jin Jang. "Why the Giant Sleeps So Deeply: Political Consequences of Individual-Level Latino Demographics." *Social Science Quarterly* 92, no. 4 (2011): 895–916.

De la Rosa, M., Lori K. Holleran, and Shulamith Lala Ashenberg. *Substance Abusing Latinos: Current Research on Epidemiology, Prevention, and Treatment.* Binghamton, NY: Haworth Social Work Practice Press, 2005.

Del Castillo, Bernal Diaz. *The Conquest of New Spain.* London: Penguin Group, 2003.

Delgado, M. *Alcohol Use/Abuse Among Latinos: Issues and Examples of Culturally Competent Services.* New York: Haworth Press, 1998.

———. *Latino Small Businesses and the American Dream: Community Social Work Practice and Economic and Social Development.* New York: Columbia University Press, 2011.

———. *Social Work with Latinos: Social, Economic, Political, and Cultural Perspectives.* 2nd ed. New York: Oxford University Press, 2017.

Delgado, Richard, Juan Perea, and Jean Stefancic. *Latinos and the Law: Cases and Materials.* St. Paul, MN: Thomson/West, 2008.

Delgado Bernal, Dolores. *Chicana/Latina Education in Everyday Life: Feminista Perspectives on Pedagogy and Epistemology.* Albany: State University of New York Press, 2006.

Delgado-Gaitan, C. *Involving Latino Families in Schools: Raising Student Achievement Through Home-School Partnerships.* Thousand Oaks, CA: Corwin Press, 2004.

Denner, J., and B. Guzmán. *Latina Girls: Voices of Adolescent Strength in the United States.* New York: New York University Press, 2006.

Department of Homeland Security. *Yearbook of Immigration Statistics: 2010.* Washington, DC: Department of Homeland Security, 2011.

———. *Yearbook of Immigration Statistics: 2013.* Washington, DC: Department of Homeland Security, 2014.

DeSipio, L. *Counting on the Latino Vote: Latinos as a New Electorate.* Race and Ethnicity in Urban Politics. Charlottesville: University of Virginia Press, 1996.

DeSipio, Louis, and Rodolfo O. de la Garza. "Forever Seen as New: Latino Participation in American Elections." In *Latinos: Remaking America*, edited by Marcelo Suarez-Orozco and Mariela M. Paez, 398–409. Berkeley: University of California Press, 2002.

Devos, Thierry, Kelly Gavin, and Francisco J. Quintana. "Say 'Adios' to the American Dream? The Interplay Between Ethnic and National Identity Among Latino and Caucasian Americans." *Cultural Diversity and Ethnic Minority Psychology* 16, no. 1 (2010): 37.

Diaz, Rafael M. *Latino Gay Men and HIV: Culture, Sexuality, and Risk Behavior.* New York: Routledge, 2013.

Díaz-Cotto, J. *Gender, Ethnicity, and the State: Latina and Latino Prison Politics.* SUNY Series in New Directions in Crime and Justice Studies. Albany: State University of New York Press, 1996.

Diaz-Greenberg, R. *The Emergence of Voice in Latino High School Students.* New York: Peter Lang, 2001.

Diaz Soto, Lourdes. *Latina/o Hope.* Explorations of Educational Purpose 14. Dordrecht: Springer Netherlands, 2011.

Driscoll, Anne K., M. Antonia Biggs, Claire D. Brindis, and Ekua Yankah. "Adolescent Latino Reproductive Health: A Review of the Literature." *Hispanic Journal of Behavioral Sciences* 23, no. 3 (2001): 255–326.

Duncan, Brian, Joseph Hotz, and Stephen Trejo. "Hispanics in the U.S. Labor Market." In *Hispanics and the Future of America*, edited by Marta Tienda and Faith Mitchell, 228–90. Washington, DC: National Academies Press, 2006.

Duncan, Brian, and Stephen Trejo. "Ancestry Versus Ethnicity: The Complexity and Selectivity of Mexican Identification in the United States." In *Research in Labor Economics*, edited by Amelie Constant, Konstantinos Tatsiramos, and Klaus Zimmermann, 31–66. Bingley, UK: Emerald Group, 2009.

———. "Ethnic Identification, Intermarriage, and Unmeasured Progress by Mexican Americans." In *Mexican Immigration to the United States*, edited by George Borjas, 227–69. Chicago: University of Chicago Press, 2007.

———. "Intermarriage and the Intergenerational Transmission of Ethnic Identity and Human Capital for Mexican Americans." Unpublished manuscript, 2009.

Durand, J., and D. S. Massey. "New World Orders: Continuities and Changes in Latin American Migration." *The Annals of the American Academy of Political and Social Science* 630 (2010): 6–52.

Dzidzienyo, Anani, and Suzanne Oboler, eds. *Neither Enemies nor Friends: Latinos, Blacks, Afro-Latinos.* New York: Palgrave Macmillan, 2005.

Eadington, W. R. "Analyzing the Trends in Gaming-Based Tourism for the State of Nevada: Implications for Public Policy and Economic Development." UNLV *Gaming Research & Review Journal* 15, no. 1 (2011): 37-50.

East, Patricia L., and Sharon B. Hamill. "Sibling Caretaking Among Mexican American Youth: Conditions That Promote and Hinder Personal and School Success." *Hispanic Journal of Behavioral Sciences* 35, no. 4 (2013): 542–64.

Edward Codina, G., and Frank F. Montalvo. "Chicano Phenotype and Depression." *Hispanic Journal of Behavioral Sciences* 16, no. 3 (1994): 296–306.

Edwards, M. *Queer Argentina: Movement Towards the Closet in a Global Time.* New Directions in Latino American Cultures. New York: Palgrave Macmillan/ Springer Nature, 2017.

Elliott, Katherine, and Anthony Urquiza. "Ethnicity, Culture, and Child Maltreatment." *Journal of Social Issues* 62, no. 4 (2006): 787–809.

Ellis, Mark. "Unsettling Immigrant Geographies: US Immigration and the Politics of Scale." *Tijdschrift voor economische en sociale geografie* 97, no. 1 (2006): 49–58.

Emeka, Amon. "Who Are the Hispanic, Non-Hispanics, and Why Do They Matter? Toward a More Inclusive Definition of the Hispanic Population." Unpublished manuscript, 2008.

Emeka, Amon, and Jody Agius Vallejo. "Non-Hispanics with Latin American Ancestry: Assimilation, Race, and Identity Among Latin American Descendants in the US." *Social Science Research* 40 (2011): 1547–563.

Eppler-Epstein, Sarah, Annie Gurvis, and Ryan King. "The Alarming Lack of Data on Latinos in the Criminal Justice System." The Urban Institute. 2016. http://apps .urban.org/features/latino-criminal-justice-data/.

Erickson, P. *Latina Adolescent Childbearing in East Los Angeles.* 1st ed. Austin: University of Texas Press, 1998.

Espinosa, Gastón, Virgilio P. Elizondo, and Jesse Miranda. *Latino Religions and Civic Activism in the United States.* New York: Oxford University Press, 2005.

Estrada-Martínez, Lorena M., Cleopatra Howard Caldwell, Amy J. Schulz, Ana V. Diez-Roux, and Silvia Pedraza. "Families, Neighborhood Socio-Demographic Factors, and Violent Behaviors Among Latino, White, and Black Adolescents." *Youth and Society* 45, no. 2 (2013): 221–42.

Evans, Diana, Ana Belen Franco, James P. Wenzel, and Robert D. Wrinkle. "Ethnic Concerns and Latino Party Identification." *Social Science Journal* 49, no. 2 (2012): 150–54.

Falicov, C. *Latino Families in Therapy.* 2nd ed. New York: Guilford Press, 2014.

Farabee, David, Lynn Wallisch, and Jane Carlisle Maxwell. "Substance Use Among Texas Hispanics and Non-Hispanics: Who's Using, Who's Not, and Why." *Hispanic Journal of Behavioral Sciences* 17, no. 4 (1995): 523–36.

Farley, Reynolds. "Blacks, Hispanics, and White Ethnic Groups: Are Blacks Uniquely Disadvantaged?" *American Economic Review* 80, no. 2 (1990): 237–41.

Faught, James, and Margaret Hunter. "Latinos and the Skin Color Paradox: Skin Color, National Origin, and Political Attitudes." *The Sociological Quarterly* 53, no. 4 (2012): 676–701.

Fawcett, S. B., J. A. Schultz, J. Watson-Thompson, M. Fox, and R. Bremby. "Building Multisectoral Partnerships for Population Health and Health Equity" [Research Support, Non-US Government]. *Preventing Chronic Disease* [serial online]. November 2010.

Feagin, J., and J. Cobas. *Latinos Facing Racism: Discrimination, Resistance, and Endurance.* New Critical Viewpoints on Society. Boulder, CO: Paradigm, 2014.

Feldmann, P. *Management in Latin America: Threats and Opportunities in the Globalized World.* Berlin: Springer, 2014.

Feldmeyer, Ben. "The Effects of Racial/Ethnic Segregation on Latino and Black Homicide." *The Sociological Quarterly* 51, no. 4 (2010): 600–23.

Feliciano, Cynthia. "The Benefits of Biculturalism: Exposure to Immigrant Culture and Dropping Out of School Among Asian and Latino Youths." *Social Science Quarterly* 82, no. 4 (2001): 865–79.

Felix-Ortiz, Maria, Michael D. Newcomb, and Hector Myers. "A Multidimensional Measure of Cultural Identity for Latino and Latina Adolescents." *Hispanic Journal of Behavioral Sciences* 16, no. 2 (1994): 99–115.

Fernandez, Kenneth, John P. Tuman, and Maryam Stevenson. "Transnational Ties and Political Behavior of Latin American Immigrants." Paper presented at the *Western Political Science Association*, San Antonio, Texas, 2011.

Finch, Brian Karl, Robert A. Hummer, Bohdan Kol, and William A. Vega. "The Role of Discrimination and Acculturative Stress in the Physical Health of Mexican-Origin Adults." *Hispanic Journal of Behavioral Sciences* 23, no. 4 (2001): 399–429.

Fitzgibbon, M. L., S. M. Gapstur, and S. J. Knight. "Results of Mujeres Felices por Ser Saludables: A Dietary/Breast Health Randomized Clinical Trial for Latino Women." *Annals of Behavioral Medicine* 28, no. 2 (2004): 95–104.

Fix, Michael E., Jeffrey S. Passel, and Kenneth Sucher. "Trends in Naturalization." *Immigration Studies Program Brief No. 3.* Washington, DC: The Urban Institute, 2003.

Flippen, Chenoa, and Marta Tienda. "Pathways to Retirement: Patterns of Labor Force Participation and Labor Market Exit Among the Preretirement Population by Race, Hispanic Origin, and Sex." *Journals of Gerontology Series* b 55, no. 1 (2000): s14–s27.

Flood, Sarah, Miriam King, Steven Ruggles, and J. Robert Warren. "Integrated Public Use Microdata Series, Current Population Survey: Version 4.0." [Machine-readable database]. Minneapolis: University of Minnesota, 2015.

Flores, Alejandro, and Alexander Coppock. "Do Bilinguals Respond More Favorably to Candidate Advertisements in English or in Spanish?" *Political Communication* 35, no. 4 (2018): 612–33.

Flores, Glenn, Milagros Abreu, Ilan Schwartz, and Maria Hill. "The Importance of Language and Culture in Pediatric Care: Case Studies from the Latino Community." *The Journal of Pediatrics* 137, no. 6 (2000): 842–48.

Flores, Glenn, Milagros Abreu, Mary Anne Olivar, and Beth Kastner. "Access Barriers to Health Care for Latino Children." *Archives of Pediatrics & Adolescent Medicine* 152, no. 11 (1998): 1119–1125.

Flores, H. *Latinos and the Voting Rights Act: The Search for Racial Purpose.* Lanham, MD; Boulder, CO; New York; London: Lexington Books, 2015.

Flores, Juan. *From Bomba to Hip-Hop: Puerto Rican Culture and Latino Identity.* New York: Columbia University Press, 2000.

Flores, Miguel, Mary Zey, Cinthya Caamal, and Nazrul Hoque. "NAFTA, Industrial Concentration, Employment Volatility, Wages, and Internal and International Mexican Migration: 1990–2009." In *Opportunities and Challenges for Applied Demography in the 21st Century*, edited by Nazrul Hoque and David A. Swanson, 155–72. New York: Springer, 2012.

Flores, Y. *Psychology Perspectives for the Chicano and Latino Family.* San Diego: Cognella Academic Publishing, 2015.

Flores-González, N. *Citizens but Not Americans: Race and Belonging Among Latino Millennials.* New York: New York University Press, 2017.

———. *School Kids/Street Kids: Identity Development in Latino Students.* New York: Teachers College Press, 2002.

Fontes, Angela, and Nicole Kelly. "Factors Affecting Wealth Accumulation in Hispanic Households: A Comparative Analysis of Stock and Home Asset Utilization." *Hispanic Journal of Behavioral Sciences* 35, no. 4 (2013): 565–87.

Fox, Jonathan, and Libby Haight. "Mexican Agricultural Policy: Multiple Goals and Conflicting Interests." In *Subsidizing Inequality: Mexican Corn Policy Since NAFTA*, edited by Jonathan Fox and Libby Haight, 9–50. Washington, DC: Woodrow Wilson International Center for Scholars, 2010.

Fraga, Luis R., John A. Garcia, Rodney E. Hero, Michael Jones-Correa, Valerie Martinez-Ebers, and Gary M. Segura. *Latino National Survey (LNS), 2006.* Ann Arbor, MI: Inter-university Consortium for Political and Social Research [distributor], 2013-06-05. https://doi.org/10.3886/ICPSR20862.v6.

———. *Latinos in the New Millennium: An Almanac of Opinion, Behavior, and Policy Preferences.* New York: Cambridge University Press, 2012.

———. "Su casa es nuestra casa: Latino Politics Research and the Development of American Political Science." *American Political Science Review* 100 (2006): 515–21.

Freeman, Robert, Marya Viorst Gwadz, Elizabeth Silverman, Alexandra Kutnick, Noelle R. Leonard, Amanda S. Ritchie, Jennifer Reed, and Belkis Y. Martinez. "Critical Race Theory as a Tool for Understanding Poor Engagement Along the HIV Care Continuum Among African American/Black and Hispanic Persons

Living with HIV in the United States: A Qualitative Exploration." *International Journal for Equity in Health* 16, no. 1 (2017): 54.

Frey, William H. "Hispanics, Race, and the Changing Political Landscape of the United States and the Mountain West." In *America's New Swing Region*, edited by Ruy Teixeira, 82–106. Washington, DC: Brookings Institution Press, 2012.

Fry, Richard, and Lindsay Lowell. *Work or Study: Different Fortunes of U.S. Latino Generations.* Washington, DC: Pew Hispanic Center, 2002.

Fussell, Elizabeth. "Hurricane Chasers in New Orleans: Latino Immigrants as a Source of a Rapid Response Labor Force." *Hispanic Journal of Behavioral Sciences* 31, no. 3 (2009): 375–94.

Gándara, Patricia, and Frances Contreras. *The Latino Education Crisis: The Consequence of Failed Social Policies.* Cambridge, MA: Harvard University Press, 2009.

Gándara, Patricia, and the White House Initiative on Educational Excellence for Hispanics. "Fulfilling America's Future: Latinas in the U.S., 2015." 2015. https://sites.ed.gov/hispanic-initiative/files/2015/09/Fulfilling-Americas-Future-Latinas-in-the-U.S.-2015-Final-Report.pdf.

Gann, Lewis H, and Peter Duignan. *The Hispanics in the United States: A History.* Boulder, CO: Westview Press, 1986.

Garcia, Carlos. "Buscando Trabajo: Social Networking Among Immigrants from Mexico to the United States." *Hispanic Journal of Behavioral Sciences* 27, no. 1 (2005): 3–22.

Garcia, F. *Pursuing Power: Latinos and the Political System.* Notre Dame, IN.: University of Notre Dame Press, 1997.

García, J., and Zea, M. *Psychological Interventions and Research with Latino Populations.* Boston: Allyn and Bacon, 1997.

Garcia, John A. "Understanding multiple social identities among Latinos: Social-cultural connections to Latino pan-ethnic Identity." Paper presented at the Western Political Science Association meeting, San Francisco, 2010.

———. *Latino Politics in America: Community, Culture, and Interests.* New York: Rowman & Littlefield, 2016.

García, M. *The Latino Generation.* Chapel Hill: University of North Carolina Press, 2014.

García, María Cristina. *Seeking Refuge: Central American Migration to Mexico, the United States, and Canada.* Berkeley: University of California Press, 2006.

García Bedolla, L. *Fluid Borders: Latino Power, Identity, and Politics in Los Angeles.* Berkeley: University of California Press, 2005.

García Bedolla, Lisa, and Melissa R. Michelson. *Mobilizing Inclusion: Transforming the Electorate Through Get-Out-the-Vote Campaigns.* New Haven, CT: Yale University Press, 2012.

Gasman, M. Baez, B. and V. Turner. *Understanding Minority-Serving Institutions.* New York: State University of New York, 2008.

Gasparini, Leonardo, Mariana Marchionni, Nicolás Badaracco, and Joaquín Serrano.

"Female Labor Force Participation in Latin America: Evidence of Deceleration." *Documentos de Trabajo del CEDLAS*, no. 181 (March 2015): 1–32. https://www .cedlas.econo.unlp.edu.ar/wp/wp-content/uploads/doc_cedlas181.pdf.

Gavin, Amelia R., Emily Walton, David H. Chae, Margarita Alegria, James S. Jackson, and David Takeuchi. "The Associations Between Socioeconomic Status and Major Depressive Disorder Among Blacks, Latinos, Asians, and Non-Hispanic Whites: Findings from the Collaborative Psychiatric Epidemiology Studies." *Psychological Medicine* 40, no. 1 (2010): 51–61.

Gay, Claudine. "Seeing Difference: The Effect of Economic Disparity on Black Attitudes Toward Latinos." *American Journal of Political Science* 50 (2006): 982–97.

Geron, K. *Latino Political Power*. Latinos, Exploring Diversity and Change. Boulder, CO: L. Rienner, 2005.

Gibson, Campbell, and Kay Jung. "Historical Census Statistics on Population Totals by Race, 1790 to 1990, and by Hispanic Origin, 1970 to 1990, for the United States, Regions, Divisions, and States." Population Division, US Census Bureau, Washington, DC, September 2002, Working Paper Series No. 56.

Gideon, J. *Gender, Globalization, and Health in a Latin American Context*. 1st ed. Studies of the Americas. New York: Palgrave Macmillan, 2014.

Gilbert, M. Jean, and Richard C. Cervantes. "Patterns and Practices of Alcohol Use Among Mexican Americans: A Comprehensive Review." *Hispanic Journal of Behavioral Sciences* 8, no. 1 (1986): 1–60.

Gloria, Alberta M., and Ester R. Rodriguez. "Counseling Latino University Students: Psycho-Sociocultural Issues for Consideration." *Journal of Counseling & Development* 78, no. 2 (2000): 145–54.

Gloria, Alberta M., J. Castellanos, and V. Orozco. "Perceived Educational Barriers, Cultural Congruity, Coping Responses, and Psychological Well-Being of Latina Undergraduates." *Hispanic Journal of Behavioral Science* 27, no. 2 (2005): 161–83.

Golash-Boza, Tanya. *Immigration Nation: Raids, Detentions, and Deportations in Post-9/11 America*. Boulder, CO: Paradigm, 2012.

Golash-Boza, Tanya, and P. Hondagneu-Sotelo. "Latino Immigrant Men and the Deportation Crisis: A Gendered Racial Removal Program." *Latino Studies* 11, no. 3 (2013): 271–92.

Golash-Boza, Tanya, and William Darity Jr. "Latino Racial Choices: The Effects of Skin Color and Discrimination on Latinos' and Latinas' Racial Self-Identifications." *Ethnic and Racial Studies* 31, no. 5 (2008): 899–934.

Gómez, Cynthia A., and Barbara VanOss Marin. "Gender, Culture, and Power: Barriers to HIV-Prevention Strategies for Women." *Journal of Sex Research* 33, no. 4 (1996): 355–62.

Gonzales, Alfonso. "Nuestro gramsci: Notes on Antonio Gramsci's Theoretical Relevance for the Study of Subaltern Latino Politics Research." *Rethinking Marxism* 30, no. 4 (2018): 546–67.

Gonzalez, Arturo. "Mexican Enclaves and the Price of Culture." *Journal of Urban Economics* 43, no. 2 (1998): 273–91.

González, J. *In Search of the Mexican Beverly Hills*. New Brunswick, NJ: Rutgers University Press, 2017.

Gonzalez, Juan. *Harvest of Empire: A History of Latinos in America*. New York: Penguin Group, 2001.

Gonzalez, K. P. "Campus Culture and the Experiences of Chicano Students in a Predominantly White University." *Urban Education* 37, no. 2 (2003): 193–218.

Gonzales, Manuel G. *Mexicanos: A History of Mexicans in the United States*. Bloomington: Indiana University Press, 2009.

Gonzalez, V., and University of California, Santa Barbara. *Taking a Leap to Close the Gap: Early Academic Success of Low-income Latino/a Children Facing Multiple Risks*. Santa Barbara: University of California, Santa Barbara, 2013.

Gonzalez-Barajas, Gabriela R., and Jeanne Brooks-Gunn. "Substance Use Differences Among US-Versus-Foreign-Born Adolescents: Testing Pathways Through Family and Peer Influences." *Hispanic Journal of Behavioral Sciences* 36, no. 4 (2014): 507–21.

Goodman, R. A., S. F. Posner, E. S. Huang, A. K. Parekh, and H. K. Koh. "Defining and Measuring Chronic Conditions: Imperatives for Research, Policy, Program, and Practice." *Preventing Chronic Disease*, 2013; 10:120239. http://doi.org/10.5888/pcd10.120239.

Gracia, Jorge J. E., and Pablo De Greiff. *Hispanics/Latinos in the United States: Ethnicity, Race, and Rights*. New York: Routledge, 2000.

Gratton, Brian, and Emily Klancher Merchant. "An Immigrant's Tale: The Mexican American Southwest 1850 to 1950." *Social Science History* 39, no. 4 (2015): 521–50.

Greenfield, G., and S. Maram. *Latin American Labor Organizations*. New York: Greenwood Press, 1987.

Greenwald, Howard P., Suzanne O'Keefe, and Mark DiCamillo. "Why Employed Latinos Lack Health Insurance: A Study in California." *Hispanic Journal of Behavioral Sciences* 27, no. 4 (2005): 517–32.

Greulich, Erica, John Quigley, and Steven Raphael. "The Anatomy of Rent Burdens: Immigration, Growth and Rental Housing." *Brookings Papers on Urban Affairs* 5 (2004).

Grey, Harvette, and Brittany N. Hall-Clark, eds. *Cultural Considerations in Latino American Mental Health*. Oxford, NY: Oxford University Press, 2015.

Griffin, John D., and Brian Newman. "The Unequal Representation of Latinos and Whites." *Journal of Politics* 69 (2007): 1032–46.

Griswold, Tabor, John Packham, Christopher March, and Laima Etchegoyhen. "Registered Nurse Workforce in Nevada—Findings from the 2013 National Workforce Survey of Registered Nurses, May 2014." *University of Nevada (Reno)-School of Medicine Report*. 2014. http://nvactioncoalition.org/wp-content/uploads/2015/03/Registered-Nurse-Workforce-NV.pdf.

Griswold, Tabor, Laima Etchegoyhen, and John Packham "Registered Nurse Workforce in Nevada—Findings from the 2013 National Workforce Survey of

Registered Nurses, May 2014." *University of Nevada (Reno)–School of Medicine Report.* 2014. http://nvactioncoalition.org/wp-content/uploads/2015/03/Registered-Nurse-Workforce-NV.pdf.

Grogger, Jeffrey, and Stephen Trejo. *Falling Behind or Moving Up? The Intergenerational Progress of Mexican Americans.* San Francisco: Public Policy Institute of California, 2002.

Guarnaccia, Peter J., Igda Martínez Pincay, Margarita Alegría, Patrick E. Shrout, Roberto Lewis-Fernández, and Glorisa J. Canino. "Assessing Diversity Among Latinos: Results from the NLAAS." *Hispanic Journal of Behavioral Sciences* 29, no. 4 (2007): 510–34.

Gullotta, Thomas P., and Sergio A. Aguilar-Gaxiola. *Depression in Latinos.* Issues in Children's and Families' Lives, vol. 8. Boston: Springer US, 2008.

Gutiérrez, David. *The Columbia History of Latinos in the United States since 1960.* New York: Columbia University Press, 2004.

Gutiérrez, G. *Latinos and Latinas at Risk: Issues in Education, Health, Community, and Justice.* Santa Barbara, CA: Greenwood, An Imprint of ABC-CLIO, LLC, 2015.

Gutiérrez, R., and T. Almaguer. *The New Latino Studies Reader.* Oakland: University of California Press, 2016.

Guzmán, M., and N. Carrasco. *Counseling & Diversity: Counseling Latino/a Americans.* Belmont, CA: Brooks/Cole, Cengage Learning, 2011.

Habell-Pallán, Michelle, and Mary Romero, eds. *Latino/a Popular Culture.* New York: NYU Press, 2002.

Hagan, J., B. Castro, and N. Rodriguez. "The Effects of US Deportation Policies on Immigrant Families and Communities: Cross-Border Perspectives." *North Carolina Law Review* 88 (2010): 1800–823.

Hagan, J., K. Eschbach, and N. Rodriguez. "US Deportation Policy, Family Separation, and Circulation Migration." *International Migration Review* 42, no. 1 (2008): 64–88.

Hajnal, Zoltan L., and Taeku Lee. *Why Americans Don't Join the Party: Race, Immigration, and the Failure (of Political Parties) to Engage the Electorate.* Princeton, NJ: Princeton University Press, 2011.

Halgunseth, Linda C., Jean M. Ispa, and Duane Rudy. "Parental Control in Latino Families: An Integrated Review of the Literature." *Child Development* 77, no. 5 (2006): 1282–297.

Hamann, E. T., and V. Zúñiga. "Schooling and the Everyday Ruptures Transnational Children Encounter in the United States and Mexico." In *Children, Youth, and Migration in Global Perspective,* edited by C. Coe, R. R. Reynolds, D. A. Boehm, J. M. Hess, and H. Rae-Espinoza, 141–60. Nashville, TN: Vanderbilt University Press, 2011.

Hansen, L. K., P. Feigl, M. R. Modiano, J. A. Lopez, S. E. Sluder, C. M. Moinpour, and F. L. Meyskens. "An Educational Program to Increase Cervical and Breast Cancer Screening in Hispanic Women: A Southwest Oncology Group Study." *Cancer Nursing* 28, no. 1 (2005): 47–53.

Hardwick, Susan W. "Toward a Suburban Immigrant Nation." In *Twenty-First Century Gateways: Immigrant Incorporation in Suburban America*, edited by A. Singer, S. W. Hardwick, and C. B. Brettell, 31–50. Washington, DC: Brookings Institution, 2008.

Hardy-Fanta, Carol. *Latina Politics, Latino Politics: Gender, Culture, and Political Participation in Boston*. Philadelphia: Temple University Press, 1993.

Hardy-Fanta, Carol, and Jeffrey N. Gerson. *Latino Politics in Massachusetts: Struggles, Strategies, and Prospects*. New York: Routledge, 2002.

Harper, S., S. Yang, and J. Lynch "Is There a Suicide Belt in the United States?" Paper presented at the Society for Epidemiologic Research, June 25, 2008.

Harris, Casey T., and Ben Feldmeyer. "Latino Immigration and White, Black, and Latino Violent Crime: A Comparison of Traditional and Non-Traditional Immigrant Destinations." *Social Science Research* 42, no. 1 (2013): 202–16.

Hartman, Jean M., Samuel D. Bradley, and Julian Bond. *Double Exposure: Poverty and Race in America*. New York: Routledge, 2016.

Hayduk, Ron. *Democracy for All: Restoring Immigrant Voting Rights in the United States*. New York: Routledge, 2006.

Hayes-Bautista, D. *La Nueva California: Latinos From Pioneers to Post-millennials*. 2nd ed. Revised. Oakland: University of California Press, 2017.

Hayes-Bautista, D., California Endowment, and California HealthCare Foundation. *The Health Status of Latinos in California*. Woodlands Hills: California Endowment and California HealthCare Foundation, 1997.

Hayes-Bautista, David E., Roberto Chiprut, and University of California, Los Angeles. Center for the Study of Latino Health. *The Art of Healing Latinos: Firsthand Accounts from Physicians and Other Health Advocates*. 2nd ed. Los Angeles: Published for the UCLA Center for the Study of Latino Health and Culture by the UCLA Chicano Studies Research Center Press, 2008.

Heredia, J. *Transnational Latina Narratives in the Twenty-First Century: The Politics of Gender, Race, and Migrations*. 1st ed. New York: Palgrave Macmillan, 2009.

Hernández-Wolfe, P. *A Borderlands View on Latinos, Latin Americans, and Decolonization: Rethinking Mental Health*. Lanham, MD: Jason Aronson, 2013.

Hero, Rodney. *Latinos and the US Political System: Two-Tiered Pluralism*. Philadelphia: Temple University Press, 1992.

Hirschman, Charles. "The Educational Enrollment of Immigrant Youth: A Test of the Segmented-Assimilation Hypothesis." *Demography* 38, no. 3 (2001): 317–36.

Hobson-Horton, Lisa D., and Lula Owens. "From Freshman to Graduate: Recruiting and Retaining Minority Students." *Journal of Hispanic Higher Education* 3, no. 1 (2004): 86–107.

Hoefer, M., N. Rytina, and B. C. Baker. *Estimates of the Unauthorized Immigrant Population Residing in the United States: January 2011*. Washington, DC: Department of Homeland Security, 2012.

Hollander, Justin B. *Sunburnt Cities: The Great Recession, Depopulation and Urban Planning in the American Sunbelt*. New York: Routledge, 2011.

Hondo, Carolyn, Mary E. Gardiner, and Yolando Sapien. *Latino Dropouts in Rural America: Realities and Possibilities*. Albany: State University of New York Press, 2008.

Hood, M. V., and Irwin L. Morris. "Amigo o enemigo? Context, Attitudes, and Anglo Public Opinion Toward Immigration." *Social Science Quarterly* 78 (1997): 309–23.

Hoque, Nazrul, and David A. Swanson, eds. *Opportunities and Challenges for Applied Demography in the 21st Century*. Applied Demography Series Vol. 2. New York: Springer, 2012.

Horevitz, Elizabeth, and Kurt C. Organista. "The Mexican Health Paradox: Expanding the Explanatory Power of the Acculturation Construct." *Hispanic Journal of Behavioral Sciences* 35, no. 1 (2013): 3–34.

Hovius, C. *Latino Migrant Workers: America's Harvesters*. Hispanic Heritage. Philadelphia: Mason Crest, 2006.

Howard, Tiffiany. "Afro-Latinos and the Black-Hispanic Identity: Evaluating the Potential for Group Conflict and Cohesion." *The National Political Science Review* (Special Issue) 19, no. 1 (2019): 29–50.

Howard, Tiffiany, and Roman Lewis. "Immigration and Ethnic Diversity in Nevada." *The Social Health of Nevada: Leading Indicators and Quality of Life in the Silver State*, edited by Dmitri N. Shalin, 1–27. Las Vegas: UNLV Center for Democratic Culture, December 2017. http://cdclv.unlv.edu/healthnv_2017/Immigration.pdf.

Huerta-Macías, A. *Workforce Education for Latinos: Politics, Programs, and Practices*. Westport, CN: Bergin & Garvey, 2002.

Hunter, Miranda. *Latino Americans and Immigration Laws: Crossing the Border*. Hispanic Heritage. Philadelphia: Mason Crest, 2005.

———. *The Story of Latino Civil Rights: Fighting for Justice*. Hispanic Heritage. Philadelphia: Mason Crest, 2005.

Hurtado, Sylvia. "The Institutional Climate for Talented Latino Students." *Research in Higher Education* 35, no. 1 (1994): 21–41.

Hutchings, Vincent L., and Nicholas A. Valentino. "The Centrality of Race in American Politics." *Annual Review of Political Science* 7 (2004): 383–408.

Ibarra, A., A. Carlos, and R. Torres. *The Latino Question*. London: Pluto Press.

Ibarra, Mickey, and Maria Perez-Brown. *Latino Leaders Speak: Personal Stories of Struggle and Triumph*. Houston: Arte Público Press, 2017.

Iber, Jorge. *Hispanics in the Mormon Zion, 1912–1999*. 1st ed. College Station: Texas A&M University Press, 2000.

Iber, Jorge, and Arnoldo DeLeon. *Hispanics in the American West*. Santa Barbara, CA: ABC-CLIO, 2006.

Instituto Nacional de Estadística y Geografía (INEGI). *Censo General de Población y Vivienda 1970*. Aguascalientes, Mexico: INEGI, 1970. http://www.inegi.org.mx/est /contenidos/proyectos/ccpv/cpv1970/default.aspx.

———. *Censo General de Población y Vivienda 1980*. Aguascalientes, Mexico: INEGI, 1980. https://www.inegi.org.mx/programas/ccpv/1980/.

———. *Censo General de Población y Vivienda*. Aguascalientes, Mexico: INEGI, 1990. https://www.inegi.org.mx/programas/ccpv/1990/.

———. *Censo General de Población y Vivienda*. Aguascalientes, Mexico: INEGI, 2000. https://www.inegi.org.mx/programas/ccpv/2000/.

———. *Censo General de Población y Vivienda*. Aguascalientes, Mexico: INEGI, 2010. https://www.inegi.org.mx/programas/ccpv/2010/.

Irazábal, Clara, and Ramzi Farhat. "Latino Communities in the United States: Place-Making in the Pre–World War II, Postwar, and Contemporary City." *Journal of Planning Literature* 22, no. 3 (2008): 207–28.

Itzigsohn, Jose. "The Formation of Latino and Latina Pan-Ethnic Identities." In *Not Just Black and White: Historical and Contemporary Perspectives on Immigration, Race. and Ethnicity in the United States*, edited by N. Foner and G. Fredrickson, 197–216. New York: Russell Sage Foundation, 2004.

Jelen, Ted, Danielle Roth-Johnson, and John P. Tuman. "Culture Wars in Latin America: Religion and Attitudes Toward Homosexuality and Abortion in Four Countries." *Journal of Religion and Theology* 1, no. 1 (2017): 1–7.

Jennings, J. *Blacks, Latinos, and Asians in Urban America: Status and Prospects for Politics and Activism*. Westport, CT: Praeger, 1994.

Jimenez, Luis F. "De Paisano a Paisano: Mexican Migrants and the Transference of Political Attitudes to their Country of Origin." PhD diss., University of Pittsburgh, 2008.

Jolly, Kim, Cynthia Archibald, and Patricia Liehr. "Risk Taking in First and Second Generation Afro-Caribbean Adolescents: An Emerging Challenge for School Nurses." *The Journal of School Nursing* 29, no. 5 (2013): 353–60.

Jones, Nicole, and Amanda Mortimer. "Measuring Acculturation with the ARSMA-II: Bi-Dimensional Analysis Increases Accuracy as Frequency of Use Increases Over Time." *Hispanic Journal of Behavioral Sciences* 36, no. 4 (2014): 387–412.

Jones-Correa, Michael. "Under Two Flags: Dual Nationality in Latin America and Its Consequences for Naturalization in the United States." *International Migration Review* 35, no. 4 (2001): 997–1029.

Kawahara, D., and O. Espin. *Feminist Therapy with Latina Women: Personal and Social Voices*. Women & Therapy, vol. 35, nos. 1–2. London: Routledge, 2013.

Kells, M., V. Balester, and V. Villanueva. *Latino/a Discourses: On Language, Identity & Literacy Education*. CrossCurrents. Portsmouth, NH: Boynton/Cook/ Heinemann, 2004.

Kelly, Nathan J., and Jana Morgan. "Religious Traditionalism and Latino Politics in the United States." *American Politics Research* 36, no. 2 (2007): 236–62.

Kennedy, E. "The Role of the Federal Government in Eliminating Health Disparities." *Health Affairs* 24, no. 2 (2005): 452–58.

King, Keith A., and Rebecca A. Vidourek. "Psychosocial Factors Associated with Recent Alcohol Use Among Hispanic Youth." *Hispanic Journal of Behavioral Sciences* 32, no. 3 (2010): 470–85.

Kingstone, Peter. *The Political Economy of Latin America: Reflections on Neoliberalism and Development After the Commodity Boom*. New York: Routledge, 2018.

Kiyama, Judy M., Samuel D. Museus, and Blanca E. Vega. "Cultivating Campus Environments to Maximize Success Among Latino and Latina College Students." In *College Completion for Latino/a Students: Institutional and System Approaches*, edited by Melissa L. Freeman and Magdalena Martinez. San Francisco: Jossey-Bass, 2015.

Kosmin, Barry A., and Ariela Keysar. "Party Political Preferences of U.S. Hispanics: The Varying Impact of Religion, Social Class, and Demographic Factors." *Ethnic and Racial Studies* 18, no. 2 (1995): 336–47.

Krogstad, Jens Manuel. "Reflecting a Racial Shift, 109 Counties Turned Majority-Minority Since 2000." Pew Research Center, August 21, 2019.

Kugler, Adriana, and Mutlu Yuksel. "Effects of Low-Skilled Immigration on US Natives: Evidence from Hurricane Mitch." NBER *Working Paper 14293*, 2018

Landale, N., S. McHale, A. Booth, and National Symposium on Family Issues. *Growing Up Hispanic: Health and Development of Children of Immigrants*. Washington, DC: Urban Institute Press, 2010.

Las Vegas Sun. "Solar Jobs Benefit Nevada's Hispanics." December 9, 2015. http://lasvegassun.com/news/2015/dec/09/solar-jobs-benefit-nevadas-hispanics/.

Latino Chamber of Commerce. "Our history." Accessed June 13, 2007. http://www.LVLCC.com.

Latino Task Force on Community Mental Health Training. *Latino Community Mental Health* (Monograph (Spanish Speaking Mental Health Research and Development Program [US]; no. 1). Los Angeles: Spanish Speaking Mental Health Research and Development Program, 1978.

Lavariega Monforti, Jessica, and Lisa Garcia Bedolla. "The Influence of Context and History on the Policy Positions and Partisanship of Hispanics in the United States." In *Perspectives on Race, Ethnicity, and Religion*, edited by Valerie-Martinez Ebers and Manochehr Dorraj, 138–52. New York: Oxford University Press, 2010.

Leal, David L., S.A. Nuño, J. Lee, and R.O. de la Garza. "Latinos, Immigration, and the 2006 Midterm Elections." *Political Science and Politics* 41 (2008): 309–17.

Leal, David L., and Stephen J. Trejo. *Latinos and the Economy: Immigrants and Minorities, Politics, and Policy*. New York: Springer, 2011.

Leal, David L., Valerie Martinez-Ebers, and Kenneth J. Meier. "The Politics of Latino Education: The Biases of At-Large Elections." *Journal of Politics* 66 (2004): 1224–244.

Lebron, A. "Racialization of Latinos and Implications for Health Following September 11th: Findings from a Northern Border Community." PhD diss., Department of Health Behavior and Education, University of Michigan, 2015.

Lee, Eun Sul, and Ronald N. Forthofer. *Analyzing Complex Survey Data*. Thousand Oaks, CA: Sage, 1996.

Lee, Jennifer, Frank D. Bean, Jeanne Batalova, and Sabeen Sandhu. "Immigration and the Black-White Color Line in the United States." *The Review of Black Political Economy* 31, nos. 1–2 (2003): 43–76.

Lee, S. *Building a Latino Civil Rights Movement*. Chapel Hill: University of North Carolina Press, 2014.

Lee, Taeku. "Race, Immigration, and the Identity-to-Politics Link." *Annual Review of Political Science* 11 (2008): 457–78.

Leitner, H., and C. Strunk. "Spaces of Immigrant Advocacy and Liberal Democratic Citizenship." *Annals of the Association of American Geographers* 104, no. 2 (2014): 348–56.

Leong, F., and M. Leach. *Suicide Among Racial and Ethnic Minority Groups: Theory, Research, and Practice*. New York: Routledge, 2008.

Lichter, Daniel T., Domenico Parisi, and Michael C. Taquino. "Emerging Patterns of Hispanic Residential Segregation: Lessons from Rural and Small-Town America." *Rural Sociology* 81, no. 4 (2016): 483–518.

Lichter, Daniel T., Scott R. Sanders, and Kenneth M. Johnson. "Hispanics at the Starting Line: Poverty Among Newborn Infants in Established Gateways and New Destinations." *Social Forces* 94, no. 1 (2015): 209–35.

Liebkind, Karmela, and Inga Jasinskaja-Lahti. "Acculturation and Psychological Well-Being Among Immigrant Adolescents in Finland: A Comparative Study of Adolescents from Different Cultural Backgrounds." *Journal of Adolescent Research* 15, no. 4 (2000): 446–69.

Lim, Jaewon, John P. Tuman, and David F. Damore. "Interstate Migration Among Latinos and the Foreign-Born Latino Population in Nevada, 2007–2011." Brookings Institution Mountain West Report, January 2014. 1–14. http://digitalscholar ship.unlv.edu/brookings_pubs/26.

Lindstrom, David P. "Economic Opportunity in Mexico and Return Migration from the United States." *Demography* 33, no. 3 (1996): 357–374.

Livingston, Gretchen, and Joan Kahn. "An American Dream Unfulfilled: The Limited Mobility of Mexican Americans." *Social Science Quarterly* 83, no. 4 (2002): 1003–12.

López, Antoinette Sedillo. *Latino Employment, Labor Organizations, and Immigration*. New York: Garland Pub., 1995.

Lopez, D., and A. Jiménez. *Latinos and Public Policy in California: An Agenda for Opportunity*. Berkeley, CA: Berkeley Public Policy Press, 2003.

Lopez, E., E. Ramirez, R. Rochin, and California State Library. *Latinos and Economic Development in California* (CRB-99-008). Sacramento, CA: California Research Bureau, 1999.

López, Gerardo R. *Persistent Inequality: Contemporary Realities in the Education of Undocumented Latina/o Students*. New York: Routledge, 2010.

Lopez, M. H., R. Morin, and P. Taylor. *Illegal Immigration Backlash Worries, Divides Latinos*. Washington, DC: Pew Hispanic Center, 2010.

López-Calvo, I. *Latino Los Angeles in Film and Fiction: The Cultural Production of Social Anxiety*. Tucson: University of Arizona Press, 2011.

Los Dos Méxicos. "Directorio de organizaciones." 2007. http://www.losdosmexicos .com.mx/directorio_organizaciones.htm.

Lowe, M. R., R. A. Byron, G. Ferry, and M. Garcia. "Food for Thought: Frequent Interracial Dining Experiences as a Predictor of Students' Racial Climate Perceptions." *Journal of Higher Education* 84, no. 4 (2013): 569–600.

Lozano, A. *Latina/o College Student Leadership: Emerging Theory, Promising Practice.* Lanham, MD: Lexington Books, 2015.

Lustig, Nora, Luis F. Lopez-Calva, and Eduardo Ortiz-Juarez. "The Decline in Inequality in Latin America: How Much, Since When and Why." Tulane Department of Economics Working Papers, No. 1118, November 2011. Accessed May 29, 2013. http://econ.tulane.edu/RePEc/pdf/tu11118.pdf.

Lyons, Patricia A., Lauren E. Coursey, and Jared B. Kenworthy. "National Identity and Group Narcissism as Predictors of Intergroup Attitudes Toward Undocumented Latino Immigrants in the United States." *Hispanic Journal of Behavioral Sciences* 35, no. 3 (2013): 323–35.

Maduro, Renaldo. "Curanderismo and Latino Views of Disease and Curing." *Western Journal of Medicine* 139, no. 6 (1983): 868.

Magaña, Lisa, and Erik Lee. *Latino Politics and Arizona's Immigration Law SB 1070.* Immigrants and Minorities, Politics and Policy. New York: Springer, 2013.

Manuel, Casas, J., and Ana P. Cabrera. "Latino/a Immigration: Actions and Outcomes Based on Perceptions and Emotions or Facts?" *Hispanic Journal of Behavioral Sciences* 33, no. 3 (2011): 283–303.

Marchevsky, A., and J. Theoharis. *Not Working: Latina Immigrants, Low-Wage Jobs, and the Failure of Welfare Reform.* New York: New York University Press, 2006.

Marrero, Pilar. June Tracking Poll: Immigration is a Critical Issue for Voters. Latino Decisions/ImpreMedia Poll. http://www.latinodecisions.com/blog/2011/06/10/june-tracking-poll-immigrationis-a-critical-issue-for-voters/. June 9, 2011.

Martínez, C., Z. Leonardo, and C. Tejeda. *Charting New Terrains of Chicana(o)/Latina(o) Education.* Themes of Urban and Inner-city Education. Cresskill, NJ: Hampton Press, 2000.

Martinez, Charles R., Heather H. McClure, and J. Mark Eddy. "Language Brokering Contexts and Behavioral and Emotional Adjustment Among Latino Parents and Adolescents." *The Journal of Early Adolescence* 29, no. 1 (2009): 71–98.

Martinez, Magdalena. "Hispanic Students in Nevada Public Higher Education: Emerging Hispanic-Serving Institutions and Performance-Based Funding." Nevada System of Higher Education, 2012.

Martinez, Magdalena, and Edith Fernández. "Latinos in Community Colleges." *New Directions in Student Services* 2004, no. 105 (2004): 51–62. Hoboken, NJ: Wiley and Sons.

Martinez, Rubén O. "The Impact of Neoliberalism on Latinos." *Latino Studies* 14, no. 1 (2016): 11–32.

Martinez Aleman, Ana M. "Latino Demographics, Democratic Individuality, and Educational Accountability: A Pragmatist's View" (Report). *Educational Researcher* (October 2006).

Márquez, B. *Democratizing Texas Politics: Race, Identity, and Mexican American Empowerment, 1945–2002.* Austin: University of Texas Press, 2014.

Márquez-Reiter, Rosina, and L. M. Rojo. *A Sociolinguistics of Diaspora: Latino Practices, Identities, and Ideologies.* New York; London: Routledge, 2015.

Marshall, Ray. *Back to Shared Prosperity: The Growing Inequality of Wealth and Income in America*. New York: Routledge, 2000.

Marsiglia, Flavio F., Scott T. Yabiku, Stephen Kulis, Tanya Nieri, Monica Parsai, and David Becerra. "The Influence of Linguistic Acculturation and Gender on the Initiation of Substance Use Among Mexican Heritage Preadolescents in the Borderlands." *The Journal of Early Adolescence* 31, no. 2 (2011): 271–99.

Martinez, Charles R., Heather H. McClure, J. Mark Eddy, and D. Molloy Wilson. "Time in US Residency and the Social, Behavioral, and Emotional Adjustment of Latino Immigrant Families." *Hispanic Journal of Behavioral Sciences* 33, no. 3 (2011): 323–49.

Massey, Douglas S. "Latinos, Poverty, and the Underclass: A New Agenda for Research." *Hispanic Journal of Behavioral Sciences* 15, no. 4 (1993): 449–75.

Massey, Douglas S., and Fernando Riosmena. "Undocumented Migration from Latin America in an Era of Rising US Enforcement." *Annals of the American Academy of Political and Social Science* 630 (2010): 294–321.

Massey, Douglas S., Jorge Durand, and Nolan J. Malone. *Beyond Smoke and Mirrors: Mexican Migration in an Era of Economic Integration*. New York: Russell Sage Foundation, 2002.

Massey, Douglas S., and Kristin E. Espinosa. "What's Driving Mexico-US Migration? A Theoretical, Empirical, and Policy Analysis." *American Journal of Sociology* 102, no. 4 (1997): 939-999.

Mazzolari, Francesca. "Dual Citizenship Rights: Do They Make More and Richer Citizens?" *Demography* 46, no. 1 (2009): 169–91.

McCloskey, J. "*Promotores* as Partners in a Community-Based Diabetes Intervention Program Targeting Hispanics." *Family & Community Health* 32, no. 1 (2009): 48–57.

McFarland, Joel, Jiashan Cui, Amy Rathbun, and Juliet Holmes. *Trends in High School Dropout and Completion Rates in the United States: 2018*. Compendium Report. NCES 2019–117. Washington, DC: US Department of Education, National Center for Education Statistics, 2019.

McGlynn, Provitera A. "Hispanic Girls Most Likely to Drop Out…and Stay Out: Mixed Messages and Discrepant Expectations Faulted." *The Hispanic Outlook in Higher Education* 12, no. 1 (2001): 30.

McNeill, Cervantes, Brian McNeill, and Joseph Michael Cervantes. *Latina/o Healing Practices: Mestizo and Indigenous Perspectives*. New York: Routledge, 2008.

Medina, A., H. Balcazar, M. L. Hollen, E. Nkhoma, and F. S. Mas. "Promotores de salud: Educating Hispanic Communities on Heart-Healthy Living." *American Journal of Health Education* 38, no. 4 (2007): 194–202.

Meier, Kenneth J. "Latinos and Representative Bureaucracy: Testing the Thompson and Henderson Hypothesis." *Journal of Public Administration Research and Theory* 3 (1993): 393–414.

Meier, Kenneth J., Eric Gonzalez Juenke, Robert D. Wrinkle, and J. T. Polinard. "Structural Choices and Representation Biases: The Post-Election Color of Representation." *American Journal of Political Science* 49 (2005): 758–68.

Meier, Kenneth J., and Joseph Stewart. *The Politics of Hispanic Education*. Albany: State University of New York Press, 1991.

Meissner, D., D. M. Kerwin, M. Chishti, and C. Bergeron. *Immigration Enforcement in the United States: The Rise of a Formidable Machinery*. Washington, DC: Migration Policy Institute, 2013.

Meléndez, Edwin, and Miren Uriarte, eds. *Latino Poverty and Economic Development in Massachusetts*. Mauricio Gastón Institute for Latino Community Development and Public Policy. Boston: University of Massachusetts, 1993.

Michelson, Melisa. "Does Ethnicity Trump Party? Competing Vote Cues and Latino Voting Behavior." *Journal of Political Marketing* 4, no. 4 (2005): 1–25.

Mills, Barbara J., Jeffery J. Clark, Matthew A. Peeples, W. Randall Haas, John M. Roberts, J. Brett Hill, Deborah L. Huntley, Lewis Borck, Ronald L. Breiger, and Aaron Clauset. "Transformation of Social Networks in the Late Pre-Hispanic US Southwest." *Proceedings of the National Academy of Sciences* 110, no. 15 (2013): 5785–790.

Mintzer, R. *Latino Americans in Sports, Film, Music, and Government: Trailblazers*. Hispanic Heritage. Philadelphia: Mason Crest, 2006.

Miranda, Alexis O., Jennifer M. Bilot, Paul R. Peluso, Kathleen Berman, and Luz G. Van Meek. "Latino Families: The Relevance of the Connection Among Acculturation, Family Dynamics, and Health for Family Counseling Research and Practice." *The Family Journal* 14, no. 3 (2006): 268–73.

Miranda, M. L. *A History of Hispanics in Southern Nevada*. Reno: University of Nevada Press, 1997.

Mirandé, Alfredo. *Hombres y Machos: Masculinity and Latino Culture*. New York: Routledge, 2018.

Mize, R., and G. Delgado. *Latino Immigrants in the United States*. Immigration & Society. Cambridge; Malden, MA: Polity Press, 2012.

Mladenka, Kenneth R. "Blacks and Hispanics in Urban Politics." *American Political Science Review* 83 (1989): 165–91.

Mohamed, H. *The New Americans? Immigration, Protest, and the Politics of Latino Identity*. Lawrence: University Press of Kansas, 2017.

Molina, Carlos W., and Marilyn Aguirre-Molina. *Latino Health in the US: A Growing Challenge*. Washington, DC: American Public Health Association, 1994.

Molina-Crespo, J. *La Salud de la Comunidad Latina en Chicago /The Latino Community's Health Status in Chicago*. Chicago: Chicago Commission on Latino Affairs, 1988.

Monnat, Shannon M. "Disease Prevalence and Behavioral Risk in Nevada." *The Social Health of Nevada*. 2012. https://digitalscholarship.unlv.edu/cgi/view content.cgi?article=1031&context=social_health_nevada_reports.

Monteiro, K. *Ethnicity and Psychology: African-, Asian-, Latino- and Native-American Psychologies*. Dubuque, IA: Kendall, 1995.

Montilla, R., and F. Medina. *Pastoral Care and Counseling with Latino/as*. Minneapolis: Fortress Press, 2006.

Mora, C. *Latinos in the West: The Student Movement and Academic Labor in Los Angeles*. Lanham, MD: Rowman & Littlefield, 2007.

Mora, J., and D. Diaz. *Latino Social Policy: A Participatory Research Model*. New York: Haworth Press, 2003.

Morales, Ed. "The Changing Face of Latino Politics in New York." *NACLA Report on the Americas* 46, no. 4 (2013): 27–31.

———. *Latinx: The New Force in American Politics and Culture*. London; Brooklyn, NY: Verso, 2018.

Morales, R., and F. Bonilla. *Latinos in a Changing US Economy: Comparative Perspectives on Growing Inequality*. Sage Series on Race and Ethnic Relations, vol. 7. Newbury Park, CA: Sage Publications, 1993.

Mossberger, Karen, Caroline J. Tolbert, and Christopher Anderson. "The Mobile Internet and Digital Citizenship in African-American and Latino Communities." *Information, Communication & Society* 20, no. 10 (2017): 1587–606.

Motel, Seth. "Statistical Portrait of Hispanics in the United States." Pew Research Hispanic Trends Project. Washington, DC: Pew Research Center, 2012.

Muennig, P., E. Lubetkin, H. Jia, and P. Franks. "Gender and the Burden of Disease Attributable to Obesity." *American Journal of Public Health* 96 (2006): 1662–668.

Mulder, Mark, Aida I. Ramos, and Gerardo Marti. *Latino Protestants in America: Growing and Diverse*. Lanham, MD: Rowman & Littlefield, 2017.

Munier, Nathan, Julia Albarracin, and Keith Boeckelman. "Determinants of Rural Latino Trust in the Federal Government." *Hispanic Journal of Behavioral Sciences* 37, no. 3 (2015): 420–38.

Muro, Mark. *Unify, Regionalize, Diversify: An Economic Development Agenda for Nevada*. Brookings Mountain West, November 2011.

Museus, S. D., J. N. Ravello, and B. E. Vega. "The Campus Racial Culture: A Critical Race Counterstory." In *Creating Campus Cultures: Fostering Success Among Racially Diverse Student Populations*, edited by S. D. Museus and U. M. Jayakumar, 28–45. New York: Routledge, 2012.

Naidoo, J. *Celebrating Cuentos: Promoting Latino Children's Literature and Literacy in Classrooms and Libraries*. Santa Barbara, CA: Libraries Unlimited, 2011.

National Association of Latino Elected Appointed Officials. Education Fund. *The Latino Vote During the Decade 1980–1990*. Los Angeles: NALEO Educational Fund, 1991.

National Council of La Raza. Hispanic Youth Employment Research Center. *Socioeconomic-Demographic Highlights of Hispanic Americans*, 1981.

National Heart, Lung, and Blood Institute. *Bringing Heart Health to Latinos: A Guide for Building Community Programs*. National Institutes of Health, National Heart, Lung, and Blood Institute, 1998.

———. *Hispanic Community Health Study-Study of Latinos: Data book: A Report to the Communities*. NIH publication no. 13–7951. Bethesda, MD: US Department of Health and Human Services, National Institutes of Health, National Heart, Lung, and Blood Institute, 2013.

Navarro, Armando M. *Mexicano and Latino Politics and the Quest for Self-Determination: What Needs to Be Done*. New York: Lexington Books, 2015.

Navarro, Armando M., R. Raman, L. J. McNicholas, and O. Loza. "Diffusion of Cancer Education Information Through a Latino Community Health Advisory Program." *Preventive Medicine* 45, nos. 2/3 (2007): 135–38.

Navarro, S., S. Hernandez, and Leslie A. Navarro. *Latinas in American Politics: Changing and Embracing Political Tradition.* Latinos and American Politics. Lanham, MD: Lexington Books, 2016.

Nevada by the Numbers. 2016. http://www.rcg1.com/category/nevada-by-the -numbers-blog/.

Nevada Department of Employment, Training and Rehabilitation. "Nevada Labor Market Overview." September 2016. 1–28.

———. "Nevada Occupational Employment and Wages (2012), Statewide Occupational Wage Estimates All Industries—SOC 472061(Construction Laborer)." 2012. http://www.nevadaworkforce.com/admin/uploadedPublications/2857_OES _WAGE_Statewide_2012.xls.

Nevada's Mental Health Workforce: Shortages and Opportunities. Kenny Guinn Center for Policy Priorities. 2014. https://guinncenter.org/wp-content/uploads /2014/10/Guinn-Center-Policy-Brief_Mental-Health-Workforce-Final.pdf.

Nevada State Health Needs Assessment. 2015. http://dpbh.nv.gov/uploadedFiles /dpbhnvgov/content/Programs/OPHIE/Docs/Part%20I_FV_final%20Nov%20 2015.pdf.

Nevarez, Griselda. "GOP 2016 Win Will Need More Than 40 Percent of Latino Vote, Says Study." *NBC News Latino.* July 15, 2015. http://www.nbcnews.com/news /latino/gop-2016-win-will-needmore-40-percent-latino-vote-n394006.

Newby, C. Alison, and Julie A. Dowling. "Black and Hispanic: The Racial Identification of Afro-Cuban Immigrants in the Southwest." *Sociological Perspectives* 50, no. 3 (2007): 343–66.

Newman, Benjamin J. "Acculturating Contexts and Anglo Opposition to the Immigration in the US." *American Journal of Political Science* 57 (2013): 374–90.

Nicholson, Stephen P., Adrian D. Pantoja, and Gary M. Segura. "Political Knowledge and Issue Voting Among the Latino Electorate." *Political Research Quarterly* 59 (2006): 259–71.

Nicholson, Stephen P., and Gary Segura. "Issue Agendas and the Politics of Latino Partisan Identification." In *Diversity in Democracy: Minority Representation in the United States,* edited by Gary M. Segura and Shaun Bowler, 51–71. Charlottesville: University of Virginia Press, 2005.

Nieri, Tanya, and Monica Bermudez-Parsai. "Gap or Overlap? Parent-Child Acculturation Differences in Mexican Immigrant Families." *Hispanic Journal of Behavioral Sciences* 36, no. 4 (2014): 413–34.

Nunez, S. Hurtado, and E. C. Galdeano, eds. *Hispanic-Serving Institutions: Advancing Research and Transformative Practice.* New York: Routledge, 2015.

Nuño, Stephen A. "Latino Mobilization and Vote Choice in the 2000 Presidential Election." *American Politics Research* 35, no. 2 (2007): 273–93.

Ochoa, Enrique, and Gilda L. Ochoa. *Latino Los Angeles: Transformations, Communities, and Activism.* Tucson: University of Arizona Press, 2005.

Office of Disease Prevention and Health Promotion. *The Social Determinants of Health*. 2016. https://www.healthypeople.gov/2020/topics-objectives/topic/social-determinants-of-health.

Olivarez, Adriana. "Studying Representations of US Latino Culture." *Journal of Communication Inquiry* 22, no. 4 (1998): 426–37.

Ono, Hiromi. "Assimilation, Ethnic Competition, and Ethnic Identities of US-Born Persons of Mexican Origin." *International Migration Review* 36, no. 3 (2002): 726–45.

Opie, F. *Upsetting the Apple Cart: Black-Latino Coalitions in New York City from Protest to Public Office*. Columbia History of Urban Life. New York: Columbia University Press, 2014.

Organista, K. *HIV Prevention with Latinos: Theory, Research, and Practice*. New York: Oxford University Press, 2012.

———. *Solving Latino Psychosocial and Health Problems: Theory, Practice, and Populations*. Hoboken, NJ: John Wiley & Sons, 2007.

Orleck, Annelise. *Storming Caesars Palace: How Black Mothers Fought Their Own War on Poverty*. Boston: Beacon Press, 2005.

Orozco, Graciela L. "Understanding the Culture of Low-Income Immigrant Latino Parents: Key to Involvement." *School Community Journal* 18, no. 1 (2008): 21–37.

Orr, M., and D. Morel. *Latino Mayors: Political Change in the Postindustrial City*. Philadelphia: Temple University Press, 2018.

Ottaviano, Gianmarco, and Giovanni Peri. "Rethinking the Effects of Immigration on Earnings." *NBER Working Paper 12497*. 2006.

Ovink, Sarah M. *Race, Class, and Choice in Latino/a Higher Education: Pathways in the College-For-All Era*. New York: Palgrave-Macmillan, 2017.

Pachon, H. "U.S. Citizenship as a Strategy for Latino Political Empowerment." Los Angeles, NALEO Background Paper No. 13. 1990.

Padilla, Yolanda C. "Determinants of Hispanic Poverty in the Course of the Transition to Adulthood." *Hispanic Journal of Behavioral Sciences* 19, no. 4 (1997): 416–32.

Padilla, Yolanda C., and Jennifer E. Glick. "Variations in the Economic Integration of Immigrant and U.S.-Born Mexicans." *Hispanic Journal of Behavioral Sciences* 22, no. 2 (2000): 179–93.

Palladino, Grace. *Skilled Hands, Strong Spirits: A Century of Building Trades History*. Ithaca, NY: Cornell University Press, 2007.

Pallares, Amalia, and Nolda Flores-González. *¡Marcha! Latino Chicago and the Immigrant Rights Movement*. Latinos in Chicago and the Midwest. Urbana, IL: University of Illinois Press, 2010.

Pantoja, Adrian D., Ricardo Ramirez, and Gary Segura. "Citizens by Choice and Voters by Necessity: Patterns in Political Mobilization by Naturalized Latinos." *Political Research Quarterly* 54, no. 4 (2001): 729–50.

Parsai, Monica, Sarah Voisine, Flavio F. Marsiglia, Stephen Kulis, and Tanya Nieri. "The Protective and Risk Effects of Parents and Peers on Substance Use, Attitudes, and Behaviors of Mexican and Mexican American Female and Male Adolescents." *Youth & Society* 40, no. 3 (2009): 353–76.

Passel, Jeffrey S., and D'Vera Cohn. "US Unauthorized Immigration Flows Are Down Sharply Since Mid-Decade." Pew Hispanic Center, Washington DC, 2011.

Passel, Jeffrey S., D'Vera Cohn, and Ana Gonzalez-Barrera. "Net Migration from Mexico Falls to Zero—Perhaps Less." Pew Latino Center, Washington DC, 2012.

Pedraza, P., M. Rivera, and National Latino/a Education Research Policy Project. *Latino Education: An Agenda for Community Action Research.* Mahwah, NJ: Lawrence Erlbaum Associates, 2005.

Peragallo, Nilda. "Latino Women and AIDS Risk." *Public Health Nursing* 13, no. 3 (1996): 217–22.

Perez, Anthony. "Who is Hispanic? Shades of Ethnicity among Latino/a Youth." In *Racism in Post-Race America: New Theories, New Directions*, edited by Charles Gallagher, 17–35. Morrisville, NC: Social Forces, 2008.

Pérez, G. *Citizen, Student, Soldier: Latina/o Youth, JROTC, and the American Dream.* Social Transformations in American Anthropology. New York: New York University Press, 2015.

Perez, Rose M., and Ilona Arnold-Berkovits. "A Conceptual Framework for Understanding Latino Immigrant's Ambiguous Loss of Homeland." *Hispanic Journal of Behavioral Sciences* 40, no. 2 (2018): 91–114.

Perez, Sonia M. *Moving Up the Economic Ladder: Latino Workers and the Nation's Prosperity.* Washington, DC: National Council of La Raza, 2000.

Perez, William. *Americans by Heart: Undocumented Latino Students and the Promise of Higher Education.* New York: Teachers College Press, 2015.

Pérez-Escamilla, Rafael, and Hugo Melgar-Quiñonez. *At Risk: Latino Children's Health.* Houston: Arte Público Press, 2011.

Pérez Rosenbaum, R. *Migration and Integration of Latinos into Rural Midwestern Communities: The Case of Mexicans in Adrian, Michigan.* Julian Samora Research Institute, Research Report No. 19. East Lansing, MI: Julian Samora Research Institute, 1997.

Perilla, Julia L., Roger Bakeman, and Fran H. Norris. "Culture and Domestic Violence: The Ecology of Abused Latinas." *Violence and Victims* 9, no. 4 (1994): 325–39.

Perlmann, Joel. *Italians Then, Mexicans Now: Immigrant Origins and Second-Generation Progress, 1890–2000.* New York: Russell Sage Foundation, 2005.

Perlmann, Joel, and Mary Waters. "Intermarriage Then and Now: Race, Generation, and the Changing Meaning of Marriage." In *Not Just Black and White: Historical and Contemporary Perspectives on Immigration, Race, and Ethnicity in the United States*, edited by Nancy Foner and George Fredrickson, 262–77. New York: Russell Sage Foundation, 2004.

Perreira, Krista M., Kathleen Mullan Harris, and Dohoon Lee. "Immigrant Youth in the Labor Market." *Work and Occupations* 34, no. 1 (2007): 5–34.

Pew Hispanic Center. Statistical Portrait of Hispanics in the United States, Washington, DC: Pew Hispanic Center, 2010.

Pew Research Center. "The Shifting Religious Identity of Latinos in the United States: Nearly One-in-Four Latinos Are Former Catholics." May 2014. https://

www.pewforum.org/2014/05/07/the-shifting-religious-identity-of-latinos-in-the
-united-states/.

Pharr, Jennifer, Courtney Coughenour, and Shawn Gerstenberger. "Healthcare Access and Health Outcomes in Southern Nevada." *Nevada Journal of Public Health* 11, no. 1, article 4 (2014): 14. https://digitalscholarship.unlv.edu/cgi/view content.cgi?article=1043&context=njph.

Philip, G. *Democracy in Latin America: Surviving Conflict and Crisis?* Cambridge, UK: Malden, MA: Polity; Distributed in the USA by Blackwell Pub., 2003.

Phillips, Janice M., and Beverly Malone. "Increasing Racial/Ethnic Diversity in Nursing to Reduce Health Disparities and Achieve Health Equity." *Public Health Reports* 129, no. 1 (2014): 45–50.

Poblete Troncoso, M., and B. Burnett. *The Rise of the Latin American Labor Movement.* New York: Bookman Associates, 1960.

Portales, M. *Crowding Out Latinos: Mexican Americans in the Public Consciousness.* Philadelphia: Temple University Press, 2000.

Portes, Alejandro, and Ruben Rumbaut. *Legacies: The Story of the Immigrant Second Generation.* Berkeley, CA: University of California Press, 2001.

Portnoy, S. *Food, Health, and Culture in Latino Los Angeles.* Studies in Food and Gastronomy. Lanham, MD: Rowman & Littlefield, 2016.

Price, M. "Cities Welcoming Immigrants: Local Strategies to Attract and Retain Immigrants in US Metropolitan Areas." *World Migration Report 2015,* 2–30. Background Paper for International Organization for Migration, Geneva, Switzerland. https://www.iom.int/sites/default/files/our_work/ICP/MPR/WMR-2015-Back ground-Paper-MPrice.pdf.

Pulido, J. *Resistance to Learning by Latino Males* [sic] *Students: Cultural and Assimilation Response Patterns and Resistance of Fifth Grade Latino Male Students.* Saarbrücken, Germany: VDM Verlag, 2008.

Qian, Zhenchao, Daniel T. Lichter, and Dmitry Tumin. "Divergent Pathways to Assimilation? Local Marriage Markets and Intermarriage Among US Hispanics." *Journal of Marriage and Family* 80, no. 1 (2018): 271–88.

Quandt, S., T. A. Arcury, J. Early, J. Tapia, J. D. Davis. "Household Food Security among Latino Migrant and Seasonal Farmworkers in North Carolina." *Public Health Reports* 119, no. 6 (Nov–Dec 2004): 568–576. doi: 10.1016/j.phr.2004.09 .006. PMID: 15504448; PMCID: PMC1497674.

Quandt, Sara A., and Thomas A. Arcury. *Latino Farmworkers in the Eastern United States: Health, Safety and Justice.* New York: Springer New York, 2009.

Quesada, James, Laurie Kain Hart, and Philippe Bourgois. "Structural Vulnerability and Health: Latino Migrant Laborers in the United States." *Medical Anthropology* 30, no. 4 (2011): 339–62.

Quesada, Uriel, Leticia Gomez, and Salvador Vidal-Ortiz. *Queer Brown Voices: Personal Narratives of Latina/o LGBT Activism.* 1st ed. Austin: University of Texas Press, 2015.

Rack, C. *Latino-Anglo Bargaining: Culture, Structure, and Choice in Court Mediation.* New York: Routledge, 2006.

Ramírez, Ricardo. *Mobilizing Opportunities: The Evolving Latino Electorate and the Future of American Politics*. Charlottesville: University of Virginia Press, 2013.

Ramos-Zayas, A. "The Role of the Spanish Language on Political Messages for the Latino Audience." Paper presented at the Southern Political Science Association Conference. New Orleans, 2015.

———. *Street Therapists: Race, Affect, and Neoliberal Personhood in Latino Newark*. Chicago; London: University of Chicago Press, 2012.

Redes En Acción. "Latino Cancer Report: Summary Recommendations for a National Hispanic/Latino Cancer Control Agenda." The National Hispanic/ Latino Cancer Network, 2004. http://www.redesenaccion.org/sites/www .redesenaccion.org/files/LatinoCancerRptSummary.pdf.

Reff, Daniel T. *Disease, Depopulation, and Culture Change in Northwestern New Spain, 1518–1764*. Salt Lake City: University of Utah Press, 1991.

Reyes, Daisy Verduzco. "Inhabiting Latino Politics: How Colleges Shape Students' Political Styles." *Sociology of Education* 88, no. 4 (2015): 302–19.

Rios, Diana I. "US Latino Audiences of Telenovelas." *Journal of Latinos and Education* 2, no. 1 (2003): 59–65.

Rios, M., L. Vazquez, and L. Miranda. *Diálogos: Placemaking in Latino Communities*. London; New York: Routledge, 2012.

Rios, Vigil, and James Diego Vigil. *Human Targets: Schools, Police, and the Criminalization of Latino Youth*. Chicago; London: University of Chicago Press, 2017.

Rivera, Fernando I., Peter J. Guarnaccia, Norah Mulvaney-Day, Julia Y. Lin, Maria Torres, and Margarita Alegría. "Family Cohesion and Its Relationship to Psychological Distress Among Latino Groups." *Hispanic Journal of Behavioral Sciences* 30, no. 3 (2008): 357–78.

Rocco, R. *Transforming Citizenship*. East Lansing: Michigan State University Press, 2014.

Rocha, Rene R. "Black-Brown Coalitions in Local School Board Elections." *Political Research Quarterly* 60 (2007): 315–27.

Rocha, Rene R., Thomas Longoria, Robert D. Wrinkle, Benjamin R. Knoll, J. L. Polinard, and James P. Wenzel. "Ethnic Context and Immigration Policy Preferences Among Latinos and Anglos." *Social Science Quarterly* 92 (2011): 1–19.

Rodriguez, Clara E. *Changing Race: Latinos, the Census, and the History of Ethnicity in the United States*. New York: New York University Press, 2000.

———. "Race, Culture, and Latino 'Otherness' in the 1980 Census." *Social Science Quarterly* 73, no. 4 (1992): 930–37.

Rodríguez, D. *Latino National Political Coalitions: Struggles and Challenges*. Latino Communities. New York: Routledge, 2002.

Rodriguez, Daniel A. *A Future for the Latino Church: Models for Multilingual, Multigenerational Hispanic Congregations*. Downers Grove, IL: IVP Academic, 2011.

Rodriguez, G. *Raising Nuestros Niños: Bringing up Latino Children in a Bicultural World*. New York: Fireside, 1999.

Rodriguez, J. *Contemporary Nutrition for Latinos: Latino Lifestyle Guide to Nutrition and Health*. New York: Writers Advantage, 2003.

Rodríguez, Joseph A. "Becoming Latinos: Mexican Americans, Chicanos, and the Spanish Myth in the Urban Southwest." *Western Historical Quarterly* 29, no. 2 (1998): 65–185.

Rodriguez, Louie F. *Intentional Excellence: The Pedagogy, Power, and Politics of Excellence in Latina/o Schools and Communities.* New York: Peter Lang, 2015.

———. *The Time Is Now: Understanding and Responding to the Black and Latina/o Dropout Crisis in the US.* New York: Peter Lang, 2014.

Rodriguez, R. *Latino Talent: Effective Strategies to Recruit, Retain, and Develop Hispanic Professionals.* Hoboken, NJ: John Wiley & Sons, 2008.

Rodriguez y Gibson, Hernández, and Ellie D. Hernández. *The Un/making of Latina/o Citizenship: Culture, Politics, and Aesthetics.* New York: Palgrave Macmillan, 2014.

Romo, Harriett, IUP/SSRC Committee for Public Policy Research on Contemporary Hispanic Issues, and Lyndon Baines Johnson Library. *Latinos & Blacks in the Cities: Policies for the 1990s.* Symposia. Austin: University of Texas, 1990.

Rosenblum, M. R., and K. McCabe. *Deportation and Discretion: Reviewing the Record and Options for Change.* Washington, DC: Migration Policy Institute, 2014.

Rudolph, J. *Embodying Latino Masculinities: Producing Masculatinidad.* New York: Palgrave Macmillan, 2012.

Rugh, Jacob S., and Douglas S. Massey. "Racial Segregation and the American Foreclosure Crisis." *American Sociological Review* 75, no. 5 (2010): 629–51.

Ryan, Camille L., and Julie Siebens. "Education Attainment in the United States: 2009." *Current Population Reports.* US Census Bureau, Report P20-566, 2012.

Saavedra, Cisneros Angel. *Latino Identity and Political Attitudes: Why Are Latinos Not Republican?* London: Palgrave Macmillan, 2017.

Sáenz, R., and M. C. Morales. *Latinos in the United States: Diversity and Change.* Malden, MA: Polity Press, 2015.

Saenz, Rogelio. "Population Bulletin Update: Latinos in the United States 2010." *Population Reference Bureau.* https://www.prb.org/latinosupdate2/.

Saiz, Albert, and Elena Zoido. "Listening to What the World Says: Bilingualism and Earnings in the US." *Review of Economics and Statistics* 87, no. 3 (2005): 523–38.

Salas, S., and P. Portes. *US Latinization: Education and the New Latino South.* Albany: State University of New York Press, 2017.

Salas-Wright, Christopher P., Eden H. Robles, Michael G. Vaughn, David Córdova, and Rafael E. Pérez-Figueroa. "Toward a Typology of Acculturative Stress: Results Among Hispanic Immigrants in the United States." *Hispanic Journal of Behavioral Sciences* 37, no. 2 (2015): 223–42.

Salinas, L. *US Latinos and Criminal Injustice.* East Lansing: Michigan State University Press, 2015.

Samers, Michael. *Migration.* London and New York: Routledge, 2010.

Sampson, W. *Poor Latino Families and School Preparation: Are They Doing the Right Things?* Lanham, MD: Scarecrow Press, 2003.

Sanabria, Harry. *The Anthropology of Latin America and the Caribbean.* New York: Routledge, 2015.

Sanchez, G. *Latinos and the 2012 Election: The New Face of the American Voter*. East Lansing: Michigan State University Press, 2015.

Sanchez, Gabriel R., Jillian Medeiros, and Shannon Sanchez-Youngman. "The Impact of Health Care and Immigration Reform on Latino Support for President Obama and Congress." *Hispanic Journal of Behavioral Sciences* 34, no. 1 (2012): 3–22.

Sanchez, Mariana, Eduardo Romano, Christyl Dawson, Patria Rojas, Marcos Martinez, Tan Li, Elena Cyrus, and Mario De La Rosa. "Cultural Correlates of DUI Risk Perceptions Among Documented and Undocumented Recent Latino Immigrants in South Florida." *Hispanic Journal of Behavioral Sciences* 39, no. 2 (2017): 211–37.

Sánchez Molina, Raul, and Lucy M. Cohen. *Latinas Crossing Borders and Building Communities in Greater Washington: Applying Anthropology in Multicultural Neighborhoods*. Lanham, MD: Lexington Books, 2016.

Sanchez, Gabriel R., and Natalie Masuoka. "Brown-Utility Heuristic? The Presence and Contributing Factors of Latino Linked Fate." *Hispanic Journal of Behavioral Sciences* 32, no. 4 (2010): 519–31.

Sanchez, Landy, and Edith Pacheco. "Rural Population Trends in Mexico: Demographic and Labor Changes." *International Handbooks of Population* 3 (2012): 155–168.

Sanders, D., and R. Fortinsky. *Dementia Care with Black and Latino Families: A Social Work Problem-Solving Approach*. New York: Springer, 2012.

Sandoval, Moises. *On the Move: A History of the Hispanic Church in the United States*. New York: Orbis Books, 2006.

Santiago, Anne M. "Patterns of Puerto Rican Segregation and Mobility." *Hispanic Journal of Behavioral Sciences* 14, no. 1 (1992): 107–33.

Santiago, Deborah A., Emily Galdeano, and Morgan Taylor. *Factbook 2015: The Condition of Latinos in Education*. Washington, DC: Excelencia in Education, 2015.

Scarpetta, Stefano, Anne Sonnet, and Thomas Manfredi. "Rising Youth Unemployment During the Crisis." OECD *Social, Employment, and Migration*, Working Papers-Paris, No. 106, 1-27. 2010. Accessed November 11, 2013. https://ideas.repec .org/p/oec/elsaab/106-en.html.

Schleef, Cavalcanti, and H. B. Cavalcanti. *Latinos in Dixie: Class and Assimilation in Richmond, Virginia*. Albany, NY: SUNY Press, 2009.

Schmal, J. *Latino Political Representation in the United States*. Santa Monica, CA: John P. Schmal, 2005.

Schneider, B. *Hierarchical Capitalism in Latin America: Business, Labor, and the Challenges of Equitable Development*. Cambridge: Cambridge University Press, 2013.

Schultze, G. *Strangers in a Foreign Land: The Organizing of Catholic Latinos in the United States*. Lanham, MD: Lexington Books, 2007.

Schwartz, E. *Latino Economics in the United States: Job Diversity*. Hispanic Heritage. Philadelphia: Mason Crest, 2005.

Secretaría del Trabajo y Previsión Social. "Salario de cotización al IMSS por sector de actividad económica—pesos por día—construcción." Accessed April 5, 2013.

http://www.stps.gob.mx/bp/secciones/conoce/areas_atencion/areas_atencion/web/menu_infsector.html.

Segal, Elizabeth A., Karen E. Gerdes, Jennifer Mullins, M. Alex Wagaman, and David Androff. "Social Empathy Attitudes: Do Latino Students Have More?" *Journal of Human Behavior in the Social Environment* 21, no. 4 (2011): 438–54.

Segura, Gary, and Helena Alves Rodrigues. "Comparative Ethnic Politics in the United States: Beyond Black and White." *Annual Review of Political Science* 9 (2006): 375–95.

Segura, Gary, and Shaun Bowler. *Diversity in Democracy: Minority Representation in the United States.* Charlottesville: University of Virginia Press, 2005.

Sepúlveda-Pulvirenti, E. *From Border Crossings to Campaign Trail: Chronicle of a Latina in Politics.* Falls Church, VA: Azul Editions, 1998.

Shalin, Dmitri N., ed. *The Social Health of Nevada: Leading Indicators and Quality of Life in the Silver State.* UNLV: Center for Democratic Culture Publications, 2012.

Shannon, Sheila M., and Kathy Escamilla. "Mexican Immigrants in U.S. Schools: Targets of Symbolic Violence." *Educational Policy* 13, no. 3 (1999): 347–70.

Sheridan, Thomas E. *Arizona: A History.* Tucson: University of Arizona Press, 2012.

Shihadeh, Edward S., and Raymond E. Barranco. "Latino Employment and Black Violence: The Unintended Consequence of US Immigration Policy." *Social Forces* 88, no. 3 (2010): 1393–1420.

Simich, Jerry L., and Thomas C. Wright, eds. *The Peoples of Las Vegas: One City, Many Faces.* Reno: University of Nevada Press, 2005.

———. *More Peoples from Las Vegas: One City, Many Faces.* Reno: University of Nevada Press, 2010.

Singer, A., J. H. Wilson, and B. DeRenzis. "Immigrants, Politics, and Local Response in Suburban Washington." Brookings Metropolitan Policy Program Report, February 2009. Washington, DC: Brookings Institution.

Singer, A., N. P. Svajlenka, and J. H. Wilson. "Local Insights from DACA Implementation." *Brookings Metropolitan Policy Program report, June 2015.* Washington, DC: Brookings Institution, 2015.

Singer, A., S. Hardwick, and C. Brettell. *Twenty-First Century Gateways: Immigrant Incorporation in Suburban America.* Washington, DC: Brookings Institution, 2008.

Skeados, Dorothy B., ed. "Pathways to Nursing Careers for Minority Youth." New York: 1199SEIU Training and Upgrading Fund (The Fund), 2007.

Small, Mario Luis. "Culture, Cohorts, and Social Organization Theory: Understanding Local Participation in a Latino Housing Project." *American Journal of Sociology* 108, no. 1 (July 2002): 1–54.

Smith, James. "Assimilation Across the Latino Generations." *American Economic Review* 93, no. 2 (2003): 315–19.

Smith, R., and R. Montilla. *Counseling and Family Therapy with Latino Populations: Strategies That Work.* Family Therapy and Counseling. New York: Routledge, 2006.

Smokowski, P., and M. Bacallao. *Becoming Bicultural: Risk, Resilience, and Latino Youth.* New York: New York University Press, 2011.

Smokowski, Paul R., and Martica L. Bacallao. "Acculturation, Internalizing Mental Health Symptoms, and Self-Esteem: Cultural Experiences of Latino Adolescents in North Carolina." *Child Psychiatry and Human Development* 37, no. 3 (2007): 273–92.

Solórzano, D., and University of California, Los Angeles. Chicano Studies Research Center. *Latina Equity in Education: Gaining Access to Academic Enrichment Programs.* Latino Policy & Issues Brief. No. 4. Los Angeles: UCLA Chicano Studies Research Center, February 2003.

Solorzano, D. G., M. Ceja, and T. Yosso. "Critical Race Theory, Racial Micro-aggressions, and Campus Racial Climate: The Experiences of African-American College Students." *Journal of Negro Education* 69, no. 1 (2000): 60–73.

Sommers, Ira, Jeffrey Fagan, and Deborah Baskin. "Sociocultural Influences on the Explanation of Delinquency for Puerto Rican Youths." *Hispanic Journal of Behavioral Sciences* 15, no. 1 (1993): 36–62.

Sosa, L. *The Americano Dream: How Latinos Can Achieve Success in Business and in Life.* New York: Dutton, 1998.

Spagat, E., and O. Millan. "Deported Mexicans Find New Life at Call Centers." Associated Press, August 22, 2014.

Stavans, I. *Latinos in the United States (What Everyone Needs to Know).* New York: Oxford University Press, 2018.

Steidel, Angel G. Lugo, and Josefina M. Contreras. "A New Familism Scale for Use with Latino Populations." *Hispanic Journal of Behavioral Science* 25, no. 3 (2003): 312–30.

Strait, Saki Cabrera. "Drug Use Among Hispanic Youth: Examining Common and Unique Contributing Factors." *Hispanic Journal of Behavioral Sciences* 21, no. 1 (February 1999): 89–103.

Stuesse, A. *Scratching Out a Living.* Oakland: University of California Press, 2016.

Suarez, R. *Latino Americans: The 500-Year Legacy that Shaped a Nation.* New York: A Celebra Book, 2013.

Suarez-Orozco, Marcelo M., and M. Paez. *Latinos: Remaking America.* Berkeley: University of California Press, 2002.

Subervi-Vélez, and Frederico A. Subervi-Vélez. *The Mass Media and Latino Politics: Studies of U.S. Media Content, Campaign Strategies and Survey Research: 1984–2004.* LEA's Communication. New York: Routledge, 2008.

Sulkowski, Michael L., Sheri Bauman, Savannah Wright, Charisse Nixon, and Stan Davis. "Peer Victimization in Youth from Immigrant and Non-Immigrant US Families." *School Psychology International* 35, no. 6 (2014): 649–69.

Sun, I., and Y. Wu. *Race, Immigration, and Social Control.* Palgrave Studies in Race, Ethnicity, Indigeneity and Criminal Justice. London: Palgrave Macmillan UK, 2018.

Suro, Roberto, Gabriel Escobar, Gretchen Livingston, Shirin Hakimzadeh, Luis Lugo, Sandra Stencel, and S. Chaudhry. "Changing Faiths: Latinos and the Transformation of American Religion." Pew Research Center 45, no. 8 (2007): 1–154.

Sussner, Katarina M., Ana C. Lindsay, Mary L. Greaney, and Karen E. Peterson. "The Influence of Immigrant Status and Acculturation on the Development of Overweight in Latino Families: A Qualitative Study." *Journal of Immigrant and Minority Health* 10, no. 6 (2008): 497–505.

Takahashi, Bruno, Juliet Pinto, Manuel Chavez, and Mercedes Vigón. *News Media Coverage of Environmental Challenges in Latin America and the Caribbean.* Palgrave Studies in Media and Environmental Communication. Cham, Switzerland: Springer International Publishing, 2018.

Telles, Edward, Mark Sawyer, and Gaspar Rivera-Salgado, eds. *Just Neighbors? Research on African American and Latino Relations in the United States.* New York: Russell Sage Foundation, 2011.

Telles, Edward Eric. *Pigmentocracies: Ethnicity, Race, and Color in Latin America.* Chapel Hill: University of North Carolina Press, 2014.

Terriquez, Veronica. "Trapped in the Working Class? Prospects for the Intergenerational (Im)mobility of Latino Youth." *Sociological Inquiry* 84, no. 3 (2011): 382–411.

Terry, Rodney L., and Marissa Fond. "Experimental U.S. Census Bureau Race and Hispanic Origin Survey Questions: Reactions from Spanish Speakers." *Hispanic Journal of Behavioral Sciences* 35, no. 4 (2013): 524–41.

Teruya, Stacey A., and Shahrzad Bazargan-Hejazi. "The Immigrant and Hispanic Paradoxes: A Systematic Review of Their Predictions and Effects." *Hispanic Journal of Behavioral Sciences* 35, no. 4 (2013): 486–509.

Thompson, G. *Up Where We Belong: Helping African American and Latino Students Rise in School and in Life.* 1st ed. Jossey-Bass Education Series. San Francisco: Jossey-Bass, 2007.

Tienda, Marta. "Latinos and the American Pie: Can Latinos Achieve Economic Parity?" *Hispanic Journal of Behavioral Sciences* 17, no. 4 (1995): 403–29.

Timmins, C. L. "The Impact of Language Barriers on the Health Care of Latinos in the United States: A Review of the Literature and Guidelines for Practice." *Journal of Midwifery & Women's Health* 47, no. 2 (2002): 80–96.

Torres, Jacqueline M., and Steven P. Wallace. "Migration Circumstances, Psychological Distress, and Self-Rated Physical Health for Latino Immigrants in the United States." *American Journal of Public Health* 103, no. 9 (2013): 1619–627.

Torres, Lucas. "Predicting Levels of Latino Depression: Acculturation, Acculturative Stress, and Coping." *Cultural Diversity and Ethnic Minority Psychology* 16, no. 2 (2010): 256.

Torres, R. "Chartbook on Health of Latinos in the Midwest." Julian Samora Research Institute, no. 3. East Lansing: Julian Samora Research Institute, 1990.

Tran, Van C., and Nicol M. Valdez. "Second-Generation Decline or Advantage? Latino Assimilation in the Aftermath of the Great Recession." *International Migration Review* 51, no. 1 (2017): 155–90.

Trejo, Stephen. "Intergenerational Progress of Mexican-Origin Workers in the US Labor Market." *Journal of Human Resources* 38, no. 3 (2003): 467–89.

Trust for America's Health and Robert Wood Johnson Foundation. *The State of Obesity: Better Policies for a Healthier America.* Washington, DC. 2017. https://stateofobesity.org/wp-content/uploads/2018/08/stateofobesity2017.pdf.

Tuman, John P. "The Impact of the COVID-19 Pandemic on Labor Market Conditions in Nevada: A Preliminary Assessment." *Journal of Labor and Society* 23, no. 3 (2020): 367–81.

——. "Labor Markets and Economic Reform in Latin America: A Review of Recent Research." *Latin American Research Review* 35, no. 3 (2000): 173–87.

——. *Latin American Migrants in the Las Vegas Valley: Civic Engagement and Political Participation.* Washington, DC: Woodrow Wilson International Center for Scholars, 2009.

——. *Reshaping the North American Automobile Industry: Restructuring, Corporatism, and Union Democracy in Mexico.* London and New York: Routledge, 2003.

Tuman, John P., Danielle Roth-Johnson, and Ted Jelen. "Conscience and Context: Attitudes Toward Abortion in Mexico." *Social Science Quarterly* 94, no. 1 (2013): 100–112.

Tuman, John P., David F. Damore, and Maria José Flor Ágreda. "Immigration and the Contours of Nevada's Latino Population." *Brookings Mountain West Report.* June 2013. Accessed August 25, 2013. https://digitalscholarship.unlv.edu/cgi/viewcontent.cgi?article=1021&context=brookings_pubs. 1–18.

——. "The Impact of the Great Recession on the Latino Community in Nevada." *Brookings Mountain West Report.* 1–14. https://digitalscholarship.unlv.edu/brookings_pubs/28/.

Tuman, John P., and Dawn Gearhart. "The Guatemalans." In Jerry L. Simich and Tom Wright, *More Peoples From Las Vegas,* 213–30.

Tuman, John P., Sheniz Moonie, and Danielle Roth-Johnson. "The Administrative Prevalence of Autism Spectrum Disorders in Nevada School Districts: A Pooled Time Series Analysis, 1994–2004." *Nevada Journal of Public Health* 5, no. 1 (2008): 15–24.

Uhlaner, Carole J., and F. Chris Garcia. "Learning Which Party Fits: Experience, Ethnic Identity, and the Demographic Foundations of Latino Party Identification." In *Diversity in Democracy,* edited by Gary Segura and Shaun Bowler, 72–101. Charlottesville: Virginia University Press, 2005.

Uhlaner, Carole, Mark Gray, and F. Chris García. "Ideology, Issues and Partisanship Among Latinos." Paper presented at the annual meeting of the Western Political Science Association, San Jose, CA. March 24–26, 2000.

Umaña-Taylor, Adriana J., and Kimberly A. Updegraff. "Latino Adolescents' Mental Health: Exploring the Interrelations Among Discrimination, Ethnic Identity, Cultural Orientation, Self-Esteem, and Depressive Symptoms." *Journal of Adolescence* 30, no. 4 (2007): 549–67.

University of Wisconsin Population Health Institute. County Health Rankings-Nevada. 2012. http://www.countyhealthrankings.org/sites/default/files/states/CHR2012_NV.pdf.

Urbina, Martin G., and Sofia Espinoza Álvarez. *Ethnicity and Criminal Justice in the Era of Mass Incarceration: A Critical Reader on the Latino Experience.* Springfield, IL: Charles C. Thomas Publisher, 2017.

———. *Latino Police Officers in the United States: An Examination of Emerging Trends and Issues.* Springfield, IL: Charles C. Thomas Publisher, 2015.

———. "Neoliberalism, Criminal Justice and Latinos: The Contours of Neoliberal Economic Thought and Policy on Criminalization." *Latino Studies* 14, no. 1 (2016): 33–58.

US Census Bureau. Current Population Survey, Annual Social and Economic Supplement. Washington, DC. 2012.

———. "American Community Survey: Guide to Data Users, Hispanic Origin."

———. "American Community Survey: History." Accessed April 17, 2013. http://www.census.gov/history/www/programs/demographic/american_community_survey.html.

———. "Profile of General Population and Housing Characteristics: 2010 Demographic Profile Data, Nevada."

———. "Profile of General Population and Housing Characteristics: 2010 Demographic Profile Data. Geography: Clark County."

———. "2000 Census. File DP-1. Profile of General Demographic Characteristic: Census 2000 Summary File (SF1), Nevada."

———. "2000 Census. QT-P9. Hispanic or Latino by Type: 2000 Census. Geographic Area, Clark County." 2010 Census. File DP-1.

———. "2011 American Community Survey, 1-year Estimates. File S0506, Selected Characteristics of the Foreign-Born Population by Region and Birth: Latin America. Geography: Nevada."

———. "2011 American Community Survey, 1-year Estimates. File B010011. Sex by Age (Hispanic or Latino). Geography: Nevada."

US Department of Homeland Security. Immigration Statistics. "Profiles of Legal Permanent Residents, by Metropolitan Statistical Area of Reference, 2005." Accessed September 9, 2007. http://www.dhs.gov/ximgtn/statistics/data/DSLPRo5m.shtm.

———. "Profiles on Naturalized Citizens, by Metropolitan Statistical Area of Reference, 2005." Accessed September 9, 2007. http://www.dhs.gov/ximgtn/statistics/data/DSNato5m.shtm.

US Department of Labor. "The Latino Labor Force in the Recovery." 2011. https://ecommons.cornell.edu/handle/1813/78877.

US Immigration and Naturalization Service. "Estimates of the Unauthorized Immigrant Population Residing in the United States: 1990 to 2000." 2003. http://www.uscis.gov/graphics/shared/aboutus/statistics/Ill_Report_1211.pdf.

Valdez, Carmen R., Brian Padilla, and Jessa Lewis Valentine. "Consequences of Arizona's Immigration Policy on Social Capital Among Mexican Mothers with

Unauthorized Immigration Status." *Hispanic Journal of Behavioral Sciences* 35, no. 3 (2013): 303–22.

Valencia, Elvia Y., and Valerie Johnson. "Latino Students in North Carolina: Acculturation, Perceptions of School Environment, and Academic Aspirations." *Hispanic Journal of Behavioral Sciences* 28, no. 3 (2006): 350–67.

Valle, R., W. Vega, and California Department of Mental Health. *Hispanic Natural Support Systems: Mental Health Promotion Perspectives*. Sacramento, CA: Department of Mental Health, 1980.

Varela, R. Enrique, and Lauren Hensley-Maloney. "The Influence of Culture on Anxiety in Latino Youth: A Review." *Clinical Child and Family Psychology Review* 12, no. 3 (2009): 217–33.

Vargas, Zaragosa. *Crucible of Struggle: A History of Mexican Americans from Colonial Times to the Present Era*. Oxford: Oxford University Press, 2011.

Vargas-Ramos, Carlos, and Anthony M. Stevens Arroyo. *Blessing la Política: The Latino Religious Experience and Political Engagement in the United States*. Santa Barbara, CA: Praeger, 2012.

Varsanyi, M. W. "Rescaling the 'Alien,' Rescaling Personhood: Neoliberalism, Immigration, and the State." *Annals of the Association of American Geographers* 98, no. 4 (2008): 877–96.

Vasquez, Francisco H., and Rodolfo D. Torres. *Latino/a Thought: Culture, Politics, and Society*. New York: Rowman & Littlefield Publishers, 2003.

Vázquez, Josefina Zoraida, and Lorenzo Meyer. *México Frente a Estados Unidos: Un Ensayo Histórico 1776–2000*. México, DF: Fondo de Cultura Económica, 2013.

Vega, S. *Latino Heartland*. New York: NYU Press, 2015.

Vega, William, Kyriakos S. Markides, Jacqueline Lowe Angel, Fernando M. Torres-Gil. Conference Series on Aging in the Americas. *Challenges of Latino Aging in the Americas*. Austin, TX: Springer, 2015.

Vélez-Ibañez, Carlos G., and Anna Sampaio, Anna. *Transnational Latina/o Communities: Politics, Processes, and Cultures*. Latin American Perspectives in the Classroom. Lanham, MD: Rowman & Littlefield, 2002.

Verdaguer, M. *Class, Ethnicity, Gender and Latino Entrepreneurship*. New York: Routledge, 2009.

Villarreal, R., and N. Hernandez. *Latinos and Political Coalitions: Political Empowerment for the 1990s*. New York: Greenwood Press, 1991.

Villarruel, Antonia M., Loretta S. Jemmott, and John B. Jemmott III. "Designing a Culturally Based Intervention to Reduce HIV Sexual Sisk for Latino Adolescents." *Journal of the Association of Nurses in AIDS Care* 16, no. 2 (2005): 23–31.

Villarruel, Antonia M., Mary Canales, and Sara Torres. "Bridges and Barriers: Educational Mobility of Hispanic Nurses." *Journal of Nursing Education* 40, no. 6 (2001): 245–51.

Villarruel, Francisco A., Gustavo Carlo, Josefina M. Grau, Margarita Azmitia, Natash J. Cabrera, and T. Jaime Cain, eds. *Handbook of US Latino Psychology: Developmental and Community-Based Perspectives*. Los Angeles: SAGE, 2009.

Waddoups, Jeffrey, and Vincent Eade. "Hotels and Casinos: Collective Bargaining During a Decade of Instability." In *Collective Bargaining Under Duress: Case Studies of Major US Industries, Urbana,* edited by Paul Clark and Anne Frost. Labor and Employment Relations Association. Ithaca: Cornell University Press, 2013.

Wals Aparicio, Sergio C. "Immigrants' Political Suitcases: A Theory of Imported Socialization." PhD diss., University of Illinois Urbana-Champaign, 2009.

Wasserman, M., D. Bender, and S. D. Lee. "Use of Preventive Maternal and Child Health Services by Latina Women: A Review of Published Interventions Studies." *Medical Care Research and Review* 64 (2007): 4–45.

Watt, Toni Terling, and Jesse McCoy Rogers. "Factors Contributing to Differences in Substance Use Among Black and White Adolescents." *Youth & Society* 39, no. 1 (2007): 54–74.

Wei, Iris I., Beth A. Virnig, Dolly A. John, and Robert O. Morgan. "Using a Spanish Surname Match to Improve Identification of Hispanic Women in Medicare Administrative Data." *Health Services Research* 21 (2006): 1469–481.

Welch, Susan, and Lee Sigelman. "The Politics of Hispanic Americans: Insights from National Surveys, 1980–1988." *Social Science Quarterly* 74, no. 1 (1993): 76–94.

Welch, Susan, Lee Sigelman, Timothy Bledsoe, and Michael Combs. *Race & Place: Race Relations in an American City.* New York: Cambridge University Press, 2001.

Western, Bruce, and Becky Pettit. "Incarceration and Social Inequality." *Daedalus* 139, no. 3 (2010): 8–19.

Wheatley, C. "Push Back: US Deportation Policy and the Reincorporation of Involuntary Return Migrants in Mexico." *The Latin Americanist* 55, no. 4 (2011): 35–60.

Wides-Munoz, Laura. "Jeb Bush Guides GOP Outreach to Latinos." *Washington Times,* January 13, 2011. Accessed May 25, 2015. http://www.washingtontimes.com /news/2011/jan/13/jeb-bush-guides-gop-outreach-latinos/?page=all.

Wilkinson, Betina Cutaia. "Perceptions of Commonality and Latino-Black, Latino-White Relations in a Multiethnic US." *Political Research Quarterly* 67 (2014): 905–16.

Winders, J. "Changing Politics of Race and Region: Latino Migration to the US South." *Progress in Human Geography* 29, no. 6 (2005): 683–99.

Wong, Janelle S. "The Effects of Age and Political Exposure on the Development of Party Identification Among Asian American and Latino Immigrants in the United States." *Political Behavior* 22 (2000): 341–71.

Woolley, Michael E., Kelli L. Kol, and Gary L. Bowen. "The Social Context of School Success for Latino Middle School Students: Direct and Indirect Influences of Teachers, Family, and Friends." *The Journal of Early Adolescence* 29, no. 1 (2009): 43–70.

World Bank. *World Development Indicators.* Data Series: "Fertility rate, total (births per woman)." Online statistical database. Accessed February 24, 2013. http://data bank.worldbank.org/.

Wortham, S., E. Murillo, and E. Hamann. *Education in the New Latino Diaspora:*

Policy and the Politics of Identity. Sociocultural Studies in Educational Policy Formation and Appropriation, vol. 2. Westport, CT: Ablex Pub., 2002.

Wray, Matt, Tatiana Poladko, Misty Vaughan. "Suicide Trends and Prevention in Nevada." *The Social Health of Nevada: Leading Indicators and Quality of Life in the Silver State*. Center for Democratic Culture, UNLV, 2012. 1–2. http://digital scholarship.unlv.edu/social_health_nevada_reports\30.

Wright, Kevin A., Jillian J. Turanovic, and Nancy Rodriguez. "Racial Inequality, Ethnic Inequality, and the System Involvement of At-Risk Youth: Implications for the Racial Invariance and Latino Paradox Theses." *Justice Quarterly* 33, no. 5 (2016): 863–89.

Wright, R., and M. Ellis. "Race, Region, and the Territorial Politics of Immigration in the U.S." *International Journal of Population Geography* 6 (2000): 197–211.

Wright, Thomas C., and Jesse Dinno Moody. "The Salvadorans." In *The Peoples of Las Vegas*, edited by Thomas C. Wright and Jerry L. Simich, 247–68. Reno: University of Nevada Press, 2005.

Wright, Thomas C., John P. Tuman, and Maryam T. Stevenson. "Immigration and Ethnic Diversity in Nevada." In *The Social Health of Nevada: Leading Indicators and Quality of Life in the Silver State*, edited by Dmitri N. Shalin. UNLV: Center for Democratic Culture Publications, 2012.

Wright-Salas, Christopher P., Eden H. Robles, Michael G. Vaughn, David Córdova, and Rafael E. Pérez-Figueroa. "Toward a Typology of Acculturative Stress: Results Among Hispanic Immigrants in the United States." *Hispanic Journal of Behavioral Sciences* 37, no. 2 (2015): 223–42.

Wrinkle, Robert D., Joseph Stewart, J. L., Kenneth J. Meier, and John R. Arvizu. "Ethnicity and Nonelectoral Political Participation." *Hispanic Journal of Behavioral Sciences* 18, no. 2 (1996): 142–53.

Yamada, Ann Marie, Ramón Valle, Concepción Barrio, and Dilip Jeste. "Selecting an Acculturation Measure for Use with Latino Older Adults." *Research on Aging* 28, no. 5 (2006): 519–61.

Yancey, G. *Who is White? Latinos, Asians, and the New Black/Nonblack Divide*. Boulder, CO: L. Rienner, 2003.

Yáñez-Chávez, Aníbal. *Latino Politics in California*. San Diego: Center for U.S.-Mexican Studies, University of California, San Diego, 1996.

Yinger, John. "Racial Prejudice and Racial Residential Segregation in an Urban Model." *Journal of Urban Economics* 3, no. 4 (1974): 383–96.

York, S. *Standing in the Gap: A Study of College-Bound Latinas' Resilience in Completing High School Within an At-Risk Environment*. Ann Arbor, MI: UMI, 2012.

Zalaya, Siboney, Patricia T. Alpert, Yu Xu, Ann McDonough, and Barbara Stover Gingerich. "The Need for Hispanic Nurses in Nevada: An Underrepresented Ethnic Group in the Nursing Workforce." *Home Health Care Management and Practice* 23, no. 5 (2011): 329–35.

Zambrana, R. *Latinos in American Society: Families and Communities in Transition*. Ithaca, NY: Cornell University Press, 2011.

———. *Understanding Latino Families: Scholarship, Policy, and Practice.* Understanding Families, vol. 2. Thousand Oaks, CA: Sage Publications, 1995.

Zapata, Alexander. "Quest for Greater Hispanic Representation in Nevada's Halls of Power Isn't Always Easy, Candidates Say." *The Nevada Independent.* 2019. https://thenevadaindependent.com/article/quest-for-greater-hispanic-representation-in-nevadas-halls-of-power-isnt-always-easy-candidates-say.

Zayas, Luis H., Kalina M. Brabeck, Laurie Cook Heffron, Joanna Dreby, Esther J. Calzada, J. Rubén Parra-Cardona, Alan J. Dettlaff, Lauren Heidbrink, Krista M. Perreira, and Hirokazu Yoshikawa. "Charting Directions for Research on Immigrant Children Affected by Undocumented Status." *Hispanic Journal of Behavioral Sciences* 39, no. 4 (2017): 412–35.

Zentella, A. *Building on Strength: Language and Literacy in Latino Families and Communities.* Language and Literacy. New York; Covina, CA: Teachers College Press; California Association for Bilingual Education, 2005.

Zimmermann, Klaus. "Migrant Ethnic Identity: Concept and Policy Implications." Institute for the Study of Labor (IZA) Discussion Paper 3056. 2007.

Index

Page numbers in italics refer to figures, maps, and tables.

About the Authors

JOHN P. TUMAN is a professor of political science and associate dean of faculty in the College of Liberal Arts at the University of Nevada, Las Vegas. He received his PhD from the University of California, Los Angeles, his MA from the University of Chicago, and his BA (High Honors) from the University of California, Berkeley. His research has engaged a number of topics on the political economy of Latin America and Latinos in the US. Tuman is the past president of the Pacific Coast Council of Latin American Studies, and he also served previously as the department chair of political science and as the director of the Institute for Latin American Studies for many years. He is the author, coauthor, and coeditor of several books and edited several volumes. In addition, he has published articles in a number of journals.

DAVID F. DAMORE, PhD, is a professor of political science at the University of Nevada, Las Vegas, where he teaches undergraduate and graduate courses in American politics and research methods and serves as department chair. Damore's research focuses on electoral politics and applied public policy. In addition to his position at UNLV, Damore is a nonresident senior fellow in the Brookings Institution's Governance Studies Program, a key vote advisor for Project Vote Smart, and a senior analyst at *Latino Decisions*. He is also the outgoing president of the Southwestern Political Science Association (2018–19). Damore regularly comments on Nevada governmental and political issues for local, national, and international media outlets. He earned his PhD from the University of California, Davis (2000), his MA from the University of Georgia (1995), and his BA from the University of California, San Diego (1992), all in political science.

TIFFIANY O. HOWARD, PhD, is an associate professor of political science and the director of the Center for Migration, Demography, and Population Studies (CMDP) at the University of Nevada, Las Vegas. She earned her joint doctorate in political science and public policy from the University of Michigan-Ann Arbor in 2006 and joined the UNLV faculty in 2008. Her fields of specialization include international security, political violence, and terrorism, immigration and refugee policy, and race, ethnicity, and gender. She has been awarded nationally recognized visiting scholar and research fellow positions, including the Department of Defense-DARPA Research Fellowship (2009), the Ford Foundation Postdoctoral Scholar Fellowship (2013–2014), the APSA Centennial Center Visiting Scholar Fellowship (2014), the Black Mountain Institute Faculty Fellowship (2015), and the Congressional Black Caucus Foundation–Center for Policy Analysis and Research–Small Business and Entrepreneurship Senior Research Fellowship (2019). Howard is the author of *The Tragedy of Failure* (Praeger Security International/ABC-CLIO, 2010) and *Failed States and the Origins of Violence* (Routledge, 2014), the coauthor of *Sex, Power and Politics: Exploring Gender Roles, Identities and Influence throughout History* (Palgrave Macmillan: 2016), and series coeditor of *Migration, Demography and Environmental Change: Global Challenges* (University of Nevada Press). Other notable peer reviewed publications appear in *Civil Wars, Studies in Conflict and Terrorism,* the *National Political Science Review,* the *Journal of Political Science Education,* and *Immigrants and Minorities.*

NERSES KOPALYAN, PhD, is an assistant professor-in-residence of political science at the University of Nevada, Las Vegas. His fields of specialization include international relations, political theory, and philosophy of science. Kopalyan has conducted extensive research on analytic philosophy, feminist theory, and paradigm building. Kopalyan is the author of *World Political Systems After Polarity* (Routledge, 2017), and the coauthor of *Sex, Power, and Politics* (Palgrave Macmillan, 2016). His current research concentrates on political violence and terrorism and its impact on geopolitical and great power relations.